Cooperative Learning &
French

Cynthia Chiupka-Jozin

Kagan

Kagan Publishing
981 Calle Amanecer
San Clemente, CA 92673
1 (800) 933-2667
www.KaganOnline.com

ISBN: 978-1-933445-29-8

Table of Contents

Dans la communauté.................1
(In the community)

Canadian French Vocabulary

In the Vocabulaire sections of this book, when an alternate Canadian French term is used (e.g., used in Canada) in place of a standard French term, the Canadian French usage is listed below the French term. The Canadian French term is preceded with a Canadian maple leaf icon as shown in the example term below.

- **Un costume** (Suit)
- ❦ **Un complet** (Suit)

Table of Contents

(continued)

Table of Contents

Table of Contents

Cooperative Learning & French • Chiupka-Jozin
Kagan Publishing • 1 (800) 933-2667 • www.KaganOnline.com

Table of Contents

(continued)

Table of Contents

(continued)

Cooperative Learning & French • Chiupka-Jozin
Kagan Publishing • 1 (800) 933-2667 • www.KaganOnline.com

Table of Contents

(continued)

Table of Contents

(continued)

Cooperative Learning & French • Chiupka-Jozin
Kagan Publishing • 1 (800) 933-2667 • www.KaganOnline.com

Table of Contents

(continued)

able of Contents

(continued)

Featured Structures

ntroduction

My oldest daughter, now nineteen and off to post-secondary education in another city, is a passionate soccer player. I think this is where my youngest daughter has developed her interest in the sport; watching her older sister. Bohdana, the senior of the two girls, plays defense. She's quite good at it too. Not just from a mother's perspective, but from an advocate of cooperative learning.

I see her out there on the pitch, playing her position, passing to other players, watching where the adversaries are placing themselves so that when she has a throw-in, she can place it just in front of her own teammate but not to the advantage of the other team.

I watch the rest of the team moving like restless water—with an ebb and flow—each responding to the other's position and movement on the field. When one teammate moves the ball toward the opposing net, to a position to score a goal, the rest move up in support and get ready to receive the ball. Each player needs the others to be successful on the field. None is able to play the game alone and no one would even attempt to try! I admire their teamwork and the success it brings them. I am in awe of the communication that is happening on the field between players and the support coming from off the field.

I admire the supporting teammates who are on the sidelines ready to "sub in" when needed. I admire the coach who yells encouragement and makes players aware of different movements and better positioning on the pitch. We can learn a lot about cooperative learning for the classroom by watching organized team sports in action.

What Is Cooperative Learning?

Cooperative learning is based on social interdependence theory: The outcome of the activity is affected by the individual's as well as others' actions. Two elements that are critical to the success of cooperative learning teams are positive interdependence and individual accountability. Without these elements, the effectiveness of cooperative learning is weakened.

Cooperative learning, as a teaching methodology, is a helpful tool to use in a classroom. It creates student interdependence, whereby students work with each other toward a common goal. When students are working together on a common goal, social skills and academic achievement increase.

Cooperative Learning Structures and PIES

Dr. Spencer Kagan bases his Cooperative Learning Structures on four essential elements: **P**ositive Interdependence, **I**ndividual Accountability, **E**qual Participation, and **S**imultaneous Interaction (**PIES**). As Dr. Kagan states in his book, *Kagan Cooperative Learning*, "learning and change come about best by a combination of pressure and support: Individual accountability creates the pressure, positive interdependence creates the support."

Cooperative Learning & French • Chiupka-Jozin
Kagan Publishing • 1 (800) 933-2667 • www.KaganOnline.com

Positive Interdependence

Positive interdependence means providing structure to a task in which students have vested interest in working together. Through the nature and structure of a task, students are encouraged to cooperate to meet certain goals that individuals could not reach on their own. Positive interdependence is the first element necessary to ensure the success of cooperative learning. The student will receive the needed support prior to individual performance. Members of a group or team gain a sense of security when they know that they can get help from peers. Positive interdependence can be created using goals, incentives, sharing resources, teammates having specific roles, sequencing subunits within the task, and role playing or simulation activities.

Positive interdependence can also be developed through competing against other teams; having teams group their desks together (physical environment); and team names, cheers, and mottos (mutual identity). Having teams working together with their heads "in the game," all actively engaged in the task can be very rewarding—both for the individual student, who is feeling a sense of belonging, and also for the teacher who is witnessing the results of a well-designed lesson.

Individual Accountability

Individual accountability is the measurable display of an individual student's knowledge or behavior. It is evident when every group member contributes to the accomplishment of group goals, can individually demonstrate what was learned from the cooperative endeavor, and supportively helps all members of the group learn successfully. As Dr. Kagan states, "the acid test for classroom success is the success of each individual student." Cooperative learning tasks must be designed to be challenging enough for all to be engaged and can be interwoven successfully so that all students must partake to reach the stated outcomes. At the end of the task, each student is able to perform some type of assessment of learning to prove that they have actually learned something while working with their group. Students may be accountable in many ways: to a partner, their group, the teacher, or their parents (e.g., a report home). If both positive interdependence and individual accountability are present, students have a more positive experience in their cooperative learning groups.

Equal Participation

Equal participation means students are participating in the task approximately equally. Equal participation allows students to develop trust, confidence, and interdependence within the group. This participation is necessary in order for students to succeed and have a positive experience in the cooperative learning

(continued)

environment. Students are able to learn from each other because they are able to speak "at their own level" of understanding. Students are able to use analogies and examples that are relevant to themselves thus aiding in the explanation to their peers. In explaining the material to a peer, the "explainer," gains a better understanding of the material. Students develop communication and social skills as they include and encourage lesser-skilled teammates and those not participating to their ability level. With well-structured cooperative instructions, students support those needing the extra help and encourage those who are slacking.

When students have a good experience in their cooperative learning group, they comment about how everyone does equal shares of the work, that group members like each other, they all remain on task and they are having fun in the process.

Teachers who use cooperative learning as a teaching methodology experience many instructional benefits. These benefits include more time to work with individuals; more time to observe the class so that teaching can be restructured or learning can be redirected if necessary; an opportunity to give more students feedback on their learning; less marking; and a more positive learning environment.

Cooperative learning can change teacher-student relationships, but the role of the teacher is still as significant as it would be in conventional pedagogy. Teachers are needed to guide, monitor, and frame students' group activities while students are engaged in cooperative learning activities.

Simultaneous Interaction

A cooperative learning classroom promotes simultaneous interaction. Simultaneous interaction means students are interacting in pairs or groups simultaneously. It's distinguishable from teacher-directed classrooms by its hub of activity in contrast to a sequential structure where one student participates at a time. To peek your head into a classroom that has students motivated and interacting in groups is a compelling site. Children in cooperative learning classrooms are active in the building of their own understanding and the outcomes are as important as the processes of learning. We see students who may sit quietly in a regular classroom, hoping not to be called on by the teacher, interacting and having a great time in their cooperative learning groups.

Emerging evidence tells us that social interaction literally changes the human brain. Students' brains will be altered by their experiences with others. We need to provide our students with positive social experiences that engage them in structured academic experiences, as well as allow for a balance of individual experiences, so that students experience a positive educational environment.

Introduction

(continued)

Teaching in the Cooperative Learning Classroom

As teachers, we want our classrooms to be filled with learning activities that are engaging for our students. We would like students to find purpose in what we are teaching. We want the curriculum to make sense for our students and for them to get a personal answer as to what is in it for them. As sensitive educators, we adapt our instruction to what our students respond to and how we understand their different abilities to learn. Classrooms do not need to have teachers as the "keepers of knowledge." Students can be simultaneously sharing their knowledge with each other and learning from each other. When more heads are involved—the more information is being shared.

Cognitive psychology research shows that if information is to be retained in the memory, it needs to be related to information that is already stored. For deep learning, the learner must engage in reorganizing, restructuring, or elaboration of the material. The most effective means of elaboration is explaining the information to someone else.

Putting the Elements Together

Having students working with other students and talking about what they are learning develops positive interdependence (the task is structured so each student contributes and every student helps teammates learn) and individual accountability (each person must share some information).

Cooperative learning practice increases student achievement. Practice can involve teams doing exploratory activities, simulations, or practicing together (coaching each other through a variety of exercises). This allows more direct contact with the material and a deeper learning experience.

Cooperative learning allows students to engage in the process of learning with other students. They are socially interacting—which is one of the primary reasons students want to attend school: to see their friends. By allowing structured social interaction through cooperative learning activities, students are permitted to talk and work together with classmates. Success is achieved through elaborate rehearsal. Students are accountable for their own learning and are more successful because of pressure for the whole group to succeed.

Cooperative Teamwork

Cooperative teamwork is the process by which learning is enhanced and teams work together so that all teammates learn the material. When cooperative learning is done well, students feel safe in their groups and are not afraid to ask questions, try out a foregin language, and take risks. Teammates readily help each other and explain at an understandable level. When students can share personal anecdotes or examples relating to content area, they are connecting to the subject in a way perhaps teachers have not (or perhaps could not have) considered.

As educators, we need to be creative in making our curriculum more attainable

Introduction

for all learners. Cooperative learning is a way of achieving this. When teachers have a variety of interests and capabilities, they can depart from the prespecified activities found in textbooks and offer more choice and usefulness by incorporating cooperative learning strategies.

Engaging Students

One of my personal goals for my classroom is to effectively design tasks that contribute to the ebb and flow of the interactions of students within cooperative learning teams. I believe in using cooperative learning strategies as a method to deliver curriculum in a more engaging manner. Students get what they need out of the activities: socialization, a sense of belonging, more and deeper understanding of the material, and a personal connection to the topic through engagement.

In the process, I develop a better understanding of the ways I need to move with the curriculum: perhaps faster in some areas, perhaps spending more time in others. I can talk with individuals, give extra support where needed and provide more useful feedback on their learning. The classroom hums with activity, where students are having fun, engaged, and motivated to learn.

Ensuring Students' Success

Through reading many articles and books on cooperative learning, I have developed a deeper understanding of the importance of positive interdependence and individual accountability.

All elements of cooperative learning (positive interdependence, individual accountability, equal participation, simultaneous interaction) are essential for success. I see how to incorporate more teambuilding and classbuilding strategies that will strengthen the atmosphere of "connectivity" and safety in the classroom, so students will feel comfortable and capable of asking and answering questions of their classmates.

The transfer of power that accompanies students working in groups versus a teacher-directed class makes many students initially uncomfortable. Their past negative experiences, which include a variety of negative interdependent behaviors (e.g., the students who are going to let others in the group do the work or students who decide they must control the group) have affected the success of group work.

With practice and skill development, cooperative learning is an effective tool. I know that I have had students in groups who have turned to me and said, "How come you didn't explain it that way?" when referring to a teammate's explanation of material!

Well, I had thought I was being clear and concise, but obviously that student response tells me that I don't know everything! This experience has encouraged me to use more cooperative learning strategies that allow students to reflect and also coach each other on learning tasks. I will remind students that "I don't know everything" and that they have the answers: to have confidence in each other's abilities.

Introduction

(continued)

Enhancing Subject Content

Structuring cooperative learning activities to enhance subject content is of utmost importance. If a teacher fails to make certain that all elements are contained in the activity, the effectiveness of the learning is diminished. Dr. Spencer Kagan has more than 250 cooperative learning structures available for any variety of learning or skill development. These boost the social interdependence of the classroom and learning the material of the curriculum.

Teachers must be conscious creators of cooperative learning activities that will engage learners. They must not use cooperative learning as "fillers" but incorporate tasks that have true meaning and goals to learning, otherwise students will be acutely aware of a teacher's intentions and will adjust their involvement accordingly. As instructors, we must excite our students by our awareness of their different learning styles and meet their individual needs by adding variety to our lessons.

Curriculum can be presented, but when it becomes interactive, students learn more. We can engage our students by motivating them through social interaction and being accountable for their learning. We recognize their abilities to interact with what we are presenting to them; that they are not just "passive recipients" of information. In turn, they become capable of analyzing and synthesizing the material presented to them. If we continue "teacher talk"—where we lecture and may have one or two students respond during class—we may in fact, be inhibiting their learning.

Accountable Learning Equals Achievement

Future success for students depends on their involvement in the classroom. Two major reasons for dropping out of college have been related to a student's failure to establish a social network of friends and classmates, and failure to become academically involved in classes.

Students need opportunities to develop social skills that are essential to their success outside of the classroom. We need to make them accountable for their learning and help them develop their skills for working with others. It is important that when seniors graduate they have developed skills in talking through material with peers, are skillful listeners, know how to build trust in a working relationship, and are knowledgeable as to how to provide leadership to group efforts.

Students are hesitant to speak French in the classroom. Some feel uncomfortable speaking French and feel that there is a lack the social support. In cooperative learning, each learner is held accountable for his or her own learning and is motivated to increase the learning of others.

Introduction

Cooperative Learning in the French as a Second Language Course

Students must obtain the experience of practicing the language by actually producing it. If they are not engaged in classroom activity, they will not benefit from the full experience of the language class. Cooperative learning groups encourage students to produce the target language, French, which is safe, due to not having to talk in front of the class, and fun to be a part of. Students who are willing to communicate are more successful in the French as a Second Language (FSL) course.

The power of cooperative learning is in the method of students working and teaching each other. As they teach and work together, they are in turn learning. When students are able to communicate the content themselves, successful learning is occurring within the Zone of Proximal Development. Scaffolding lessons brings them closer to the desired speech production and helps them develop confidence to carry on simple to complex conversation in class. As students develop language skills in the classroom, they feel more confident and then try language production on their own. As students work together, they can take more chances speaking the language.

Strategies and Activities to Captivate Students

I have created a variety of activities based on cooperative learning strategies, which help to engage students and encourage the use and learning of French. I feel that if students gain positive experience in producing the language, they will be more inclined to continue their FSL courses past grade nine and possibly until they graduate from high school.

Engaging students to actively participate in the FSL classroom requires an environment where students feel safe to explore activities. These activities meet their perceived ability and a level of social interdependence whereby students must rely on each other to complete an activity. Developing a feeling of safety in the classroom also allows for some student control so that they feel a sense of belonging and involvement in their learning.

The use of cooperative learning strategies will engage students and create a "safe" (social and psychological) environment to speak in the target language (FSL) more often in the classroom. Engaging students in discussion and encouraging them to communicate is a challenging task faced by many FSL teachers. For me, I am constantly trying to engage my students using different strategies and topics of study. Students want to learn how to communicate in the target language but are not being challenged by the work that is provided.

Introduction

(continued)

The new curriculum in Canada includes requirements based upon the Common European Framework. This new structure of assessment will take the focus away from the heavy emphasis on grammar and incorporate the grammatical structures into a more communicative approach. They need authentic learning experiences as well as lessons that will lead them to feeling confident and capable speaking French.

Teamwork Creates Individual Success

We can all learn from watching team sports. The way the coach directs, but does not get out on the field and play for their team; the manner in which teammates support each other; the flow of the game and movement on the field—each player watching his or her teammates' moves and making corrections to their own movements in response—and the opposition moving to improve their advantage in the game.

The support provided by teammates on the field can be implemented in the classroom. It must be encouraged by an effective coach, so that once out there (on their own in their respective groups), they can support and help each other. Coaches, or teachers, can provide feedback, extra practice, and/or a supportive presence, while cooperative learning groups take control of their own learning to reach the goal of the curriculum with a sense of ownership, pride, and personal achievement.

References

Bennett, B., C. Rolheiser-Bennett, and L. Stevahn. 1991. *Cooperative Learning: Where Heart Meets Mind.* Toronto, ON: Educational Connections.

Freeman, L. A. 2011. "An Examination of Socially Destructive Behaviors in Group Work." *Journal of Marketing Education 33* (1), 5–17.

Gillies, R. M. 2003. "The Behaviours, Interactions, and Perceptions of Junior High School Students During Small-Group Learning." *Journal of Educational Psychology 95* (1), 137–147.

Jensen, E. 2005. "Managing the Social Brain." In E. Jensen, *Teaching with the Brain in Mind* (pp. 94–101). Alexandria, VA: Association for Supervision and Curriculum Development.

Johnson, D. W. 2009. "An Educational Psychology Success Story: Social Interdependence Theory and Cooperative Learning." *Educational Researcher 38* (5), 365–379.

eferences

(continued)

Kagan, S. 2003. "A Brief History of Kagan Structures." *Kagan Online Magazine* (Spring).

Kagan, S. 2004. "From Lessons to Structures: A Paradigm Shift for 21st Century Education." *Kagan Online Magazine* (Spring).

Kagan, S. 2009. "Structures Optimize Engagement." In S. Kagan, *Kagan Cooperative Learning* (pp. I:37–I:49). San Clemente, CA: Kagan Publishing.

Kagan, S. and M. Kagan. 2009. *Kagan Cooperative Learning.* San Clemente, CA: Kagan Publishing.

Lopata, C. M. 2003. "Survey of Actual and Preferred Use of Cooperative Learning Among Exemplar Teachers." *The Journal of Educational Research 96* (4), 232–239.

McNeil, J. D. 2009. *Contemporary Curriculum: In Thought and Action.* Hoboken, NJ: John Wiley & Sons.

Millis, B. J. 2009. "Becoming an Effective Teacher Using Cooperative Learning: A Personal Odyssey." *Peer Review* (Spring): 17–21.

Shimazoe, J. A. 2010. "Group Work Can Be Gratifying: Understanding & Overcoming Resistance to Cooperative Learning." *College Teaching 58*, 52–57.

Slavin, R. E. 1995. *Research on Cooperative Learning and Achievement: What We Know, What We Need to Know.* Center for Research on the Education of Students Placed at Risk, John Hopkins University.

Smith, K. A., S. D. Sheppard, R. T. Johnson, and D. W. Johnson. 2005. "Pedagogies of Engagement: Classroom-Based Practices." *Journal of Engineering Education* (January): 1–15.

About the Author

Cynthia Chiupka-Jozin

I started teaching FSL in Moose Factory Ontario and migrated south to my hometown of Wawa where I have been teaching with the Algoma District School Board since 1998. I developed an interest in brain-compatible classrooms and differentiated instruction, which led me to read profusely on these subjects and use these methods in my many areas of teaching. Teaching in a small high school in Northern Ontario, Canada, has me teaching a variety of subjects which has included the social sciences, English, and French as a second language. I have held a variety of positions which have included Student Success and School Success Lead teacher. I am the department head for Languages, Arts, Healthy Active Living, and the Social Sciences. I am constantly in colleagues' classrooms to see how I can support them in their teaching. I have held many professional development workshops to introduce both primary and secondary teachers to cooperative learning strategies.

When I began teaching French, there was a feeling of something missing: students were filling in worksheets, but not communicating in French. The rows all faced the front of the classroom and speaking French was limited to answering homework questions or the odd partner-dialogue presentation. The classroom was bustling but many were off-task and feeling anxious about speaking French. So the challenge was how to get students to talk (in French) to classmates and not just me, the teacher! I realized that I was the only one moving around and engaged in the class—I was learning—but what about my students? How do I get them up and interacting in the class?! This led me to developing games and activities which would require students to interact in French. I came across a treasure chest of activities offered by Kagan Publishing. I went online, did a massive search and bought almost every book and took every graduate course offered by Kagan. Many of the activities were easily modified to be used in the French language classroom.

In a conversation with Miguel Kagan at the Cooperative Learning Winter Academy in Las Vegas, 2010, I mentioned to Miguel that Kagan Publishing really needed a French as a Second Language resource! The *Spanish* book was great, the *Second Language* book was helpful too—but French was needed! He told me to submit an idea, I did, and the rest is history!

I am also in the process of completing my Master's in Education. The focus is on cooperative learning in the French as a second language classroom.

My classrooms are now lively environments where I am constantly exploring new and differentiated instructional strategies.

# About the Author

This book is the work of many years and many students who were willing to partake in another of "Mrs. Jozin's activities!" I admit, some students were not so willing, but soon became convinced of the effectiveness once they saw how well they did on tests and projects as well as how easy it was to remember course material. I am indebted to all the great students I have had the pleasure of teaching, the many supportive colleagues who have themselves taken the leap to cooperative learning strategies at both the elementary and secondary levels.

My family has been my strength. My children, Bohdana, Davin and Annika, and husband, Steve, have encouraged me to continue on—have taken care of themselves while I wandered away to write or pursue my studies away from home.

Thank you to Miguel who guided me along this book design process and Becky Herrington, the wonderful editor who endured my stories of snow and cold in the spring as we worked through the editing journey. I am also indebted to former teachers who showed me that learning could and can be fun! Merci mille-fois to monsieur Claude Paradis, my former teacher, and vice-principal (retired as the principal of a French high school), who listened to my adventures and then spent time at his kitchen table reading through the rough draft for 'anglicisms' and 'things that just didn't sound right'! The discussions around French grammar and teaching French as a second language versus first language instruction were a lesson for both of us! To my new friend and Kagan trainer, who lives and works in Red Deer Alberta, (Canada!), Julia Rheaume, who spent time looking at the book from the trainer/French teacher perspectives: grand merci! I am indebted to you for your translation work and 'fresh eyes'!

This book will make the step to incorporating cooperative learning into your classroom easy, painless and fun for all! I always look forward to trying a new activity as much as my students do. They are the ones who always come to class asking, *"What are we doing today, Miss?"* and are always so helpful in letting me know what works and how we need to tweak something so that it works better. Many students come into my French class with a negative attitude due to their previous fears of speaking and learning French. This fear vanishes quickly once they are highly engaged and having fun!

Cynthia Chiupka-Jozin

Acknowledgments

Thanks go to Miguel Kagan for the feedback and opportunity to write this French book for Kagan. Many thanks to Cathy Nguyen for making this book come alive with the design and her contributions; Jeremie Rujanawech for contributing design; Becky Herrington for managing the publication; Alex Core for cover design and color; Erin Kant for illustrations; Julia Rheaume and Justin Frieman for reviewing the book; and Ginny Harvey for copyediting.

Chapter 1
Dans la communauté
(In the community)

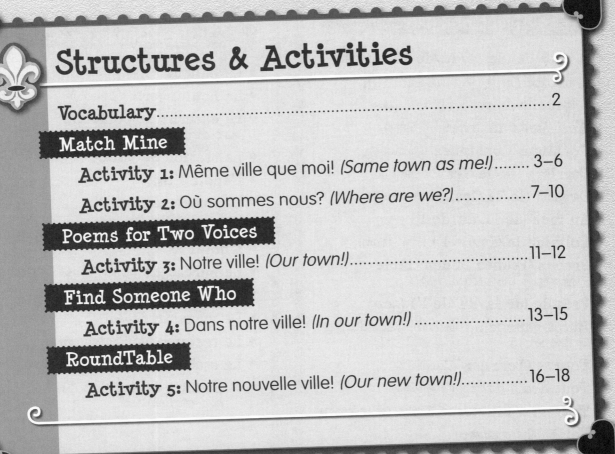

Structures & Activities

Vocabulaire

Dans la communauté
(In the community)

Les rues (Streets)

- **La rue** (Street)
- **L'avenue** (Avenue)
- **Le boulevard** (Boulevard)
- **Le chemin** (Road)

Les directions (Directions)

- **À côté de (de la/du/de l')** (Next to)
- **À droite** (On the right)
- **À gauche** (On the left)
- **C'est juste là** (It's right there)
- **Continue/Continuez** (Continue)
- **Derrière (le/la/les)** (Behind)
- **Devant (le/la/les)** (In front of)
- **En face (de la/du/de l')** (Across from)
- **Loin (de la/du/de l')** (Far from)
- **Prends/Prenez la deuxième** (Take/take the second one)
- **Près de (de la/du/de l')** (Near)
- **Rue à gauche...** (Take the second street on the left...)
- **Tourne/Tournez** (Turn)
- **Tout droit** (Straight ahead)
- **Traverse/Traversez** (Cross (go across))
- **Voilà** (There is/are)

La conversation (Talking)

- **Merci** (Thank you)
- **Où se trouve...** (Where is... located?)
- **Oui! Bien sûr!** (Yes! Of course!)
- **S'il vous plaît, pour aller au...?** (Can you tell me how I get to...?)

Les lieux (Places)

- **La banque** (Bank)
- **La boulangerie** (Bakery)
- **La caserne de pompiers** (Fire station)
- **La station de police** (Police station)
- **L'école** (School)
- **L'épicerie** (Grocery store)
- **L'hôpital** (Hospital)
- **L'hôtel** (Hotel)
- **Le bureau de poste** (Post office)
- **Le centre commercial** (Mall)
- **Le magasin** (Store)
- **Le restaurant** (Restaurant)
- **La station-service** (Service/gas station)
  - ❦ **Station de service** (Service/gas station)

Cooperative Learning & French • Chiupka-Jozin
Kagan Publishing • 1 (800) 933-2667 • www.KaganOnline.com

Même ville que moi!
(Same town as me!)

Match Mine

Partners sit on opposite sides of a barrier. Both partners have identical game boards (a map with streets) and game pieces (different buildings to be placed on the street map). One partner (the Sender) places buildings at different addresses on the map, then must describe to the other partner (the Receiver) where the buildings are located. Their goal is to use vocabulary and clear communication to make a match.

Steps

 Students Pair Up
The teacher creates a barrier between two students (this can be two folders connected by paper clips so that partners cannot see each other's creations).

 Distribute Materials
Each partner needs one game board (the street map) and a sheet with the game pieces (buildings). Students cut out the buildings so each student has an identical set of pieces. **Hint:** They may choose a small set of buildings to start out with: e.g., only three buildings to place—then work up to more as they improve their ability to describe locations to each other.

 Place Your Buildings
Behind the barrier, Partner A (the Sender) uses the game pieces to add to the street map.

 Make a Match
Partner A describes the placement of buildings to Partner B (Receiver). Partner A must clearly describe the information so that Partner B can match the exact location of each building. For example, Partner A directs Partner B to the location of school by saying, *"L'école est au coin de la rue Principale et l'avenue du Paradis"* or the address of a building: *La banque est au 104 rue Principale.*

(continued)

Même ville que moi!
(Same town as me!)

Match Mine

Steps

5 **Check and Celebrate**
Once the pair thinks they have a match, they compare their maps. They celebrate if they made a match and all buildings are in the same places.

6 **Switch Roles**
Partners switch roles so that Partner B now creates a new location for their buildings. Partner B is the Sender and Partner A is the Receiver.

Variations

- **Play as Partners.** Two players play together on one side of the barrier and two players play on the other side.

- **RoundTable.** As a team, students decide where the buildings will be located by taking turns adding buildings to the street map. They verbalize the locations as they take their turn adding buildings.

- **RoundTable Consensus.** Teams come up with the name of their town and four building locations by using RoundTable Consensus. All must contribute an idea and the team must all agree with the idea before they proceed. Other teammates can coach, helping with the French sentences!

Même ville que moi!
(Same town as me!)

Directions: Make one copy of the game board for each student playing (two game boards per pair).

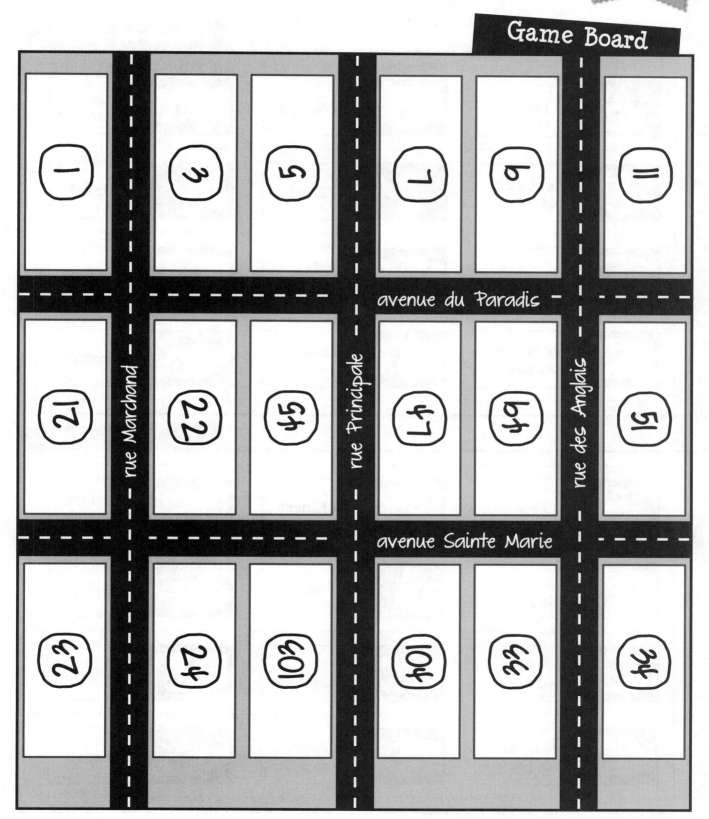

Game Board

avenue du Paradis

rue Marchand

rue Principale

rue des Anglais

avenue Sainte Marie

1   3   5   7   9   11
21   22   45   47   49   51
23   24   103   104   33   34

Même ville que moi!
(Same town as me!)

Directions: Teacher makes a copy of identical game pieces for each partner. Students cut out game pieces along the dotted line, making sure each partner has one of each piece.

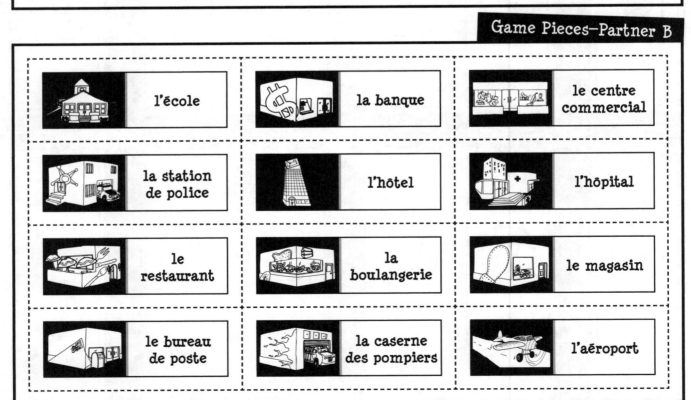

Game Pieces—Partner A

l'école	la banque	le centre commercial
la station de police	l'hôtel	l'hôpital
le restaurant	la boulangerie	le magasin
le bureau de poste	la caserne de pompiers	l'aéroport

Game Pieces—Partner B

l'école	la banque	le centre commercial
la station de police	l'hôtel	l'hôpital
le restaurant	la boulangerie	le magasin
le bureau de poste	la caserne des pompiers	l'aéroport

Où sommes nous?
(Where are we?)

Match Mine

Partners sit on opposite sides of a barrier. Both partners have identical game boards (a map with streets and buildings) and direction cards (directions to different locations.) One partner, the Sender, picks a direction card. The Sender must describe to the other partner, the Receiver, how to get to the location to which they are providing the directions. Their goal is to use vocabulary and clear communication to get to the correct location.

Steps

1 Students Pair Up
Create a barrier between two students (this can be two folders connected by paper clips so that partners cannot see each other's creations).

2 Distribute Materials
Each partner needs one game board (the street map). Each team needs a set of direction cards. Students cut out the direction cards and place them face down on the table.

3 Give the Directions
Behind the barrier, Partner A (the Sender) picks one of the directives cards.

4 Follow the Directions
Partner A reads the directions on the card to Partner B (Receiver). Partner A must clearly read the information so that Partner B can match the exact location to where they are being sent. Partner B must be able to ask questions to clarify where they are being sent. Partner A must be able to confirm or correct Partner B's movement to the given location.

5 Check and Celebrate
Once the pair thinks it has a match, Partner B announces where the pair has stopped. Partner A checks and they celebrate if they made it to the right place!

6 Switch Roles
Partners switch roles so that Partner B now selects a direction card. Partner B is now the Sender and Partner A is the Receiver.

(continued)

Où sommes nous?
(Where are we?)

Match Mine

Variations

- **Play as Partners.** Two players play together on one side of the barrier and two players play on the other side.

- **Create Your Own!** Players work together to create new directions to same or different locations and can play using their own directions.

- **RoundTable Consensus.** Teams come up with the directions to different locations by using RoundTable Consensus. All must contribute an idea and the team must all agree with the idea before they proceed. Other teammates can coach, helping with the French sentences.

- **How Can I Get There?** *S'il vous plaît, pour aller au...?* (Can you tell me how I get to...?) Teams create locations to find—asking directions from a specific location on the map.

- **Send-A-Problem.** Teams write directions to a location and send their directions to another team to find the location.

- **Dialogues!** *S'il vous plaît, pour aller au....?* (Can you tell me how I get to...?) Teams create conversations asking directions and giving the simplest route to the destination. This can be done as a partner activity for stronger students.

Où sommes nous?
(Where are we?)

Directions: Make one copy of the game board for each student playing (two game boards per pair).

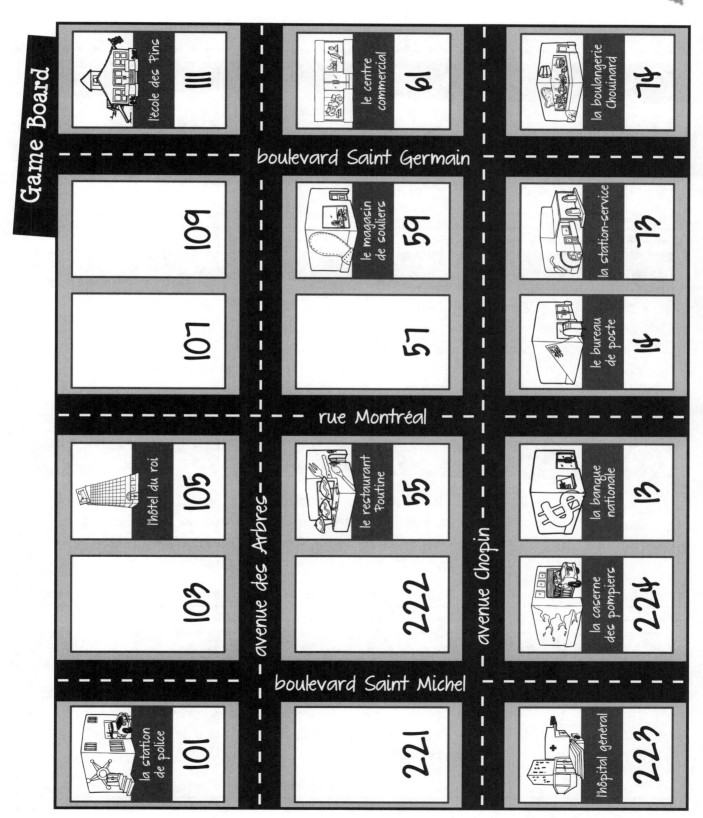

Où sommes nous?
(Where are we?)

Directions: Cut out Directives Cards along the dotted line and lay face down on the table for each team to use.

1  Directives #1

Commence à la station-service au 73 boulevard Saint Germain. Tourne à gauche sur le boulevard Saint Germain. Va tout droit jusqu'à l'avenue des arbres. Tourne à droite. Ta destination est à la gauche. Quelle est ta destination finale?

Destination finale: L'école des Pins au 111 avenue des arbres

2  Directives #2

Commence à l'école des Pins au 111 avenue des arbres. Tourne à droite sur l'avenue des arbres. Tourne à gauche sur le boulevard Saint Germain. Tourne à droite sur l'avenue Chopin. Traverse la rue Montréal. Ta destination est au coin à la droite. Quelle est ta destination finale?

Destination finale: le restaurant Poutine au 55 avenue Chopin

3  Directives #3

Commence à l'hôtel du roi au 105 avenue des arbres. Tourne à droite sur l'avenue des arbres. Tourne à gauche sur le boulevard Saint Michel. Continue tout droit. Traverse l'avenue Chopin. Ta destination est à la droite. Quelle est ta destination finale?

Destination finale: l'hôpital général au 223 boulevard Saint Michel

4  Directives #4

Commence au restaurant Poutine au 55 avenue Chopin. Tourne à gauche sur l'avenue Chopin. Traverse la rue Montréal. Puis traverse le boulevard Saint Germain. Ta destination est à la gauche. Quelle est ta destination finale?

Destination finale: le centre commercial au 61 avenue Chopin

Cooperative Learning & French • Chiupka-Jozin
Kagan Publishing • 1 (800) 933-2667 • www.KaganOnline.com

Notre ville!
(Our town!)

Poems for Two Voices

Partners create and present a poem *(cinquain)*. They recite it as one voice, the other voice, or both together.

Steps

1 Poem Design
The teacher explains to class the *cinquain* design of the poem they will create about their town (see the next page).

2 Partners Work Together
Partners write their poem together.

3 Label Parts
Partners label each line of their poem, A, B, or AB representing who will read each line (Partner A, Partner B or both partners together).

4 Practice Reading
Partners practice reading their poem.

5 Recite
Partners recite their poems to another pair or to the class.

6 Celebrate
Provide positive feedback and celebrate the successes of the class! *Bravo!*

(continued)

Notre ville!
(Our town!)

Directions: Partners create and present a poem they recite, using either one voice, taking turns, or both together.

Une strophe de cinq vers sur votre municipalité
Faites trois listes de mots:
• Liste A: les mots descriptifs: les adjectifs (propre, sécuritaire, sain, merveilleux)
• Liste B: les verbes qui se terminent en «er» (habiter, marcher, acheter, déménager, aimer, etc.)
• Liste C: les expressions qui décrivent votre municipalité (une ville vivante, une grande ville ou une petite ville)

Voici la formule pour votre poème.
Utilisez les mots de vos listes:
Ligne 1—1 mot de Liste A
Ligne 2—2 mots de Liste A
Ligne 3—3 mots de Liste B
Ligne 4—1 expression de Liste C
La ligne 5—écrivez le nom de votre communauté

Exemple: **MONTRÉAL**
Propre,
vieille, vivante.
Se promener, visiter, aimer,
une grande ville,
Montréal.

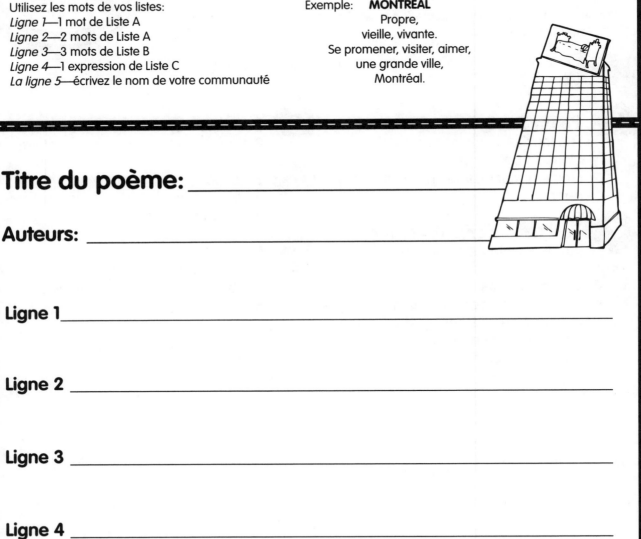

Titre du poème: _____

Auteurs: _____

Ligne 1 _____

Ligne 2 _____

Ligne 3 _____

Ligne 4 _____

Ligne 5 _____

Dans notre ville!
(In our town!)

Find Someone Who

Students circulate around the classroom forming and reforming pairs trying to "find someone who" knows the correct word to match the image.

Steps

> **Setup:** The teacher prepares the *Dans notre ville!* worksheet for students to use.

1 Distribute Worksheet
Students are given a worksheet to review vocabulary.

2 Students Pair Up
Students circulate around the class. Students keep a hand raised until they find a partner.

3 Ask
In pairs, students take turns asking partners for the correct vocabulary word to match the image on the worksheet: Partner A asks Partner B. Partner B responds. Partner A records the answer on his or her own worksheet and expresses appreciation. For example, the interaction between Partner A and

Partner B may look like:
A: *Qu'est-ce que c'est au #5?*
B: *C'est la caserne de pompiers.*
A: *Oui, excellent! Peux-tu mettre tes initiales?*

4 Check
Partner B checks and initials the answer.

5 Reverse Roles
Partner B now asks a question and Partner A responds. Partner B records the answer on his or her own worksheet and expresses appreciation.

(continued)

Dans notre ville!
(In our town!)

Find Someone Who

Steps

6 Check
Partner A checks and initials the answer.

7 Praise and Part
Partners high five—and raise a hand as they search for a new partner.

8 Repeat
Students repeat the process until their worksheets are complete.

9 Experts
Experts are students who have completed their worksheets. Once their worksheet is completed, they return to their desks and can be approached by others as a resource.

10 Teams Compare
Students compare answers in teams. If there is a disagreement or uncertainty, students simultaneously raise hands to ask a team question. Teacher responds to a team question.

Dans notre ville!
(In our town!)

Directions: Circulate around the classroom forming and re-forming pairs trying to "find someone who" can correctly identify the name of one of the images on the *Dans notre ville!* worksheet. Circle the correct answer provided by your partner and have your partner initial the answer.

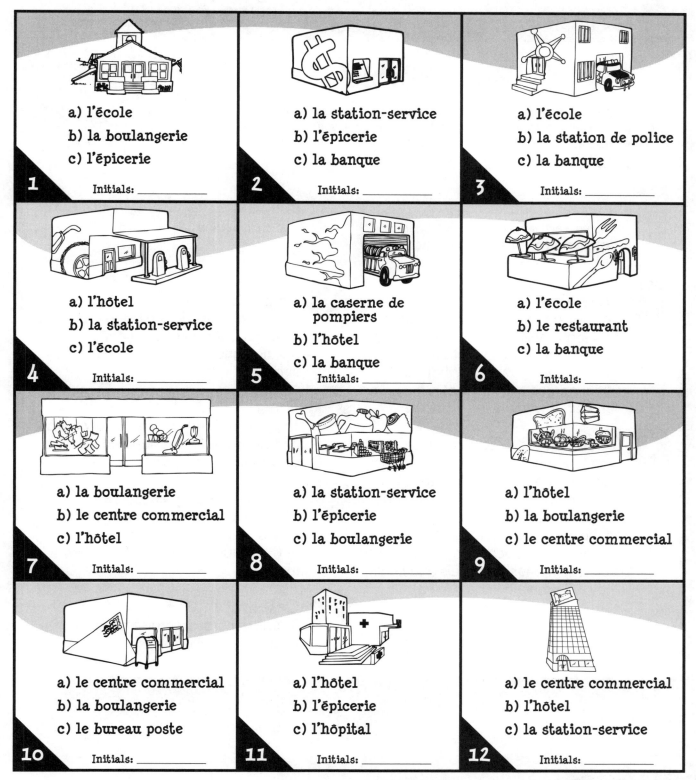

1
a) l'école
b) la boulangerie
c) l'épicerie
Initials: _____

2
a) la station-service
b) l'épicerie
c) la banque
Initials: _____

3
a) l'école
b) la station de police
c) la banque
Initials: _____

4
a) l'hôtel
b) la station-service
c) l'école
Initials: _____

5
a) la caserne de pompiers
b) l'hôtel
c) la banque
Initials: _____

6
a) l'école
b) le restaurant
c) la banque
Initials: _____

7
a) la boulangerie
b) le centre commercial
c) l'hôtel
Initials: _____

8
a) la station-service
b) l'épicerie
c) la boulangerie
Initials: _____

9
a) l'hôtel
b) la boulangerie
c) le centre commercial
Initials: _____

10
a) le centre commercial
b) la boulangerie
c) le bureau poste
Initials: _____

11
a) l'hôtel
b) l'épicerie
c) l'hôpital
Initials: _____

12
a) le centre commercial
b) l'hôtel
c) la station-service
Initials: _____

Notre nouvelle ville!
(Our new town!)

RoundTable

Teams create their own town, adding ideas using RoundTable. Teams then create a drawing/sketch of their new town adding details. After some planning, teams share their new towns with other teams, each student taking a turn sharing.

Steps

Setup: Each team has one pen/pencil and one paper. Have gridded chart paper and colored markers/pencils ready for drawing their new town.

1 New Town
The teacher announces to the class that teams will create their own new towns. (1) Start with what buildings will be in the new town. (2) What will the street names be? (3) What is the name for their new town?

2 Describe the Town
Team members plan their town. One paper and pen/pencil is used. Each team member records an idea and passes the paper and pen/pencil to the next team member. Team members each add to the list a type of building, names for streets and finally, they will name their new town.

3 Team Consensus
Team members decide using group consensus the location of each building and the location of each street.

4 Draw
Teams draw and label their new town on the gridded chart paper to be displayed in the classroom.

5 Teams Stand-N-Share
After deciding who will share what, teams partner up with another team and take turns describing their new towns.

6 Celebrate
Teams generously praise each other for their creativity!

(continued)

5

Notre nouvelle ville!
(Our new town!)

RoundTable

Variations

- **Town/City of the Future!** Team members use RoundRobin to describe what a city of the future will look like.

- **Simultaneous RoundTable.** Each student has a paper and pen. Each paper has one of the following titles: buildings, street names, town names, recreation spaces. Students simultaneously write on their paper, then pass the paper clockwise for the next teammate to add an idea. For example, the student with the "Recreation Spaces" paper may write "park" on the page and pass it. The next student may write "golf course." Students simultaneously write ideas matching the title of the paper. When done, they use their ideas to create their town.

Notre nouvelle ville!
(Our new town!)

Directions: Each team member helps plan the new town by creating a list of buildings, names of streets and other recreational places in the space below. Using team consensus, teams draw on the chart paper and decide on the location of buildings, names of streets, and the name of the town.

Chapter 2
Les vêtements et la température
(Clothing and temperature)

Structures & Activities

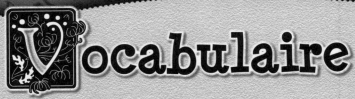

Vocabulaire

Les vêtements et la température
(Clothing and temperature)

Le temps (Weather)

- **Il fait beau** (It's nice out)
- **Il fait chaud** (It's hot out)
- **Il fait du brouillard** (It's foggy)
- **Il fait du soleil/il fait soleil** (It's sunny)
- **Il fait du vent/il vente** (It's windy)
- **Il fait frais/c'est frais** (It's cool)
- **Il fait froid** (It's cold out)
- **Il fait mauvais** (It's bad weather)
- **Il neige** (It's snowing)
- **Il pleut** (It's raining)
- **La température** (The weather)
- **Quel temps fait-il?** (What's the weather like?)
- **Qu'est-ce que tu portes quand...** (What do you wear when...)

Les vêtements (Clothing)

- **Des bottes** (Boots)
- **Des boucles d'oreille** (Earrings)
- **Des chaussettes** (Socks)
- **Des mitaines** (Mittens)
- **Des sandales** (Sandals)
- **Des souliers** (Shoes)
- **Je porte** (I wear, am wearing)
- **Un blouson** (Jacket)
- **Un chandail** (Sweater)
- **Un chapeau** (Hat)

- **Un collier** (Necklace)
- **Un costume** (Suit)
- **Un coupe-vent** (Windbreaker/jacket)
- **Un foulard** (Scarf)
- **Un imperméable** (Raincoat)
- **Un jean** (Jeans)
- **Un maillot de bain** (Bathing suit/swimsuit)
- **Un manteau** (Coat)
- **Un pantalon** (Pants)
- **Un pull** (Pullover)
  - ❧ **Un pullover** (Pullover)
- **Un short** (Shorts)
- **Un t-shirt** (T-shirt)
- **Une bague** (Ring)
- **Une chemise** (Shirt)
- **Une cravate** (Tie)
- **Une jupe** (Skirt)
- **Une robe** (Dress)

On s'habillé (Getting dressed)

- **Il/Elle met** (He or she puts on/is putting on)
- **Il/Elle porte** (He or she wears, is wearing)
- **Il fait du soleil** (It's sunny)
- **Je mets** (I put on)
- **Tu mets** (You put on/are putting on)
- **Tu portes** (You wear (singular-one person))

Les vêtements!
(Clothing!)

Flashcard Game

Partners proceed through three rounds as they quiz each other with flashcards, mastering the name of each piece of clothing to win cards.

Steps

Setup: The teacher gives each student his or her own set of flashcards.

1 Pair Up
In pairs, the Tutee gives his or her flashcards to the Tutor.

2 Round 1: Maximum Cues
The Tutor shows the question/picture on the first cards, asks, *"Qu'est-ce que c'est?"* and shows and reads the answer written on the back of the card. The Tutor then turns the card back over and again asks the question, *"Qu'est-ce que c'est?"* and the Tutee is to answer from memory.

3 Tutee Answers
If correct answer is given, Tutee wins the card back and receives delightful praise from the Tutor. If wrong, the Tutor shows the Tutee the answer side of the card and coaches. The card is then returned to the stack to try again later. **Hint:** Tutor can ask, *"How can I help you remember that?"* The pair can discuss ways of remembering answers.

4 Switch
When the Tutee wins all cards, partners switch roles. When the new Tutee wins all his or her cards, partners advance to Round 2.

5 Round 2: Few Cues
The process is repeated, except the Tutor shows only the picture side of the card and asks the Tutee to answer from memory. If wrong, the Tutor shows the Tutee the answer side, and card is returned to stack to try again.

(continued)

Les vêtements!
(Clothing!)

Flashcard Game

Steps

6 Round 3: No Cues
Again, the process is repeated, except the Tutor quizzes Tutee on each question without showing the Tutee the answer side of the card.

Hints

- Limit each round. Students can pick out no more than five cards to remember. If a student has won all cards, he or she can add more cards.

- Color-code cards for masculine and feminine words.

Variations

- **Hide the English.** To increase difficulty and avoid having students translate the vocabulary from English, hide the English terms by covering them up or whiting them out before copying the cards. If you cover up the English, be sure to teach students the French for each illustration in advance to ensure students know and use the target vocabulary.

- **Word Wall.** Enlarge the cards, cut them out, and post them on a classroom Word Wall to familiarize students with the chapter vocabulary.

Les vêtements!
(Clothing!)

Directions: Cut out the *Les vêtements!* cards along the dotted line. Then fold each in half so the clothing is on the front and the name is on the back. Keep picture and name on opposite sides.

1
Flashcard Game
Les vêtements!
jeans
Question

1
Flashcard Game
un jean
Réponse

2
Flashcard Game
Les vêtements!
t-shirt
Question

2
Flashcard Game
un t-shirt
Réponse

3
Flashcard Game
Les vêtements!
pants
Question

3
Flashcard Game
un pantalon
Réponse

4
Flashcard Game
Les vêtements!
boots
Question

4
Flashcard Game
des bottes
Réponse

Les vêtements!

(Clothing!)

Directions: Cut out the *Les vêtements!* cards along the dotted line. Then fold each in half so the clothing is on the front and the name is on the back. Keep picture and name on opposite sides.

5 — Les vêtements! — Flashcard Game — *sandals* — Question

5 — Flashcard Game — des sandales — Réponse

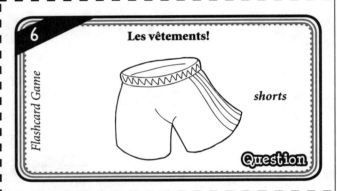

6 — Les vêtements! — Flashcard Game — *shorts* — Question

6 — Flashcard Game — un short — Réponse

7 — Les vêtements! — Flashcard Game — *shirt* — Question

7 — Flashcard Game — une chemise — Réponse

8 — Les vêtements! — Flashcard Game — *pullover* — Question

8 — Flashcard Game — un pull — Réponse

Les vêtements!
(Clothing!)

Directions: Cut out the *Les vêtements!* cards along the dotted line. Then fold each in half so the clothing is on the front and the name is on the back. Keep picture and name on opposite sides.

9 Flashcard Game — Les vêtements! — *bathing suit* — Question
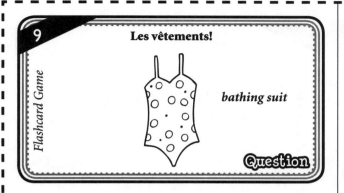

9 Flashcard Game — un maillot de bain — Réponse

10 Flashcard Game — Les vêtements! — *suit* — Question

10 Flashcard Game — un costume — Réponse

11 Flashcard Game — Les vêtements! — *tie* — Question
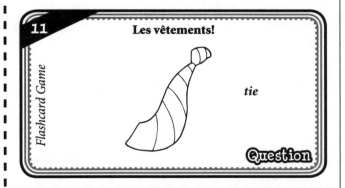

11 Flashcard Game — une cravate — Réponse

12 Flashcard Game — Les vêtements! — *dress* — Question

12 Flashcard Game — une robe — Réponse

Les vêtements!
(Clothing!)

Directions: Cut out the *Les vêtements!* cards along the dotted line. Then fold each in half so the clothing is on the front and the name is on the back. Keep picture and name on opposite sides.

13 Les vêtements!

Flashcard Game

skirt

Question

13

Flashcard Game

une jupe

Réponse

14 Les vêtements!

Flashcard Game

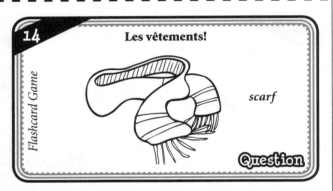

scarf

Question

14

Flashcard Game

un foulard

Réponse

15 Les vêtements!

Flashcard Game

sweater

Question

15

Flashcard Game

un chandail

Réponse

16 Les vêtements!

Flashcard Game

socks

Question

16

Flashcard Game

des chaussettes

Réponse

Les vêtements!
(Clothing!)

Directions: Cut out the *Les vêtements!* cards along the dotted line. Then fold each in half so the clothing is on the front and the name is on the back. Keep picture and name on opposite sides.

17   *Flashcard Game*   **Les vêtements!**

shoes

Question

17   *Flashcard Game*

des souliers

Réponse

---

18   *Flashcard Game*   **Les vêtements!**

coat

Question

18   *Flashcard Game*

un manteau

Réponse

---

19   *Flashcard Game*   **Les vêtements!**

raincoat

Question

19   *Flashcard Game*

un imperméable

Réponse

---

20   *Flashcard Game*   **Les vêtements!**

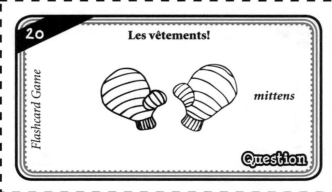

mittens

Question

20   *Flashcard Game*

des mitaines

Réponse

Flashcard Game

Les vêtements!
(Clothing!)

Directions: Cut out the *Les vêtements!* cards along the dotted line. Then fold each in half so the clothing is on the front and the name is on the back. Keep picture and name on opposite sides.

21 | Les vêtements!

Flashcard Game

hat

Question

21

Flashcard Game

un chapeau

Réponse

22 | Les vêtements!

Flashcard Game

← earrings

Question

22

Flashcard Game

des boucles d'oreille

Réponse

23 | Les vêtements!

Flashcard Game

ring

Question

23

Flashcard Game

une bague

Réponse

24 | Les vêtements!

Flashcard Game

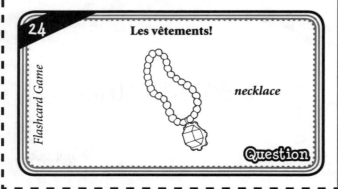

necklace

Question

24

Flashcard Game

un collier

Réponse

  Cooperative Learning & French • Chiupka-Jozin
Kagan Publishing • 1 (800) 933-2667 • www.KaganOnline.com

Quel temps fait-il?
(What's the weather like?)

Quiz-Quiz-Trade

Students quiz a partner, get quizzed by a partner, and then trade their cards to repeat the process with a new partner.

Steps

Setup: The teacher prepares the set of *Quel temps fait-il?* Question Cards for the class.

1 Distribute Cards
The teacher cuts out the cards and distributes them to the class, one card per student.

2 Students Pair Up
Students stand up, hand up, pair up, and face each other.

3 Students Quiz Each Other
Students take turns asking questions about the card. Questions can be simply, *"Quel temps fait-il?."* His or her partner responds by answering with the correct term for the weather. **Hint:** If his or her partner does not know the correct response, the answer is immediately shown to

him or her and then questioned again, *"Quel temps fait-il?."* Partners celebrate the correct response! Then, the other partner quizzes his or her partner about the card.

4 Trade Cards and Find New Partners
After partners have asked and answered each other's questions, they give each other a high five, trade cards, and find a new partner.

5 Continue Quizzing
This activity can go on for an allotted amount of time, or for a number of trades.

(continued)

Quel temps fait-il?
(What's the weather like?)

Quiz-Quiz-Trade

Variations

- **Increase Difficulty.** More advanced students can create questions based on true and false, or specific details on the card. For example:
    1. *"Quel temps fait-il?"* Pictured on the card is a person dressed in weather of a certain climate.
    2. Multiple-choice response.
    3. Questions generated by students about what a person would wear in that climate/weather.

- **Hide the English.** To increase difficulty and avoid having students translate the vocabulary from English, hide the English terms by covering them up or whiting them out before copying the cards. If you cover up the English, be sure to teach students the French for each illustration in advance to ensure students know and use the target vocabulary.

- **Word Wall.** Enlarge the cards, cut them out, and post them on a classroom Word Wall to familiarize students with the chapter vocabulary.

Quel temps fait-il?
(What's the weather like?)

Directions: Cut out the *Quel temps fait-il?* cards along the dotted line. Then fold the card in half so the question is on the front and the answer is on the back. Glue or tape cards together to keep the answers and questions on opposite sides.

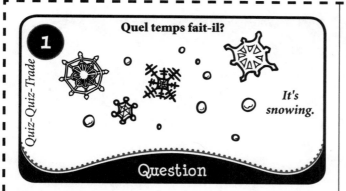

1 Quel temps fait-il?
It's snowing.
Quiz-Quiz-Trade
Question

1 Réponse
Il neige.
Quiz-Quiz-Trade

2 Quel temps fait-il?
It's windy.
Quiz-Quiz-Trade
Question

2 Réponse
Il fait du vent/
Il vente.
Quiz-Quiz-Trade

3 Quel temps fait-il?
It's bad weather.
Quiz-Quiz-Trade
Question

3 Réponse
Il fait mauvais.
Quiz-Quiz-Trade

4 Quel temps fait-il?
It's cool.
Quiz-Quiz-Trade
Question

4 Réponse
Il fait frais/
c'est frais.
Quiz-Quiz-Trade

Quel temps fait-il?
(What's the weather like?)

Directions: Cut out the *Quel temps fait-il?* cards along the dotted line. Then fold the card in half so the question is on the front and the answer is on the back. Glue or tape cards together to keep the answers and questions on opposite sides.

5 — Quiz-Quiz-Trade — Quel temps fait-il? — *It's nice out.* — Question

Réponse — **5** — Quiz-Quiz-Trade — Il fait beau.

6 — Quiz-Quiz-Trade — Quel temps fait-il? — *It's foggy.* — Question

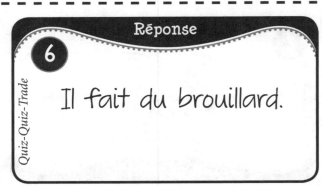

Réponse — **6** — Quiz-Quiz-Trade — Il fait du brouillard.

7 — Quiz-Quiz-Trade — Quel temps fait-il? — *It's hot out.* — Question

Réponse — **7** — Quiz-Quiz-Trade — Il fait chaud.

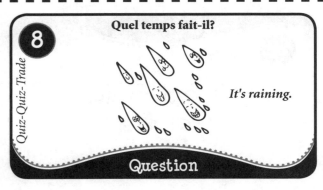

8 — Quiz-Quiz-Trade — Quel temps fait-il? — *It's raining.* — Question

Réponse — **8** — Quiz-Quiz-Trade — Il pleut.

Quel temps fait-il?
(What's the weather like?)

Directions: Cut out the *Quel temps fait-il?* cards along the dotted line. Then fold the card in half so the question is on the front and the answer is on the back. Glue or tape cards together to keep the answers and questions on opposite sides.

9 — Quiz-Quiz-Trade — **Quel temps fait-il?** — *It's cold out.* — Question

9 — Quiz-Quiz-Trade — Réponse — **Il fait froid.**

10 — Quiz-Quiz-Trade — **Quel temps fait-il?** — *It's windy.* — Question

10 — Quiz-Quiz-Trade — Réponse — **Il fait du vent/ Il vente.**

11 — Quiz-Quiz-Trade — **Quel temps fait-il?** — *It's bad weather.* — Question

11 — Quiz-Quiz-Trade — Réponse — **Il fait mauvais.**

12 — Quiz-Quiz-Trade — **Quel temps fait-il?** — *It's cool.* — Question

12 — Quiz-Quiz-Trade — Réponse — **Il fait frais.**

Quel temps fait-il?
(What's the weather like?)

Directions: Cut out the *Quel temps fait-il?* cards along the dotted line. Then fold the card in half so the question is on the front and the answer is on the back. Glue or tape cards together to keep the answers and questions on opposite sides.

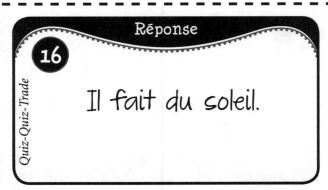

Cooperative Learning & French • Chiupka-Jozin
Kagan Publishing • 1 (800) 933-2667 • www.KaganOnline.com

Qu'est-ce que tu portes quand...?
(What do you wear when...?)

Pairs Compare

Pairs create a list of possible ideas or answers to a question or statement posed to them about what they would wear. Pairs pair and compare their answers with another pair. Finally, pairs work as a team to create additional answers or ideas.

Steps

Setup: The teacher gives each team two sheets of paper, one for each set of partners. Each team member has a pen or pencil to write his or her answers.

1 Teacher Provides a Question
The teacher provides the question, *"Qu'est-ce que tu portes quand il fait beau?"* Teacher provides Think Time. Teacher announces how long students will have to record their responses.

2 RallyTable
Shoulder partners share answers with each other: One partner states and records a response and then the other partner states and records a response. Pairs keep their answers "secret" from other pairs.

3 Teacher Calls Time
When time is up the teacher asks pairs to form a team of four.

4 Pairs Compare
Pairs pair and share their answers using RoundRobin. For each answer, the face partner in the other pair adds an answer to their list or checks it off if they already have it.

5 Team Challenge
As a team, students generate new answers, taking turns within pairs recording answers on their pair list.

(continued)

Qu'est-ce que tu portes quand...?
(What do you wear when...?)

Pairs Compare

Ideas

Here are a variety of questions you can use to have students generate many responses to practice their clothing vocabulary.

Qu'est-ce que tu portes quand...

1. Il fait beau?
2. Il fait froid?
3. Il neige?
4. Il pleut?
5. Il fait mauvais?
6. Tu vas à la plage?
7. Tu vas à un party?
8. Tu vas à une danse?
9. Tu vas en Alaska?
10. Tu vas en Jamaïque?

Qu'est-ce que tu portes quand...?
(What do you wear when...?)

Directions: In pairs, take turns creating a list of clothing items. Compare your list with another pair and see if you come up with the same items. Then, as a team, see if you can all come up with new clothing items.

Question ou phrase:

_____
_____
_____

1. _____
2. _____
3. _____
4. _____
5. _____
6. _____
7. _____
8. _____
9. _____
10. _____
11. _____
12. _____
13. _____
14. _____
15. _____

On voyage!
(We're traveling!)

Match Mine

Partners sit on opposite sides of a barrier. Both partners have identical game boards (a page with an open suitcase) and game pieces (clothing and accessories). One partner (the Sender) describes what they are packing in their suitcase. Their goal is to use vocabulary and clear communication to make a match, so that the Receiver has "packed" the same items.

Steps

Setup: The teacher copies the Suitcase game boards and game pieces for each student.

1 Students Pair Up
Create a barrier between two students (this can be two folders connected by paper clips so that partners cannot see each other's creations).

2 Distribute Materials
Each partner needs one game board (the suitcase) and a sheet with the game pieces (clothing and accessories). Students cut out the clothing/accessories so each student has an identical set of pieces.

3 Dress the Player
Behind the barrier, Partner A (the Sender) uses the game pieces to pack their suitcase.

4 Make a Match
Partner A describes what they have put into their suitcase to Partner B (the Receiver). Partner A must clearly describe the information so Partner B can match the packed suitcase exactly! Partner A states: *"Dans ma valise, je mets…"*

5 Check and Celebrate
Once the pair thinks they have a match, they compare suitcases. They celebrate if they made a match.

6 Switch Roles
Partners switch roles so that Partner A now packs their suitcase. Partner B is the Sender and Partner A is the Receiver.

(continued)

On voyage!
(We're traveling!)

Match Mine

Variations

- **Play as Partners.** Two players play together on one side of the barrier and two players play on the other side.

- **RoundTable.** As a team, students decide what to pack by taking turns adding items to the suitcase. They verbalize the items as they add them.

- **RoundTable Consensus.** Teams come up with the trip destination and weather of that location to pack the appropriate items by using RoundTable Consensus. All must contribute an idea and the team must all agree with the idea before they proceed. Other teammates can coach, helping with the French sentences.

On voyage!
(We're traveling!)

Directions: Make one copy of the game board for each student playing (two game boards per pair).

On voyage!
(We're traveling!)

4

Match Mine

Directions: The teacher makes a copy of identical game pieces for each partner. Students cut out game pieces along the dotted line, making sure each partner has one of each piece.

On s'habille!
(Getting dressed!)

Match Mine

Partners sit on opposite sides of a barrier. Both partners have identical game boards (a page with a boy in his boxers or a girl in her shorts and tee!) and game pieces (clothing and accessories). One partner (the Sender) dresses the boy or girl with clothing and accessories, then must describe to the other partner (the Receiver) how the person is dressed. Their goal is to use vocabulary and clear communication to make a match.

Steps

1 Students Pair Up
Create a barrier between two students (this can be two folders connected by paper clips so that partners cannot see each other's creations).

2 Distribute Materials
Each partner needs one game board (the person) and a sheet with the game pieces (clothing and accessories). Students cut out the clothing/accessories so each student has an identical set of pieces.

3 Dress the Boy or Girl
Behind the barrier, Partner A (the Sender) uses the game pieces to dress the boy or girl.

4 Make a Match
Partner A describes the outfit to Partner B (Receiver). Partner A must clearly describe the information so Partner B can match the boy's or girl's outfit exactly!

5 Check and Celebrate
Once the pair thinks they have a match, they compare persons. They celebrate if they made a match.

6 Switch Roles
Partners switch roles. Partner B now creates a new outfit and is the Sender, and Partner A is the Receiver.

(continued)

On s'habille!
(Getting dressed!)

Match Mine

Variations

• **Play as Partners.** Two players play together on one side of the barrier and two players play on the other side.

• **RoundTable.** As a team, students decide what the boy will wear by taking turns adding on items. They verbalize the clothing items as they dress the boy.

• **RoundTable Consensus.** Teams come up with the city the boy lives in and the weather in the city. The team uses RoundTable Consensus to take turns to dress the boy appropriately for the day. Each teammate takes a turn adding a piece of clothing and the team must all agree with the article of clothing before they proceed. Other teammates can coach, helping with the French Sentences!

On s'habille!
(Getting dressed!)

Directions: The teacher makes one copy of the game board for each student playing (two game boards per pair).

On s'habille!
(Getting dressed!)

Directions: The teacher makes a copy of identical game pieces for each partner. Students cut out game pieces along the dotted line, making sure each partner has one of each piece.

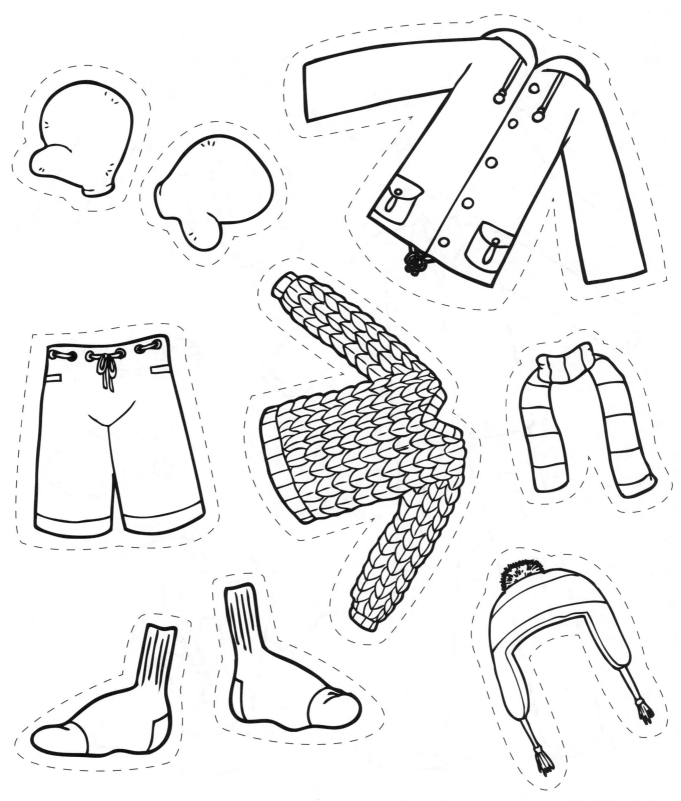

On s'habille!
(Getting dressed!)

Directions: The teacher makes a copy of identical game pieces for each partner. Students cut out game pieces along the dotted line, making sure each partner has one of each piece.

On s'habille!
(Getting dressed!)

Directions: The teacher makes a copy of identical game pieces for each partner. Students cut out game pieces along the dotted line, making sure each partner has one of each piece.

On s'habille!
(Getting dressed!)

Directions: The teacher makes one copy of the game board person for each student playing (two game boards per pair).

On s'habille!
(Getting dressed!)

Directions: The teacher makes a copy of identical game pieces for each partner. Students cut out game pieces along the dotted line, making sure each partner has one of each piece.

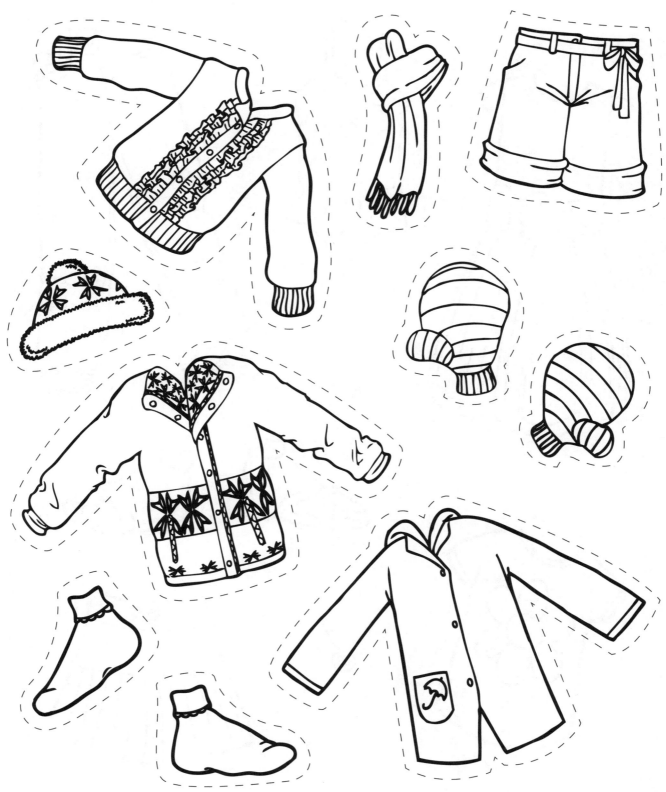

On s'habille!
(Getting dressed!)

Directions: The teacher makes a copy of identical game pieces for each partner. Students cut out game pieces along the dotted line, making sure each partner has one of each piece.

Je veux voyager!
(I want to travel!)

Jot Thoughts

Teammates cover the team table writing their ideas on slips of paper, writing ideas about what clothing they will pack to take with them on their trip!

Steps

Setup: Students each have many slips of paper (sticky notes or cut-up paper).

1 **The Teacher Names a Place**
Teacher names a location to travel to and provides Think Time. The teacher announces how much time the team has to brainstorm ideas.

2 **Teams Say and Write**
Teammates announce a piece of clothing they will pack for their trip in one idea per slip of paper.

3 **Place Your Papers**
When a teammate writes an item of clothing, his or her slip of paper is placed in the center of the team table so that everyone can see it (no overlapping slips of paper). Teams attempt to cover the table with the names of as many different pieces of clothing as they can think of.

(continued)

Je veux voyager!
(I want to travel!)

Jot Thoughts

Variations

- **Time/Limits.** Teacher can set a time for the activity or can determine the number of slips per student.

  Examples:
  Qu'est-ce que je mets dans ma valise? Je veux voyager…

  1. *En Alaska…*
  2. *En Jamaïque…*
  3. *Au Canada en décembre…*
  4. *En Floride…*
  5. *En Angleterre…*

- **Draw the Clothing.** Students draw the clothing item and say what it is as they place their slip of paper in the center of the table.

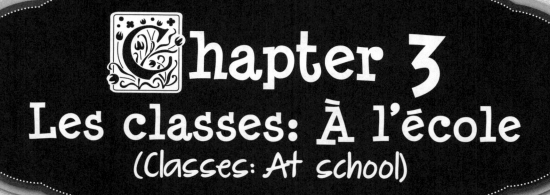

Chapter 3
Les classes: À l'école
(Classes: At school)

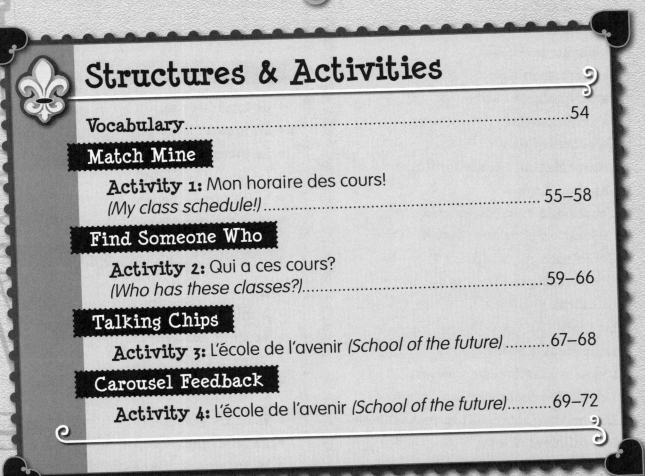

Structures & Activities

Vocabulaire

Les classes: À l'école
(Classes: At school)

Les sujets (Subjects)

- **La biologie** (Biology)
- **La chimie** (Chemistry)
- **La comptabilité** (Accounting)
- **La géographie** (History)
- **La musique** (Music)
- **La physique** (Physics)
- **La récréation** (Recess)
- **La technologie** (Technology)
- **La trigonométrie** (Trigonometry)
- **L'algèbre** (Algebra)
- **L'alimentation** (Food and nutrition)
- **L'anglais** (English)
- **L'économie** (Business/economics)
- **L'éducation physique** (Physical education)
- **L'électronique** (Electronics)
- **L'informatique** (Computer science)
- **Le calcul** (Calculus)
- **Le droit** (Law)
- **Le français** (French)
- **Les arts plastiques** (Visual arts)
- **Les études sociales** (Social studies)
- **Les mathématiques (Les maths)** (Math)
- **Les sciences** (Science)

Pour parler des cours
(Talking about classes)

- **J'ai...** (I have)
- **Quel cours as-tu?** (What class do you have?)
- **Quels cours as-tu ce semestre?** (What classes (courses) do you have this semester?)
- **Quand est-ce que tu as...** (When do you have...)

L'horaire (Schedule)

- **Le lundi** (Mondays)
- **Le mardi** (Tuesdays)
- **Le mercredi** (Wednesdays)
- **Le jeudi** (Thursdays)
- **Le vendredi** (Fridays)
- **Mon horaire** (My schedule)

L'heure (Time)

- **À** (At)
- **À midi** (At noon)
- **Aujourd'hui** (Today)
- **Demain** (Tomorrow)
- **Et demie** (Thirty e.g., Une heure et demie = one thirty = 1:30)
- **Et quart** (0:15)
- **Le lendemain** (The day after tomorrow)
- **Moins quart** (:45 = quarter to/quarter of e.g., Trois heures moins quart = quarter to three = 2:45)
- **Une heure** (One o'clock)

Mon horaire des cours!
(My class schedule!)

Match Mine

Partners sit on opposite sides of a barrier. Both partners have identical game boards (a page with a timetable). One partner (the Sender) plans their weekly class schedule, then must describe to the other partner (the Receiver) when they have classes. Their goal is to use vocabulary and clear communication to make a match.

Steps

1 Students Pair Up
Create a barrier between two students (this can be two folders connected by paper clips so that partners cannot see each other's creations).

2 Distribute Materials
Each partner needs one game board (the schedule) and a set of game pieces (the classes).

3 Create Your Schedule
Behind the barrier, Partner A (the Sender) creates their weekly class schedule.

4 Make a Match
Partner A describes their schedule to Partner B (Receiver). Partner A must clearly describe their information so that Partner B can match their partner's weekly class schedule.

5 Check and Celebrate
Once the pair thinks it has a match, the pair compares schedules. They celebrate if they made a match.

6 Switch Roles
Partners switch roles so that Partner B now creates a new weekly schedule and is the Sender, and Partner A is the Receiver.

(continued)

Mon horaire des cours!
(My class schedule!)

Match Mine

Variations

- **Play as Partners.** Two players play together on one side of the barrier and two players play on the other side.

- **RoundTable.** As a team, students decide what the weekly schedule will be by taking turns adding on items. They verbalize the classes as they place them on the schedule.

- **Create Your Own Schedule!** Students create their own timetable and pairs compare their schedules asking and answering questions in French.

Hint

- Laminate the class schedule game board (or put the page into a plastic page protector) so that students can write on the page with erasable markers.

Mon horaire des cours!
(My class schedule!)

Directions: The teacher makes one copy of the game board for each student playing (two game boards per pair).

	lundi	mardi	mercredi	jeudi	vendredi
8:00–9:00					
9:00–10:00					
10:00–11:00					
11:00–12:00					
12:00–1:00					
1:00–2:00					

Mon horaire des cours!
(My class schedule!)

Directions: The teacher makes a copy of identical game pieces for each partner. Students cut out game pieces along the dotted line, making sure each partner has one of each piece.

Game Pieces

Partner A		
	l'algèbre	la trigonométrie
l'électronique	le droit	la géographie
la musique	les sciences	la biologie
l'économie	la comptabilité	le calcul
le français	l'anglais	l'informatique
les arts plastiques	l'éducation physique	la chimie
la technologie	la physique	les mathématiques (les maths)

Game Pieces

		Partner B
l'algèbre	la trigonométrie	
l'électronique	le droit	la géographie
la musique	les sciences	la biologie
l'économie	la comptabilité	le calcul
le français	l'anglais	l'informatique
les arts plastiques	l'éducation physique	la chimie
la technologie	la physique	les mathématiques (les maths)

Qui a ces cours?
(Who has these classes?)

Find Someone Who

Students circulate around the classroom forming and reforming pairs trying to "find someone who" has the same class at the same time based on their schedule of classes.

Steps

Setup: The teacher prepares the *Qui a ces cours?* worksheet for students to use. Copy enough different schedules for the class. Schedules can be printed on different colored paper.

1 Distribute Worksheet
Students are each given one of the six class schedules provided. Give different students different schedules to mix it up.

2 Students Pair Up
Students circulate around the class. Students keep a hand raised until they find a partner.

3 Ask
In pairs, students take turns asking a question about their schedule: For example, *"À quelle heure est-ce que tu as l'anglais?"* *"Quand as-tu l'éducation physique?"* *"Est-ce que tu as le français à neuf heures?"* or more specifically: *"Lundi matin, as-tu*

l'anglais à huit heures?" If Partner B answers, "the same time" *"Oui, j'ai le français à neuf heures"* (they both have that class at the same time), Partner A records Partner B's name on his or her own worksheet and expresses appreciation.

4 Check
Partner B checks and initials where Partner A wrote his or her name.

5 Reverse Roles
Partner B now asks a question and Partner A responds. Partner B records Partner A's name on his or her own worksheet and expresses appreciation.

(continued)

Qui a ces cours?
(Who has these classes?)

Find Someone Who

6 **Check**
Partner A checks and initials where Partner B wrote his or her name.

7 **Praise and Part**
Partners high five and raise a hand as they search for a new partner.

8 **Repeat**
Students repeat the process until their worksheets are complete.

9 **Experts**
Experts are students who have completed their worksheets. Once their worksheet is completed, they return to their desks and can be approached by others as a resource.

10 **Teams Compare**
Students compare answers in teams. Teams see who has similar class schedules by asking and answering in French!

Qui a ces cours?
(Who has these classes?)

Directions: Students circulate around the classroom forming and re-forming pairs trying to "find someone who" has similar classes at the same time. Students write their partner's name, partner checks and initials the box where they have the same class.

1.	lundi	mardi	mercredi	jeudi	vendredi
8:00–9:00	**l'anglais** nom de partenaire _____ initiales	**l'anglais** nom de partenaire _____ initiales	**l'anglais** nom de partenaire _____ initiales	**l'anglais** nom de partenaire _____ initiales	**l'anglais** nom de partenaire _____ initiales
9:00–10:00	**les mathématiques** nom de partenaire _____ initiales	**les mathématiques** nom de partenaire _____ initiales	**les mathématiques** nom de partenaire _____ initiales	**les mathématiques** nom de partenaire _____ initiales	**les mathématiques** nom de partenaire _____ initiales
10:00–11:00	**la géographie** nom de partenaire _____ initiales	**la géographie** nom de partenaire _____ initiales	**la géographie** nom de partenaire _____ initiales	**la géographie** nom de partenaire _____ initiales	**la géographie** nom de partenaire _____ initiales
11:00–12:00	**l'éducation physique** nom de partenaire _____ initiales	**l'éducation physique** nom de partenaire _____ initiales	**l'éducation physique** nom de partenaire _____ initiales	**l'éducation physique** nom de partenaire _____ initiales	**l'éducation physique** nom de partenaire _____ initiales
12:00–1:00	**DÎNER** nom de partenaire _____ initiales	**DÎNER** nom de partenaire _____ initiales	**DÎNER** nom de partenaire _____ initiales	**DÎNER** nom de partenaire _____ initiales	**DÎNER** nom de partenaire _____ initiales
1:00–2:00	**le français** nom de partenaire _____ initiales	**le français** nom de partenaire _____ initiales	**le français** nom de partenaire _____ initiales	**le français** nom de partenaire _____ initiales	**le français** nom de partenaire _____ initiales

Qui a ces cours?
(Who has these classes?)

Directions: Students circulate around the classroom forming and re-forming pairs trying to "find someone who" has similar classes at the same time. Students write their partner's name, partner checks and initials the box where they have the same class.

2.	lundi	mardi	mercredi	jeudi	vendredi
8:00—9:00	**les mathématiques** nom de partenaire initiales	**les mathématiques** nom de partenaire initiales	**les mathématiques** nom de partenaire initiales	**les mathématiques** nom de partenaire initiales	**les mathématiques** nom de partenaire initiales
9:00—10:00	**l'éducation physique** nom de partenaire initiales	**l'éducation physique** nom de partenaire initiales	**l'éducation physique** nom de partenaire initiales	**l'éducation physique** nom de partenaire initiales	**l'éducation physique** nom de partenaire initiales
10:00—11:00	**le français** nom de partenaire initiales	**le français** nom de partenaire initiales	**le français** nom de partenaire initiales	**le français** nom de partenaire initiales	**le français** nom de partenaire initiales
11:00—12:00	**la géographie** nom de partenaire initiales	**la géographie** nom de partenaire initiales	**la géographie** nom de partenaire initiales	**la géographie** nom de partenaire initiales	**la géographie** nom de partenaire initiales
12:00—1:00	**DÎNER** nom de partenaire initiales	**DÎNER** nom de partenaire initiales	**DÎNER** nom de partenaire initiales	**DÎNER** nom de partenaire initiales	**DÎNER** nom de partenaire initiales
1:00—2:00	**l'anglais** nom de partenaire initiales	**l'anglais** nom de partenaire initiales	**l'anglais** nom de partenaire initiales	**l'anglais** nom de partenaire initiales	**l'anglais** nom de partenaire initiales

Qui a ces cours?
(Who has these classes?)

Directions: Students circulate around the classroom forming and re-forming pairs trying to "find someone who" has similar classes at the same time. Students write their partner's name, partner checks and initials the box where they have the same class.

3.	lundi	mardi	mercredi	jeudi	vendredi
8:00–9:00	**les mathématiques** nom de partenaire initiales	**les mathématiques** nom de partenaire initiales	**les mathématiques** nom de partenaire initiales	**les mathématiques** nom de partenaire initiales	**les mathématiques** nom de partenaire initiales
9:00–10:00	**la géographie** nom de partenaire initiales	**la géographie** nom de partenaire initiales	**la géographie** nom de partenaire initiales	**la géographie** nom de partenaire initiales	**la géographie** nom de partenaire initiales
10:00–11:00	**le français** nom de partenaire initiales	**le français** nom de partenaire initiales	**le français** nom de partenaire initiales	**le français** nom de partenaire initiales	**le français** nom de partenaire initiales
11:00–12:00	**l'anglais** nom de partenaire initiales	**l'anglais** nom de partenaire initiales	**l'anglais** nom de partenaire initiales	**l'anglais** nom de partenaire initiales	**l'anglais** nom de partenaire initiales
12:00–1:00	**DÎNER** nom de partenaire initiales	**DÎNER** nom de partenaire initiales	**DÎNER** nom de partenaire initiales	**DÎNER** nom de partenaire initiales	**DÎNER** nom de partenaire initiales
1:00–2:00	**l'éducation physique** nom de partenaire initiales	**l'éducation physique** nom de partenaire initiales	**l'éducation physique** nom de partenaire initiales	**l'éducation physique** nom de partenaire initiales	**l'éducation physique** nom de partenaire initiales

Qui a ces cours?
(Who has these classes?)

Directions: Students circulate around the classroom forming and re-forming pairs trying to "find someone who" has similar classes at the same time. Students write their partner's name, partner checks and initials the box where they have the same class.

4.	lundi	mardi	mercredi	jeudi	vendredi
8:00–9:00	**le français** nom de partenaire initiales	**le français** nom de partenaire initiales	**le français** nom de partenaire initiales	**le français** nom de partenaire initiales	**le français** nom de partenaire initiales
9:00–10:00	**les mathématiques** nom de partenaire initiales	**les mathématiques** nom de partenaire initiales	**les mathématiques** nom de partenaire initiales	**les mathématiques** nom de partenaire initiales	**les mathématiques** nom de partenaire initiales
10:00–11:00	**la géographie** nom de partenaire initiales	**la géographie** nom de partenaire initiales	**la géographie** nom de partenaire initiales	**la géographie** nom de partenaire initiales	**la géographie** nom de partenaire initiales
11:00–12:00	**l'anglais** nom de partenaire initiales	**l'anglais** nom de partenaire initiales	**l'anglais** nom de partenaire initiales	**l'anglais** nom de partenaire initiales	**l'anglais** nom de partenaire initiales
12:00–1:00	**DÎNER** nom de partenaire initiales	**DÎNER** nom de partenaire initiales	**DÎNER** nom de partenaire initiales	**DÎNER** nom de partenaire initiales	**DÎNER** nom de partenaire initiales
1:00–2:00	**l'éducation physique** nom de partenaire initiales	**l'éducation physique** nom de partenaire initiales	**l'éducation physique** nom de partenaire initiales	**l'éducation physique** nom de partenaire initiales	**l'éducation physique** nom de partenaire initiales

Qui a ces cours?
(Who has these classes?)

Directions: Students circulate around the classroom forming and re-forming pairs trying to "find someone who" has similar classes at the same time. Students write their partner's name, partner checks and initials the box where they have the same class.

5.	lundi	mardi	mercredi	jeudi	vendredi
8:00–9:00	**le français** nom de partenaire initiales	**le français** nom de partenaire initiales	**le français** nom de partenaire initiales	**le français** nom de partenaire initiales	**le français** nom de partenaire initiales
9:00–10:00	**la géographie** nom de partenaire initiales	**la géographie** nom de partenaire initiales	**la géographie** nom de partenaire initiales	**la géographie** nom de partenaire initiales	**la géographie** nom de partenaire initiales
10:00–11:00	**les mathématiques** nom de partenaire initiales	**les mathématiques** nom de partenaire initiales	**les mathématiques** nom de partenaire initiales	**les mathématiques** nom de partenaire initiales	**les mathématiques** nom de partenaire initiales
11:00–12:00	**l'éducation physique** nom de partenaire initiales	**l'éducation physique** nom de partenaire initiales	**l'éducation physique** nom de partenaire initiales	**l'éducation physique** nom de partenaire initiales	**l'éducation physique** nom de partenaire initiales
12:00–1:00	**DÎNER** nom de partenaire initiales	**DÎNER** nom de partenaire initiales	**DÎNER** nom de partenaire initiales	**DÎNER** nom de partenaire initiales	**DÎNER** nom de partenaire initiales
1:00–2:00	**l'anglais** nom de partenaire initiales	**l'anglais** nom de partenaire initiales	**l'anglais** nom de partenaire initiales	**l'anglais** nom de partenaire initiales	**l'anglais** nom de partenaire initiales

Qui a ces cours?
(Who has these classes?)

Directions: Students circulate around the classroom forming and re-forming pairs trying to "find someone who" has similar classes at the same time. Students write their partner's name, partner checks and initials the box where they have the same class.

6.	lundi	mardi	mercredi	jeudi	vendredi
8:00–9:00	**l'anglais** nom de partenaire initiales	**l'anglais** nom de partenaire initiales	**l'anglais** nom de partenaire initiales	**l'anglais** nom de partenaire initiales	**l'anglais** nom de partenaire initiales
9:00–10:00	**l'éducation physique** nom de partenaire initiales	**l'éducation physique** nom de partenaire initiales	**l'éducation physique** nom de partenaire initiales	**l'éducation physique** nom de partenaire initiales	**l'éducation physique** nom de partenaire initiales
10:00–11:00	**les mathématiques** nom de partenaire initiales	**les mathématiques** nom de partenaire initiales	**les mathématiques** nom de partenaire initiales	**les mathématiques** nom de partenaire initiales	**les mathématiques** nom de partenaire initiales
11:00–12:00	**la géographie** nom de partenaire initiales	**la géographie** nom de partenaire initiales	**la géographie** nom de partenaire initiales	**la géographie** nom de partenaire initiales	**la géographie** nom de partenaire initiales
12:00–1:00	**DÎNER** nom de partenaire initiales	**DÎNER** nom de partenaire initiales	**DÎNER** nom de partenaire initiales	**DÎNER** nom de partenaire initiales	**DÎNER** nom de partenaire initiales
1:00–2:00	**le français** nom de partenaire initiales	**le français** nom de partenaire initiales	**le français** nom de partenaire initiales	**le français** nom de partenaire initiales	**le français** nom de partenaire initiales

L'école de l'avenir
(School of the future)

Talking Chips

Students take turns in teams, sharing their ideas to describe a futuristic school.

Steps

Setup: The teacher gives team member an equal number of Talking Chips. These may be pieces of paper, bingo chips, or the ready-made talking chips provided.

1 Teacher Provides Topic
The teacher challenges students to think about what school will be like in the future. What courses will be offered? What will it look like? What will be the daily schedule?

2 Share Ideas
One team member places a chip in the center of the table and begins the discussion.

3 Keep the Discussion Going
Team members use chips to continue the discussion. Each time a member has an idea, he or she places one of

his or her Talking Chips on the team table. Players can make as many statements as they have Talking Chips, but once they have used up their Talking Chips, they must wait until other team members have used up theirs.

4 Chips Used Up
Once all team Talking Chips have been placed on the team table, students collect chips and can continue their discussion. **Hint:** All students must have used up all of their Talking Chips before collecting chips and continuing the discussion.

L'école de l'avenir
(School of the future)

Directions: Cut out the *Mon tour à parler* chips along the dotted line. Give a minimum of two chips to each student for discussion to play *"Mon tour à parler."*

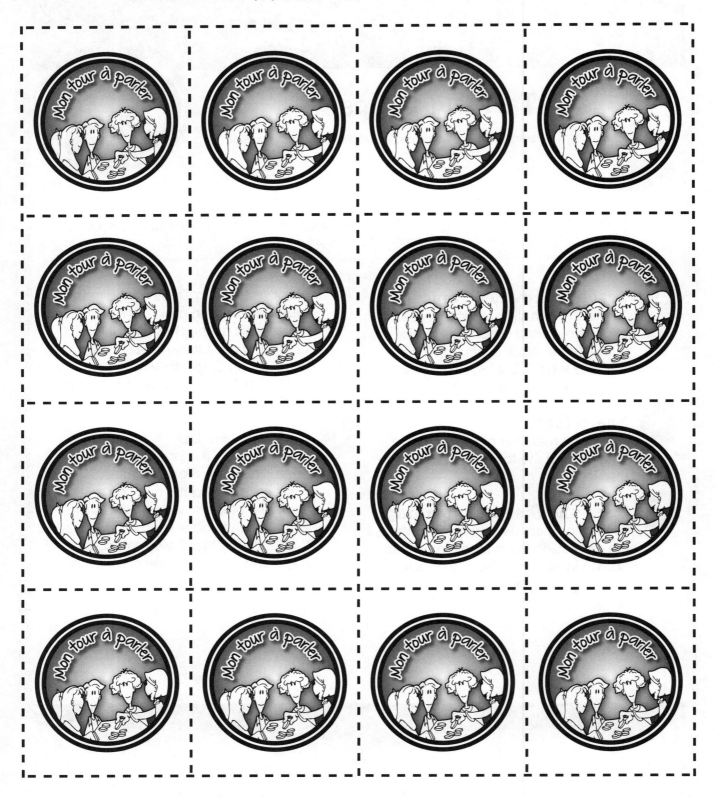

L'école de l'avenir
(School of the future)

Carousel Feedback

Teams rotate from project to project to leave feedback for other teams about their design of a futuristic school.

Steps

Setup: From the Talking Chips activity, teams design their "school of the future," drawing a floor plan, perhaps how it looks on the outside, the daily timetable for students, and any other features or benefits they feel would create an imaginative school of the future. Each team has a Feedback Form near its project for other teams to record comments.

1 Teams Stand
Teams stand in front of their projects.

2 Teams Rotate
Teams rotate clockwise to the next project.

3 Teams Discuss
For a specified amount of time, teams discuss their reactions to the other team's project, with no writing.

4 Team Records Responses
Team member #1 records feedback on the Feedback form. Students are encouraged to include positive comments (e.g., comments relating to the success criteria of the assignment).

5 Teacher Calls Time
Teacher indicates that time is up!

6 Teams Rotate
Teams move clockwise to the next team project, discuss, and give feedback on the project. A new recorder is selected for each round.

(continued)

L'école de l'avenir
(School of the future)

Carousel Feedback

7 **Teams Continue**
Teams continue to rotate, observe, discuss and record comments until they rotate back to their own project, or until teacher calls time.

8 **Teams Review**
Teams review the feedback they received from the other teams.

Variation

• **Theme Schools.** The assignment could be about a school based on a theme. For example, clown school, athletic school, school of the arts, school in the outdoors, etc.

L'école de l'avenir
(School of the future)

Directions: In teams, create a School of the Future floorplan. Students will circulate around the room and provide feedback about each of the posters.

L'école de l'avenir

L'école de l'avenir
(School of the future)

Directions: Teams use this Commentaires Form when rotating from project to project to leave feedback for other teams about their floorplan.

Commentaires

Chapter 4

Qu'est-ce que tu aimes manger?
(What do you like to eat?)

Structures & Activities

Vocabulaire

Qu'est-ce que tu aimes manger?
(What do you like to eat?)

Chapter 4

La nourritures (Food)

- **La boisson** (Drink)
- **La crevette** (Shrimp)
- **La glace** (Ice cream)
  - ❦ **La crème glacée** (Ice cream)
- **La pizza** (Pizza)
- **La poutine** (Poutine)
- **La soupe** (Soup)
- **Le boeuf** (Beef)
- **Le café** (Coffee)
- **Le dessert** (Dessert)
- **Le homard** (Lobster)
- **Les huîtres** (Oysters)
- **Le jus d'orange/de pomme/ de raisin** (orange juice/apple/grape)
- **Le poisson** (Fish)
- **Le poulet** (Chicken)
- **Le sandwich roulé** (Wrap)
- **Le taco** (Taco)
- **Le thé** (Tea)
- **La viande** (Meat)
- **L'écrivisse** (Crawfish/crayfish)
- **Le frappé aux fruits** (Smoothie)
  - ❦ **Le yogourt fouetté** (Smoothie)
- **Le lait frappé** (Milkshake)
- **Les fruits** (Fruit)

- **Les fruits de mer** (Seafood)
- **Les légumes** (Vegetables)
- **Les rouleaux de printemps** (Spring rolls)
- **Le sandwich** (Sub sandwich)
  - ❦ **Le sous-marin** (Sub sandwich)

Les repas (Meals)

- **Le petit déjeuner** (Breakfast)
  - ❦ **Le déjeuner** (Breakfast)
- **Le déjeuner** (Lunch)
  - ❦ **Le dîner** (Lunch)
- **Le dîner** (Supper)
  - ❦ **Le souper** (Supper)
- **Qu'est-ce que tu veux manger?** (What do you want to eat?)
- **Aimes-tu manger...?** (Do you like to eat...?)

Les adverbes de quantité
(Adverbs of quantity)

- **Assez (de)** (Enough (of)
- **Beaucoup (de)** (A lot (of)
- **Je veux manger** (I want to eat)
- **Un peu (de)** (A little (of))

Qu'est-ce que tu manges?
(What do you eat?)

Pairs Compare

The teacher asks students a question about food such as, *"What do you eat for breakfast?"* Pairs create a list of possible food items. Pairs pair and compare their answers with another pair. Finally, pairs work as a team to create additional answers or ideas.

Steps

 Teacher Provides Question
The teacher provides a question or statement about eating to which students can respond in a variety of ways. For example, *"Qu'est-ce que tu manges pour le souper?"* Teacher provides Think Time. Teacher announces how much time students will have to record responses.

 RallyTable
Shoulder partners create a list of answers. One partner provides a response by writing it down, passes the paper to their partner who writes their response. Pairs continue adding ideas one at a time. Pairs keep their answers "secret" from other pairs.

 Teacher Calls Time
When time is up, the teacher asks pairs to pair up with the other pair on their team.

 Pairs Compare
Pairs pair up and take turns, sharing their answers using RoundRobin. For each answer, the face partner in the other pair adds the answer to that pair's list, or checks it off if they already have it.

 Team Challenge
As a team, students generate new answers, taking turns within pairs recording answers on their pair list.

(continued)

(continued)

Activity 1

Qu'est-ce que tu manges?
(What do you eat?)

Pairs Compare

Variation

- **Use Dictionary.** Students look up new food words in the dictionary to help generate new answers!

Ideas

Here are a variety of questions you can use to have students generate many responses to practice their food vocabulary.

1. *Qu'est-ce que tu manges pour le déjeuner?*

2. *Qu'est-ce que tu manges pour le souper?*

3. *Qu'est-ce que tu manges pour le dîner?*

4. *Qu'est-ce que tu mets sur ta pizza?*

5. *Quelles sont les variétés de sous-marins?*

6. *Qu'est-ce que tu aimes sur ton sous-marin?*

7. *Qu'est-ce que tu manges au restaurant?*

Cooperative Learning & French • Chiupka-Jozin
Kagan Publishing • 1 (800) 933-2667 • www.KaganOnline.com

Qu'est-ce que tu manges?
(What do you eat?)

Directions: In pairs, take turns creating a list of food items. Compare your list with another pair and see if you come up with the same items. Then, as a team, see if you can all come up with new food items.

Teacher Question: _____

_____

_____

Réponses

1. _____
2. _____
3. _____
4. _____
5. _____
6. _____
7. _____
8. _____
9. _____
10. _____
11. _____
12. _____
13. _____
14. _____
15. _____

Qu'est-ce que tu manges?
(What do you eat?)

Talking Chips

Students talk about what they want to eat using Talking Chips to take turns sharing their ideas.

Steps

Setup: The teacher gives each teammate an equal number of Talking Chips. These may be pieces of paper, bingo chips, or the ready-made Talking Chips provided.

1 Teacher Announces Topic
Teacher provides topic about food—(e.g., What Do You Like to Eat?; Names of Famous Restaurants; Names of Fruits or Vegetables; Ingredients You Like on Your Pizza).

 2 Think and Share
One student places a chip in center of the team table to begin the discussion.

3 Take Turns
Students use chips to continue the discussion. Any team member can place a chip down when he or she has something to say. There is no set order as to when students can share their ideas.

 4 Chips Used Up
When team members use all of their Talking Chips, they have to wait until other team members have used all of their own chips. Students then collect chips and continue their discussion.

Variation

• **Set Time Limit.** The teacher sets a time limit like three minutes or sets a number of chips each student must use. For example, each student receives three chips and each must contribute three times before the discussion is over.

Qu'est-ce que tu manges?

(What do you eat?)

Directions: Cut out the *Mon tour à parler* chips along the dotted line. Give a minimum of two chips to each student for discussion to play *"Mon tour à parler."*

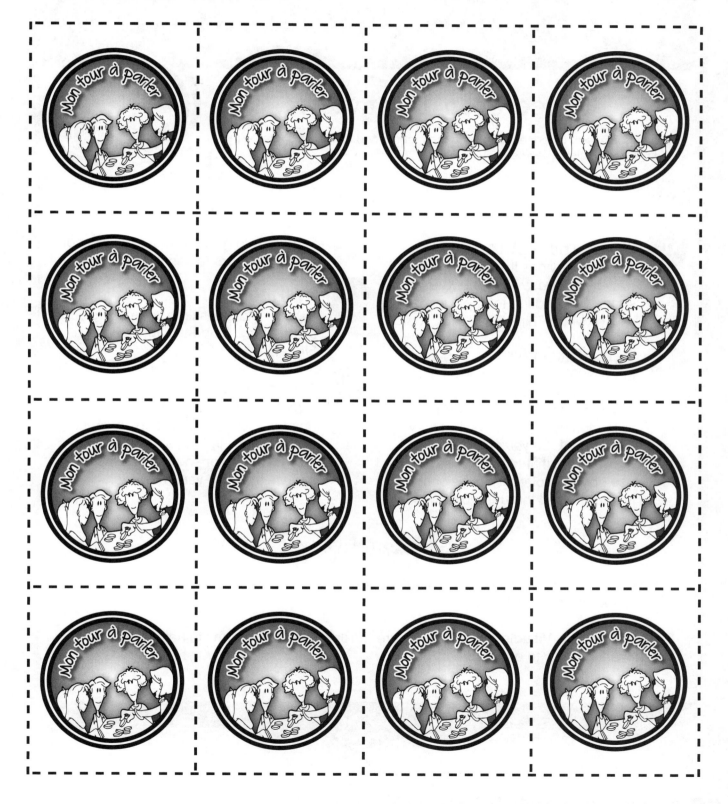

Qu'est-ce que tu veux manger?
(What do you want to eat?)

Three-Step Interview

Students interview a partner about food preferences and then each shares with teammates what they learned.

Steps

 1 Topic and Think Time
Teacher provides the interview topic *(Qu'est-ce que tu veux manger?)*, states the duration for the interview, and provides Think Time.

 2 Pairs Interview
In pairs, Student A interviews Student B. Student A asks, *"Qu'est-ce que tu veux manger?"* and Student B responds by explaining what they want to eat: *"Je veux manger…"*.
Remember: if Student B does not use up the allotted time, he or she is encouraged through questions by

Student A to give more details. It is not Student A's turn to share until time is up!

 3 Switch
Teacher indicates time is up. Pairs switch roles. Student B interviews Student A.

 4 Share Responses Using RoundRobin
Pairs pair up to form groups of four. Each student, in turn, shares with the team what he or she learned in the interview. *"Il/Elle veut manger…"*

Variations

• **Record.** Use the provided Recording Sheet to have students record what their partner and teammates like to eat.

• **Use Cards as Visuals.** Have food Picture Cards available to teams to help them select items they wish to eat.

Qu'est-ce que tu veux manger?

(What do you want to eat?)

Directions: During the interview, this Recording Sheet is to record what your partner likes to eat. Also, use this recording sheet during RoundRobin to record what your teammates like to eat.

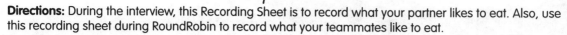

Mon/Ma partenaire veut manger

1. _____

2. _____

3. _____

4. _____

5. _____

6. _____

7. _____

8. _____

Le membre de mon équipe veut manger

1. _____

2. _____

3. _____

4. _____

5. _____

6. _____

7. _____

8. _____

Le membre de mon équipe veut manger

1. _____

2. _____

3. _____

4. _____

5. _____

6. _____

7. _____

8. _____

Activity 4

J'aime manger...et toi?
(I like to eat...and you?)

Quiz-Quiz-Trade

Students quiz a partner, get quizzed by a partner, and then trade their cards to repeat the process with a new partner.

Steps

Setup: The teacher prepares a set of Question Cards for the class.

1 Distribute Cards
The teacher cuts out the cards and distributes them to the class, one card per student.

2 Students Pair Up
Students stand up, hand up, pair up, and face each other.

3 Students Quiz Each Other
Students take turns asking questions about the card. Questions can be simply, *"Qu'est-ce que c'est?."* His or her partner may respond, *"C'est un sous-marin."* Then, the other partner quizzes his or her partner about the card.

4 Trade Cards and Find New Partners
After partners have asked and answered each other's questions, they give each other a high five, trade cards, and find a new partner.

5 Continue Quizzing
This activity can go on for an allotted amount of time, or for a number of trades.

(continued)

J'aime manger...et toi?
(I like to eat...and you?)

Quiz-Quiz-Trade

Tip

- **Increase Difficulty.** More advanced students can create questions based on true and false, or specific details on the card. For example:
  1. *"C'est un…"* partner has to say if the statement is true or if it is false, and then give the correct name for the item.
  2. Multiple-choice response.
  3. Questions generated by students about the food item— or a detail about the food.
  4. Partner A may say, *"J'aime manger la pizza, et toi, qu'est-ce que tu aimes manger?"*—the item they like to eat is pictured on the card— they must respond, *"Moi, j'aime manger..."*

J'aime manger...et toi?

(I like to eat...and you?)

Directions: Cut out the *J'aime manger...et toi?* cards along the dotted line. Then fold the card in half so the question is on the front and the answer is on the back. Glue or tape cards together to keep the answers and questions on opposite sides.

---

1 Quiz-Quiz-Trade

J'aime manger...et toi?

la poutine

Question

Réponse

1 Quiz-Quiz-Trade

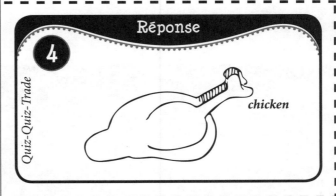

poutine

---

2 Quiz-Quiz-Trade

J'aime manger...et toi?

les légumes

Question

Réponse

2 Quiz-Quiz-Trade

vegetables

---

3 Quiz-Quiz-Trade

J'aime manger...et toi?

les fruits

Question

Réponse

3 Quiz-Quiz-Trade

fruit

---

4 Quiz-Quiz-Trade

J'aime manger...et toi?

le poulet

Question

Réponse

4 Quiz-Quiz-Trade

chicken

J'aime manger...et toi?
(I like to eat...and you?)

Directions: Cut out the *J'aime manger...et toi?* cards along the dotted line. Then fold the card in half so the question is on the front and the answer is on the back. Glue or tape cards together to keep the answers and questions on opposite sides.

5 | *J'aime manger...et toi?*
Quiz-Quiz-Trade

le boeuf

Question

5 | Réponse
Quiz-Quiz-Trade

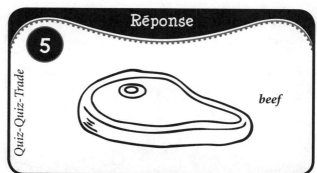

beef

6 | *J'aime manger...et toi?*
Quiz-Quiz-Trade

le poisson

Question

6 | Réponse
Quiz-Quiz-Trade

fish

7 | *J'aime manger...et toi?*
Quiz-Quiz-Trade

la soupe

Question

7 | Réponse
Quiz-Quiz-Trade

soup

8 | *J'aime manger...et toi?*
Quiz-Quiz-Trade

les fruits de mer

Question

8 | Réponse
Quiz-Quiz-Trade

seafood

J'aime manger...et toi?
(I like to eat...and you?)

Directions: Cut out the *J'aime manger...et toi?* cards along the dotted line. Then fold the card in half so the question is on the front and the answer is on the back. Glue or tape cards together to keep the answers and questions on opposite sides.

9 — Quiz-Quiz-Trade — J'aime manger...et toi?

le homard

Question

Réponse — Quiz-Quiz-Trade — **9**

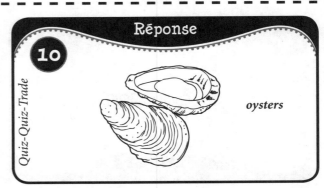

lobster

10 — Quiz-Quiz-Trade — J'aime manger...et toi?

les huîtres

Question

Réponse — Quiz-Quiz-Trade — **10**

oysters

11 — Quiz-Quiz-Trade — J'aime manger...et toi?

les crevettes

Question

Réponse — Quiz-Quiz-Trade — **11**

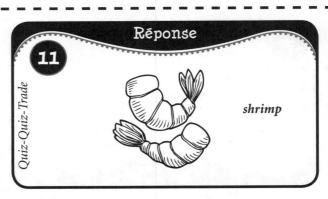

shrimp

12 — Quiz-Quiz-Trade — J'aime manger...et toi?

la pizza

Question

Réponse — Quiz-Quiz-Trade — **12**

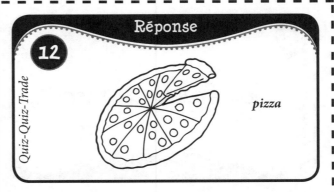

pizza

J'aime manger...et toi?
(I like to eat...and you?)

Directions: Cut out the *J'aime manger...et toi?* cards along the dotted line. Then fold the card in half so the question is on the front and the answer is on the back. Glue or tape cards together to keep the answers and questions on opposite sides.

13

Quiz-Quiz-Trade

le sandwich

Question

Réponse

13

Quiz-Quiz-Trade

sub sandwich

14

Quiz-Quiz-Trade

J'aime manger...et toi?

le sandwich roulé

Question

Réponse

14

Quiz-Quiz-Trade

wrap

15

Quiz-Quiz-Trade

J'aime manger...et toi?

la glace

Question

Réponse

15

Quiz-Quiz-Trade

ice cream

16

Quiz-Quiz-Trade

J'aime manger...et toi?

le taco

Question

Réponse

16

Quiz-Quiz-Trade

taco

Chapter 5
DRMRSVANDERTRAMP
(Dr. Mrs. Vandertramp)

Structures & Activities

Vocabulaire

DRMRSVANDERTRAMP
(Dr. Mrs. Vandertramp)

> Dr. Mrs. Vandertramp is a mnemonic device for remembering verbs that take *être* in the past tense.

Chapter 5

Les actions (Actions)

- **Devenir** (To become) — D
- **Devenu** (e) (s) (es) (Became)
- **Revenir** (To return, come home) — R
- **Revenu** (e) (s) (es) (Came home)
- **Monter** (To climb, go up) — M
- **Monté** (e) (s) (es) (Climbed, went up)
- **Retourner** (To return) — R
- **Retourné** (e) (s) (es) (Returned)
- **Sortir** (To go out, exit) — S
- **Sorti** (e) (s) (es) (Went out, exited)
- **Venir** (To come) — V
- **Venu** (e) (s) (es) (Came)
- **Aller** (To go) — A
- **Allé** (e) (s) (es) (Went)
- **Naître** (To be born) — N
- **Né** (e) (s) (es) (Was born)
- **Descendre** (To descend, go down) — D
- **Descendu** (e) (s) (es) (Descended)
- **Entrer** (To enter) — E
- **Entré** (e) (s) (es) (Entered)
- **Rentrer** (To re-enter, come home) — R
- **Rentré** (e) (s) (es) (Re-entered)
- **Tomber** (To fall) — T
- **Tombé** (e) (s) (es) (Fell)

- **Rester** (To stay) — R
- **Resté** (e) (s) (es) (Stayed)
- **Arriver** (To arrive) — A
- **Arrivé** (e) (s) (es) (Arrived)
- **Mourir** (To die) — M
- **Mort** (e) (s) (es) (Died)
- **Partir** (To leave) — P
- **Parti** (e) (s) (es) (Left)

Le verbe être (The verb to be):

- **Je suis** (I am)
- **Tu es** (You are)
- **Il est** (He is)
- **Elle est** (She is)
- **On est** (We are/one is)
- **Qui est?** (Who is?)
- **Nous sommes** (We are)
- **Vous êtes** (You are)
- **Ils sont** (They are) (masculine plural)
- **Elles sont** (They are) (feminine plural)

When conjugating this group of transitive verbs in the past tense, the past participle must agree in number and gender with the subject!

Cooperative Learning & French • Chiupka-Jozin
Kagan Publishing • 1 (800) 933-2667 • www.KaganOnline.com

Au passé composé!
(In the past tense!)

Showdown

Teams practice conjugating the past tense of the transitive verbs using pictures of activities on question cards.

Steps

Setup: The teacher demonstrates for the class how to write a past tense sentence using the Picture Cards. See the Check It page for examples.

1 Distribute Picture Cards
Question cards are placed in the center of the team table.

2 Read Question
Showdown Captain reads a question.

3 Think and Write
Students work alone and write answers on wipe-off boards or pieces of paper.

4 Thumbs Up
Teammates signal when ready.

5 Showdown
Showdown Captain calls, *"Showdown!"* or *"Montrez-moi!"* in French.

6 Show and Discuss
Teammates show and discuss their answers. The Showdown Captain then verifies the answer with the teacher who has the Check It page.

7 Celebrate
Teammates celebrate or coach.

8 Start Again
New Showdown Captain leads next round.

(continued)

Au passé composé!
(In the past tense!)

Showdown

Variations

- **Check It.** Teacher distributes the Check It page to each team. Students write complete sentences and compare during Showdown. The Showdown Captain has the Check It page so the team can check their answers.

- **Create Your Own.** Students create their own cards to pass to another team to use for Showdown. The Question Cards can be fill in the blank, answer the question, or change the verb form to the past tense.

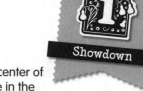

Au passé composé!
In the past tense!

Directions: Cut out the *Au passé composé!* cards along the dotted line. Teams place cards in the center of the table. The Showdown Captain picks a card and reads it aloud. Every student writes a sentence in the past tense describing the pictures. Students "Showdown" to compare sentences.

1 · Showdown

Devenir

2 · Showdown

Revenir

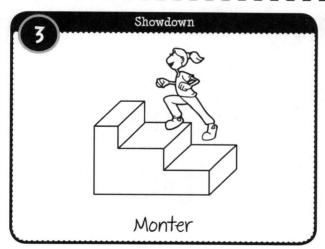

3 · Showdown

Monter

4 · Showdown

Sortir

5 · Showdown

Aller

6 · Showdown

Naître

Au passé composé!
In the past tense!

Directions: Cut out the *Au passé composé!* cards along the dotted line. Teams place cards in the center of the table. The Showdown Captain picks a card and reads it aloud. Every student writes a sentence in the past tense describing the pictures. Students "Showdown" to compare sentences.

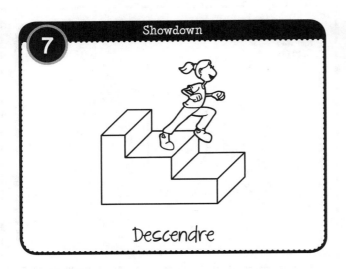

7 Showdown

Descendre

8 Showdown

Entrer

9 Showdown

Tomber

10 Showdown

Rester

11 Showdown

Mourir

12 Showdown

Partir

Au passé composé!
In the past tense!

Directions: Use this Check It page to check answers.

Check It		
Pictures	**Verbs**	**Sentences Describing Pictures in the Past Tense**
1	**1** Devenir (To become)	**1** Il est devenu médecin.
2	**2** Revenir (To return home)	**2** Elle est revenue.
3	**3** Monter (To climb)	**3** Elle est montée par l'escalier.
4	**4** Sortir (To go out, exit)	**4** Il est sorti de la maison.
5	**5** Aller (To go)	**5** Il est allé au cinéma.
6	**6** Naître (To be born)	**6** Il est né en janvier.
7	**7** Descendre (To go down)	**7** Elle est descendue par l'escalier.
8	**8** Entrer (To enter)	**8** Il est entré dans la salle de cinéma.
9	**9** Tomber (To fall)	**9** Elle est tombée de sa bicyclette.
10	**10** Rester (To stay)	**10** Il est resté dans le parc.
11	**11** Mourir (To die)	**11** Il est mort en 2012.
12	**12** Partir (To leave)	**12** Elle est partie avec ses amis.

Trouve l'erreur!
(Find the mistake!)

Find-the-Fiction

Students write three statements about their weekend in the past tense using the verbs from this chapter. Teammates try to "find" which one of the three statements is the "fiction."

Steps

Setup: The teacher provides paper for each student.

1 Think and Write
Students write down three statements on their own piece of paper.

2 Stand and Share
One student on each team stands and reads his or her statements to teammates.

3 Think and Guess
Without talking, all teammates independently write down their best guess as to which statement is the "fiction."

4 RoundRobin
Teammates RoundRobin (one student shares their guess and students continue sharing clockwise until all teammates have shared and defend their "best guess.") **Hint:** The teacher may ask teams to come to a consensus on their "best guess."

5 Announce
Teammates announce their guess/guesses.

6 Reveal
The standing student announces the false statement.

(continued)

Trouve l'erreur!
(Find the mistake!)

Find-the-Fiction

Steps

7 **Celebrate**
Students celebrate: The standing student congratulates the teammates who correctly guessed the false statement. Teammates who were "fooled" congratulate the standing student for being so "tricky!"

8 **Next**
The next teammate stands to share. The process is repeated.

Variations

• **Class Find-the-Fiction.** The class works together to find the fiction. Teacher or a student tries to outwit the class.

• **StandUp–HandUp–PairUp!** Students circulate in the class each trying to guess their classmate's fiction. Students write a checkmark on the top of the page for each student who correctly guessed the fiction. They write an X-mark at the bottom of the page for each student who guessed incorrectly. Students can count and compare how many right and wrong guesses they received.

• **Conjugation Review.** Have students write out three sentences in the past tense, one sentence will have an error (e.g., in an auxiliary verb or in the formation of the past participle). Teams or classmates must find the incorrect spelling or conjugation.

Trouve l'erreur!
(Find the mistake!)

Directions: Students write three statements about their weekend in the past tense. One of the three statements must be fiction. Teammates guess which statement is the fiction.

La fin de semain passée

1 _____

_____

_____

_____

2 _____

_____

_____

_____

_____

3 _____

_____

_____

_____

_____

Quelles sont les différences?
(What are the differences?)

Same-Different

Students compare two similar, yet different pictures. Students record similarities and differences on the Recording Sheet.

Steps

Setup: The teacher creates a barrier for each pair of students. This can be two file folders connected with a paperclip at the top. Partners receive different pictures (Picture 1 or Picture 2), and one Recording Sheet.

1 **Students Form Pairs**
Partners sit facing each other with their pictures hidden behind their barriers.

2 **Students Discover Differences**
Using the target vocabulary and basic grammatical structures, students take turns making statements about their picture that their partner either confirms or amends according to what is on their own picture. The pictures are designed to encourage students to use the chapter vocabulary.

3 **Students Record**
Partners take turns recording the similarities and differences on their Recording Sheets.

Hint

Laminate the pictures so that students can use dry-erase markers.

Variation

• **Circle the Differences.** Students make statements and circle where their pictures are different and then compare pictures when done.

Quelles sont les différences?

(What are the differences?)

Picture 1

MONSIEUR
TOUSSAUD

Quelles sont les différences?
(What are the differences?)

Picture 2

Quelles sont les différences?
(What are the differences?)

Directions: Use this Recording Sheet to record similarities and differences in the two pictures.

Similarités

1. _____
2. _____
3. _____
4. _____
5. _____
6. _____
7. _____
8. _____
9. _____
10. _____
11. _____
12. _____
13. _____
14. _____
15. _____
16. _____
17. _____
18. _____
19. _____
20. _____

Différences

1. _____
2. _____
3. _____
4. _____
5. _____
6. _____
7. _____
8. _____
9. _____
10. _____
11. _____
12. _____
13. _____
14. _____
15. _____
16. _____
17. _____
18. _____
19. _____
20. _____

Les phrases au passé composé!
(Sentences in the past tense!)

RallyCoach

Students work together to write sentences in the past tense. Teacher models the thought process and students work in pairs.

Steps

Setup: The teacher provides one worksheet for each pair of students.

1 Teacher Models
The teacher carries out examples together with the class, identifying the verb in the sentence and talks through how to change it to the past tense. Students are instructed to talk through the process with their coach.

2 Pair Up
Students sit in pairs with one worksheet between them.

3 First Sentence
Partner A rewrites the first sentence in the past tense while "talking it out;" Partner B coaches and praises.

4 Next Sentence
Partner A passes the paper to Partner B; Partner B "talks it out" and rewrites the next sentence; Partner A coaches and praises.

5 Keep Going
Partners continue taking turns rewriting each sentence, verbalizing it each time.

Variation

• **Go Solo.** Once students have completed the worksheet, students can work on a few questions on their own and hand it in to the teacher.

Les phrases au passé composé!
(Sentences in the past tense!)

Directions: One worksheet is provided per pair of students. Students rewrite the sentences using the past tense, identifying the verb. Partner A solves by talking aloud to his or her partner. Partner B coaches and praises. Roles are then reversed. Pairs continue until the page is complete.

Mettez les phrases au passé composé

Partner A ODD—Partner B EVEN

1 Il descend du train.

_____

2 Nous allons au cinéma.

_____

3 Vous partez, madame?

_____

4 Elle reste chez elle.

_____

5 'Je tombe de ma bicyclette!', crie Julie.

_____

6 Elle meurt en 2010.

_____

7 Ils sortent de la maison.

_____

8 Elles montent l'escalier.

_____

9 Quand est-ce que tu rentres chez toi?

_____

10 Paul revient aujourd' hui.

_____

Les phrases au passé composé!
(Sentences in the past tense!)

Directions: One worksheet is provided per pair of students. Students rewrite the sentences using the past tense, identifying the verb. Partner A solves by talking aloud to his or her partner. Partner B coaches and praises. Roles are then reversed. Pairs continue until the page is complete.

Mettez les phrases au passé composé
Partner A ODD—Partner B EVEN

1 Elles vont en France.

_____

2 'Je reviens chez moi', dit Pierre.

_____

3 Elle part avec ses amis.

_____

4 Nous restons chez nous.

_____

5 Ils arrivent au restaurant.

_____

6 Tu pars à huit heures.

_____

7 Est-ce que vous descendez en taxi, Paul et Louis?

_____

8 Il monte dans l'arbre dans la forêt.

_____

9 Marie sort de la maison.

_____

10 Vous tombez sur la glace, monsieur Renaud!

_____

Qu'est-ce que tu as fait...?
(What did you do...?)

RallyTable

Partners take turns writing responses to a question posed by the teacher.

Steps

> **Setup:** Students sit in pairs with one piece of paper and a pencil.

1 **Think**
The teacher provides a question to which there are multiple possible responses, and provides Think Time.

2 **Write and Pass**
Partners take turns writing their responses, then passing the paper and pencil. Each student writes one response and then passes the paper to his or her partner.

3 **Celebrate**
After the allotted time and number of responses, pairs celebrate their terrific use of the past tense and their awesome responses!

(continued)

Qu'est-ce que tu as fait...?
(What did you do...?)

RallyTable

Questions

- Questions can be selected from the following:
  - *Qu'est-ce que tu as fait hier?*
  - *Qu'est-ce que tu as fait pendant les vacances de Noël?*
  - *Qu'est-ce que tu as fait l'été passé?*
  - *Qu'est-ce que tu as fait pendant la fin de semaine?*

Variations

- **Past Tense.** Students look at a picture and come up with as many sentences in the past tense as they can think of.

- **Create a Story.** Students then create a story (either in partners or teams) based on their responses, drawing pictures (or finding images) to match the activities.

Qu'est-ce que tu as fait...?
(What did you do...?)

Directions: The teacher poses a question. In pairs, partners take turns writing their responses.

Question

Réponses

1.

2.

3.

4.

5.

6.

7.

8.

9.

10.

Chapter 6
Les professions
(Professions)

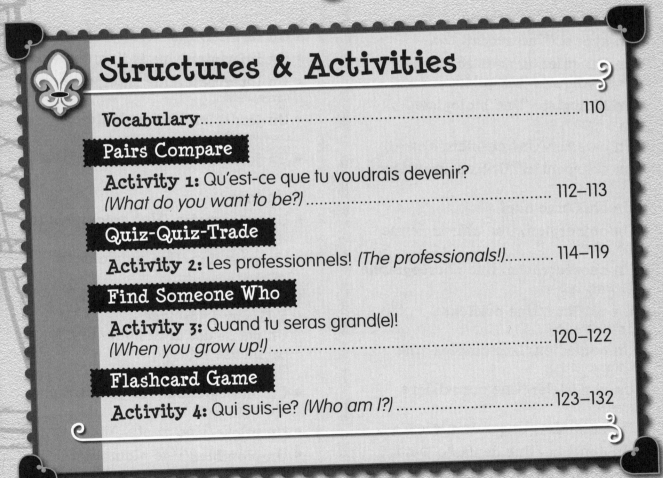

Structures & Activities

Vocabulaire

Les professions
(Professions)

Les professions (Professions)

- **Un agent de police** (Police officer)
- **Un agent de voyage** (Travel agent)
- **Un animateur/Une animatrice** (TV host/hostess)
- **Un artiste/Une artiste** (Artist)
- **Un avocat/Une avocat** (Lawyer)
- **Un banquier/banquière** (Banker) **Une banquier/banquière** (Banker)
- **Un biologiste/Une biologiste** (Biologist)
- **Un caissier/Une cassière** (Cashier)
- **Un charpentier/Une charpentière** (Carpenter)
- **Un chef/une chef** (Chef)
- **Un chirurgien/Une chirurgienne** (Surgeon)
- **Un choréographe/Une choréographe** (Choreographer)
- **Un coiffeur/Une coiffeuse** (Hair dresser)
- **Un comédien/Une comédienne** (Comedian)
- **Un conseiller/Une conseillère** (Counselor)
- **Un cuisinier/Une cuisinière** (Cook)
- **Un dentiste/Une dentiste** (Dentist)
- **Un détective/Une détective** (Detective)

- **Un écrivain/Une écrivaine** (Writer)
- **Un enseignante/Une enseignante** (School teacher)
- **Un entraineur/Une entraineuse** (Trainer/coach)
- **Un facteur, Une factrice** (Mail carrier)
- **Un fermier/Une fermière** (Farmer)
- **Un infirmier/Une infirmière** (Nurse)
- **Un interprète/Une interprète** (Interpreter)
- **Un jardinier/Une jardinière** (Gardener)
- **Un journaliste/ Une journaliste** (Journalist)
- **Un juge** (Judge)
- **Un mécanicien/Une mécanicienne** (Mechanic)
- **Un musicien/Une musicienne** (Musician)
- **Un patineur artistique/Une patineur artistique Un patineuse artistique/Une patineuse artistique** (Figure skater)
- **Un photographe/Une photographe** (Photographer)
- **Un pilote/Une pilote** (Pilot)
- **Un plombier/Une plombière** (Plumber)

Vocabulaire

Les professions
(Professions)

- **Un pompier/Une pompière**
  (Fireman/woman)
- **Un professeur/Une professeur**
  (Teacher/professor)
- **Un réalisateur/Une réalisatrice**
  (Film director)
- **Une vedette** (Rock star)
  - ♣ **Un rockeur/Une rockeuse**
    (Rock star)
- **Un scientifique** (Scientist)
- **Un secrétaire/Une secrétaire**
  (Secretary)
- **Un serveur/Une serveuse**
  (Waiter/waitress)
- **Un soldat** (Soldier)
- **Un vendeur/Une vendeuse**
  (Salesman/woman)

Pour devenir (To become)

- **J'aimerais** (Devenir)
  (I would like (to become))
- **Je deviendrai...quand je serai
  _____ ans.**
  (I'll be...when I am __ years old.)
- **Je veux devenir** (I want to become)
- **Je veux être** (I want to be)
- **Je voudrais devenir...**
  (I would like to become...)
- **Je voudrais être** (I would like to be)
- **Qu'est-ce que tu aimerais devenir
  quand tu seras grand(e)?**
  (What do you want to be when you
  are older?)
- **Qu'est-ce que tu voudrais devenir?**
  (What do you want to be/become?)

Qu'est-ce que tu voudrais devenir?
(What do you want to be?)

Pairs Compare

Pairs create a list of possible ideas or answers to the question, *"Qu'est-ce que tu voudrais devenir?"* using the professions they are studying. Pairs pair and compare their answers with another pair. Finally, pairs work as a team to create additional answers or ideas.

Steps

 1 Teacher Provides Question
The teacher provides the question: *"Qu'est-ce que tu voudrais devenir?"* and provides Think Time. Teacher announces how much time students will have to record responses.

2 RallyTable
Shoulder partners share answers with each other, responding in a complete sentence, *"Je voudrais devenir…, et toi?"* One partner provides a response by saying *"Je voudrais devenir…, et toi ?"* and then writing their choice of profession on the Pair's list. The other partner then responds, verbally expressing what they would like to become and write the profession on the Pair's list. Pairs keep their answers "secret" from other pairs.

 3 Teacher Calls Time
When time is up, the teacher asks pairs to form teams of four.

4 Pairs Compare
Pairs pair and share their answers using RoundRobin. For each answer, pairs announce, *"Nous voulons devenir..."* and state an answer. For each answer, the other pair adds an answer to their list or checks it off if they already have it.

 5 Team Challenge
As a team, students generate new answers, taking turns within pairs recording answers on their pair lists. **Hint:** Students can use the dictionary to find new and exciting professions not listed on their vocabulary lists!

Qu'est-ce que tu voudrais devenir?

What do you want to be?

Directions: In pairs, take turns creating a list of professions. Compare your list with another pair and see if you come up with the same items. Then, as a team, see if you can all come up with new professions.

Liste avec mon/ma partenaire

1. _____
2. _____
3. _____
4. _____
5. _____
6. _____
7. _____
8. _____
9. _____
10. _____

Liste de l'équipe

1. _____
2. _____
3. _____
4. _____
5. _____
6. _____
7. _____
8. _____
9. _____
10. _____

Les professionels!
(The professionals!)

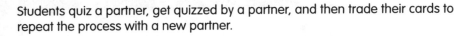

Quiz-Quiz-Trade

Students quiz a partner, get quizzed by a partner, and then trade their cards to repeat the process with a new partner.

Steps   **Setup:** The teacher prepares the set of *Les professionels!* Question Cards for the class.

1 **Distribute Cards**
The teacher cuts out the cards and distributes them to the class, one card per student.

2 **Students Pair Up**
Students stand up, hand up, pair up, and face each other.

3 **Students Quiz Each Other**
Students take turns asking, *"Qui est-ce?"* (Who is it?). Partners respond with the profession in French. Partners can provide a hint by reading where that person works. Increase the difficulty: Students can ask *"Où est-ce qu'il/elle travaille?"* (Where does he or she work?) and the partner responds. **Hint:** If a partner does not know the correct response, the answer is immediately shown to him or her and then the partner is questioned again. Partners celebrate the correct response! Then, the other partner quizzes his or her partner about the card.

4 **Trade Cards and Find New Partners**
After partners have asked and answered each other's questions, they give each other a high five, trade cards, and find a new partner.

5 **Continue Quizzing**
This activity can go on for an allotted amount of time, or for a number of trades.

Variations

- **Hide the English.** To increase difficulty and avoid having students translate the vocabulary from English, hide the English terms by covering them up or whiting them out before copying the cards. If you cover up the English, be sure to teach students the French for each illustration in advance to ensure students know and use the target vocabulary.

- **Word Wall.** Enlarge the cards, cut them out, and post them on a classroom Word Wall to familiarize students with the chapter vocabulary.

Les professionels!
(The professionals!)

Directions: Cut out the *Les professionels!* cards along the dotted line. Then fold the card in half so the question is on the front and the answer is on the back. Glue or tape cards together to keep the answers and questions on opposite sides.

Les professionels

1

Quiz-Quiz-Trade

police officer

Question

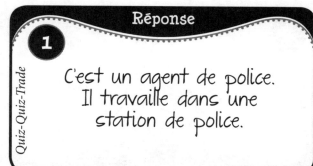

Réponse

1

Quiz-Quiz-Trade

C'est un agent de police. Il travaille dans une station de police.

Les professionels

2

Quiz-Quiz-Trade

artist

Question

Réponse

2

Quiz-Quiz-Trade

C'est un artiste. Il travaille dans un studio.

Les professionels

3

Quiz-Quiz-Trade

lawyer

Question

Réponse

3

Quiz-Quiz-Trade

C'est un avocat. Il travaille dans un bureau.

Les professionels

4

Quiz-Quiz-Trade

banker

Question

Réponse

4

Quiz-Quiz-Trade

C'est un banquier. Il travaille dans une banque.

Les professionels!
(The professionals!)

Directions: Cut out the *Les professionels!* cards along the dotted line. Then fold the card in half so the question is on the front and the answer is on the back. Glue or tape cards together to keep the answers and questions on opposite sides.

Les professionels

Quiz-Quiz-Trade

5

cashier

Question

Rēponse

Quiz-Quiz-Trade

5

C'est une caissière.
Elle travaille dans
un magasin.

Les professionels

Quiz-Quiz-Trade

6

carpenter

Question

Rēponse

Quiz-Quiz-Trade

6

C'est une charpentière.
Elle travaille dans
une maison.

Les professionels

Quiz-Quiz-Trade

7

chef

Question

Rēponse

Quiz-Quiz-Trade

7

C'est un chef.
Il travaille dans
un restaurant.

Les professionels

Quiz-Quiz-Trade

8

surgeon

Question

Rēponse

Quiz-Quiz-Trade

8

C'est une chirurgienne.
Elle travaille dans
un hôpital.

Quiz-Quiz-Trade

Les professionels!
(The professionals!)

Directions: Cut out the *Les professionels!* cards along the dotted line. Then fold the card in half so the question is on the front and the answer is on the back. Glue or tape cards together to keep the answers and questions on opposite sides.

9 | Les professionels

hair dresser

Question

9 | Rēponse

C'est une coiffeuse. Elle travaille dans un salon de coiffeur.

10 | Les professionels

nurse

Question

10 | Rēponse

C'est une infirmière. Elle travaille dans l'hôpital.

11 | Les professionels

gardener

Question

11 | Rēponse

C'est un jardinier. Il travaille dans un jardin.

12 | Les professionels

farmer

Question

12 | Rēponse

C'est un fermier. Il travaille à la ferme.

Quiz-Quiz-Trade

Quiz-Quiz-Trade (side labels)

Les professionels!
(The professionals!)

Directions: Cut out the *Les professionels!* cards along the dotted line. Then fold the card in half so the question is on the front and the answer is on the back. Glue or tape cards together to keep the answers and questions on opposite sides.

13 Les professionels

female mechanic

Question

Réponse

13 C'est une mécanicienne. Elle travaille dans un garage.

14 Les professionels

fireman

Question

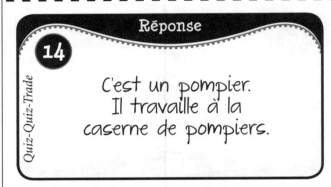

Réponse

14 C'est un pompier. Il travaille à la caserne de pompiers.

15 Les professionels

firewoman

Question

Réponse

15 C'est une pompière. Elle travaille à la caserne de pompiers.

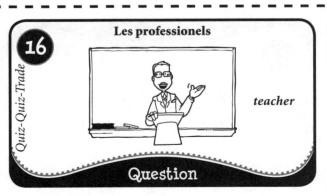

16 Les professionels

teacher

Question

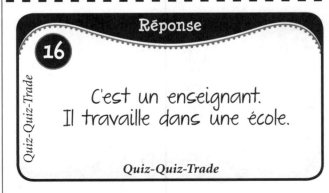

Réponse

16 C'est un enseignant. Il travaille dans une école.

Quiz-Quiz-Trade

Les professionels!
(The professionals!)

Directions: Cut out the *Les professionels!* cards along the dotted line. Then fold the card in half so the question is on the front and the answer is on the back. Glue or tape cards together to keep the answers and questions on opposite sides.

17 Quiz-Quiz-Trade

Les professionels

secretary

Question

---

17 Quiz-Quiz-Trade

Rēponse

C'est une secrétaire. Elle travaille dans un bureau.

18 Quiz-Quiz-Trade

Les professionels

waiter

Question

---

18 Quiz-Quiz-Trade

Rēponse

C'est un serveur. Il travaille dans un restaurant.

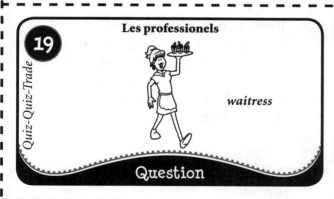

19 Quiz-Quiz-Trade

Les professionels

waitress

Question

---

19 Quiz-Quiz-Trade

Rēponse

C'est une serveuse. Elle travaille dans un restaurant.

2o Quiz-Quiz-Trade

Les professionels

salesman

Question

2o Quiz-Quiz-Trade

Rēponse

C'est un vendeur Il travaille dans un magasin.

Quiz-Quiz-Trade

Quand tu seras grand(e)!
(When you grow up!)

Find Someone Who

Students circulate around the classroom forming and re-forming pairs trying to "find someone who" can answer one of the questions.

Steps

Setup: The teacher prepares a worksheet for students to use.

1 Distribute Worksheet
Students are given the worksheet, review it, and review how to ask and answer questions about professions when they get older (e.g., *"Quand tu seras grand(e), aimerais-tu devenir..? Oui, quand je serai grand(e) j'aimerais devenir…/Non, quand je serai grand(e) je n'aimerais pas devenir…!"*).

2 Students Pair Up
Students circulate around the class. Students keep a hand raised until they find a partner.

3 Ask
In pairs, students take turns asking a question from the worksheet: Partner A asks Partner B a question and Partner B responds. Partner

A records the answer on his or her own worksheet and expresses appreciation.

4 Check
Partner B checks and initials the answer.

5 Reverse Roles
Partner B now asks a question and Partner B responds. Partner B records the answer on his or her own worksheet and expresses appreciation.

6 Check
Partner A checks and initials the answer.

7 Praise and Part
Partners high five and raise a hand as they search for a new partner.

(continued)

Quand tu seras grand(e)!
(When you grow up!)

Find Someone Who

Steps

8 **Repeat**
Students repeat the process until their worksheets are complete.

9 **Experts**
Experts are students who have completed their worksheets. Once their worksheets are completed, they return to their desks and can be approached by others as a resource.

Variations

• **Identify the future professional.** The teacher distributes a picture of a professional. Students are asked to identify the professional. For example, the teacher asks, *"Qui veut devenir artiste?"* The student with the artist picture stands and responds, *"Moi, je veux devenir artiste!"*. The teacher could ask another student, *"Est-ce que Mary veut devenir artiste"* and that student could answer in response to the picture of the professional Mary is holding.

• **StandUp–HandUp–PairUp.** Students stand up, put a hand up, and pair up. One student asks the other, *"qu'est-ce que tu veux devenir?"* (What do you want to be?) and their partner responds with the name of the profession pictured on their card, *"je veux devenir…"* They switch roles. After they ask each other and answer a question, they put a hand up and find a new partner and repeat the process.

Quand tu seras grand(e)!
(When you grow up!)

Directions: Students circulate around the classroom forming and re-forming pairs trying to "find someone who" to ask if they would want to have the profession when they grow up.

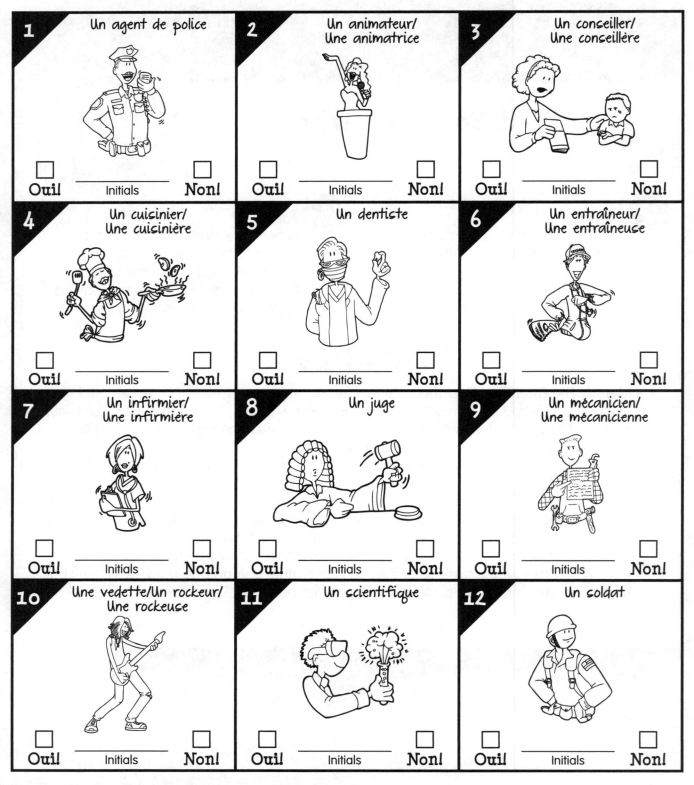

1 Un agent de police	2 Un animateur/ Une animatrice	3 Un conseiller/ Une conseillère
Oui! ___ Initials Non!	Oui! ___ Initials Non!	Oui! ___ Initials Non!
4 Un cuisinier/ Une cuisinière	5 Un dentiste	6 Un entraîneur/ Une entraîneuse
Oui! ___ Initials Non!	Oui! ___ Initials Non!	Oui! ___ Initials Non!
7 Un infirmier/ Une infirmière	8 Un juge	9 Un mécanicien/ Une mécanicienne
Oui! ___ Initials Non!	Oui! ___ Initials Non!	Oui! ___ Initials Non!
10 Une vedette/Un rockeur/ Une rockeuse	11 Un scientifique	12 Un soldat
Oui! ___ Initials Non!	Oui! ___ Initials Non!	Oui! ___ Initials Non!

Qui suis-je?
(Who am I?)

Flashcard Game

Partners proceed through three rounds as they quiz each other with flashcards, mastering the name of the professions to win cards.

Steps

Setup: The teacher makes duplicates of the *Who am I?* cards. Students receive their own set of flashcards.

1 Pair Up
In pairs, the Tutee gives his or her flashcards to the Tutor.

2 Round 1: Maximum Cues
The Tutor shows the question/picture on the first cards, asks the question, *"Qui suis-je?"* and shows and reads the answer written on the back of the card. The Tutor then turns the card back over and again asks the question on the front of the card, asking the Tutee to answer from memory.

3 Tutee Answers
If the correct answer is given, Tutee wins the card back and receives delightful praise from the Tutor. If wrong, the Tutor shows the Tutee the answer side of the card and coaches. The card is then returned to the stack to try again later. **Hint:** Tutor can ask, *"How can I help you remember that?"* The pair can discuss ways of remembering answers.

4 Switch
When the Tutee wins all the cards, partners switch roles. When the new Tutee wins all of his or her cards, partners advance to Round 2.

(continued)

Qui suis-je?
(Who am I?)

Flashcard Game

 Round 2: Few Cues
The process is repeated, except the Tutor shows only the question side of the card and asks the Tutee to answer from memory. If wrong, the Tutor shows the Tutee the answer side, and the card is returned to the stack to try again.

 Round 3: No Cues
Again, the process is repeated, except the Tutor quizzes Tutee on each question without showing the Tutee the flashcards.

Hints

- Limit each round to no more than five cards. If a student has won all the cards, he or she can add bonus cards.

- Color-code cards for masculine and feminine nouns.

Variations

- **Hide the English.** To increase difficulty and avoid having students translate the vocabulary from English, hide the English terms by covering them up or whiting them out before copying the cards. If you cover up the English, be sure to teach students the French for each illustration in advance to ensure students know and use the target vocabulary.

- **Word Wall.** Enlarge the cards, cut them out, and post them on a classroom Word Wall to familiarize students with the chapter vocabulary.

Qui suis-je?
(Who am I?)

Directions: Cut out the *Qui suis-je?* cards along the dotted line. Then fold each in half so the picture is on the front and the name is on the back. Keep picture and profession on opposite sides.

1 · Flashcard Game · Qui suis-je? · *police officer* · Question

1 · Flashcard Game · un agent de police · Réponse

2 · Flashcard Game · Qui suis-je? · *TV hostess* · Question

2 · Flashcard Game · une animatrice · Réponse

3 · Flashcard Game · Qui suis-je? · *artist* · Question

3 · Flashcard Game · un artiste · Réponse

4 · Flashcard Game · Qui suis-je? · *lawyer* · Question

4 · Flashcard Game · un avocat · Réponse

Qui suis-je?
(Who am I?)

Directions: Cut out the *Qui suis-je?* cards along the dotted line. Then fold each in half so the picture is on the front and the name is on the back. Keep picture and profession on opposite sides.

5 Flashcard Game · **Qui suis-je?** · *travel agent* · **Question**

5 Flashcard Game · un agent de voyage · **Réponse**

6 Flashcard Game · **Qui suis-je?** · *banker* · **Question**

6 Flashcard Game · un bancaire · **Réponse**

7 Flashcard Game · **Qui suis-je?** · *comedian* · **Question**

7 Flashcard Game · un comédien · **Réponse**

8 Flashcard Game · **Qui suis-je?** · *cook* · **Question**

8 Flashcard Game · un cuisinier · **Réponse**

Qui suis-je?

(Who am I?)

Directions: Cut out the *Qui suis-je?* cards along the dotted line. Then fold each in half so the picture is on the front and the name is on the back. Keep picture and profession on opposite sides.

#		
9 — Flashcard Game — **Qui suis-je?** — *female soldier* — **Question**	**9** — Flashcard Game — une soldate — **Réponse**	
10 — Flashcard Game — **Qui suis-je?** — *male soldier* — **Question**	**10** — Flashcard Game — un soldat — **Réponse**	
11 — Flashcard Game — **Qui suis-je?** — *nurse* — **Question**	**11** — Flashcard Game — une infirmière — **Réponse**	
12 — Flashcard Game — **Qui suis-je?** — *detective* — **Question**	**12** — Flashcard Game — un détective — **Réponse**	

Qui suis-je?
(Who am I?)

Directions: Cut out the *Qui suis-je?* cards along the dotted line. Then fold each in half so the picture is on the front and the name is on the back. Keep picture and profession on opposite sides.

13 Flashcard Game — Qui suis-je? — *pilot* — Question

13 Flashcard Game — un pilote — Réponse

14 Flashcard Game — Qui suis-je? — *plumber* — Question

14 Flashcard Game — un plombier — Réponse

15 Flashcard Game — Qui suis-je? — *mail carrier* — Question

15 Flashcard Game — un facteur — Réponse

16 Flashcard Game — Qui suis-je? — *scientist* — Question

16 Flashcard Game — un scientifique — Réponse

Qui suis-je?
(Who am I?)

Directions: Cut out the *Qui suis-je?* cards along the dotted line. Then fold each in half so the picture is on the front and the name is on the back. Keep picture and profession on opposite sides.

17 — Flashcard Game — Qui suis-je? — *photographer* — Question

17 — Flashcard Game — un photographe — Réponse

18 — Flashcard Game — Qui suis-je? — *journalist* — Question

18 — Flashcard Game — un journaliste — Réponse

19 — Flashcard Game — Qui suis-je? — *writer* — Question

19 — Flashcard Game — une écrivaine — Réponse

20 — Flashcard Game — Qui suis-je? — *dentist* — Question

20 — Flashcard Game — un dentiste — Réponse

Qui suis-je?
(Who am I?)

Directions: Cut out the *Qui suis-je?* cards along the dotted line. Then fold each in half so the picture is on the front and the name is on the back. Keep picture and profession on opposite sides.

21 | Flashcard Game | **Qui suis-je?**

trainer/coach

Question

21 | Flashcard Game

un entraîneur

Rêponse

22 | Flashcard Game | **Qui suis-je?**

musician

Question

22 | Flashcard Game

une musicienne

Rêponse

23 | Flashcard Game | **Qui suis-je?**

figure skater

Question

23 | Flashcard Game

une patineuse artistique

Rêponse

24 | Flashcard Game | **Qui suis-je?**

judge

Question

24 | Flashcard Game

un juge

Rêponse

Qui suis-je?
(Who am I?)

Directions: Cut out the *Qui suis-je?* cards along the dotted line. Then fold each in half so the picture is on the front and the name is on the back. Keep picture and profession on opposite sides.

25 | Flashcard Game | **Qui suis-je?**

farmer

Question

---

25 | Flashcard Game

un fermier

Rĕponse

---

26 | Flashcard Game | **Qui suis-je?**

mechanic

Question

---

26 | Flashcard Game

un mécanicien

Rĕponse

---

27 | Flashcard Game | **Qui suis-je?**

teacher/ professor

Question

---

27 | Flashcard Game

un professeur/ un enseignant

Rĕponse

---

28 | Flashcard Game | **Qui suis-je?**

film director

Question

---

28 | Flashcard Game

un réalisateur

Rĕponse

Qui suis-je?
(Who am I?)

Directions: Cut out the *Qui suis-je?* cards along the dotted line. Then fold each in half so the picture is on the front and the name is on the back. Keep picture and profession on opposite sides.

29
Flashcard Game
Qui suis-je?
gardener
Question

29
Flashcard Game
une jardinière
Rēponse

30
Flashcard Game
Qui suis-je?
firewoman
Question

30
Flashcard Game
une pompière
Rēponse

31
Flashcard Game
Qui suis-je?
rock star
Question

31
Flashcard Game
un rockeur
Rēponse

32
Flashcard Game
Qui suis-je?
waitress
Question

32
Flashcard Game
une serveuse
Rēponse

Cooperative Learning & French • Chiupka-Jozin
Kagan Publishing • 1 (800) 933-2667 • www.KaganOnline.com

Chapter 7
Les adjectifs
(Adjectives)

Structures & Activities

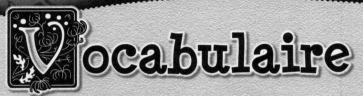

Vocabulaire

Les adjectifs
(Adjectives)

Les adjectifs (Adjectives)

- **Actif/Active** (Active)
- **Adorable** (Adorable)
- **Âgé (e)** (Old)
- **Agréable** (Pleasant)
- **Agressif/-ive** (Aggressive)
- **Ambitieux /-ieuse** (Ambitious)
- **Amiable** (Likeable)
- **Bavard (e)** (Talkative)
- **Beau/Belle** (Handsome/Beautiful)
- **Calme** (Calm)
- **Capable** (Capable)
- **Célèbre** (Famous)
- **Chic** (Stylish)
- **Content (e)** (Happy)
- **Courageux/-euse** (Courageous)
- **Créatif/ive** (Creative)
- **Cruel/Cruelle** (Cruel)
- **Curieux/-euse** (Curious)
- **Désorganisé (e)** (Disorganized)
- **Distrait (e)** (Distracted/Absent minded)
- **Doux/Douce** (Sweet)
- **Énergique** (Energetic)
- **Ennuyeux/-euse** (Boring)
- **Extraverti (e)** (Outgoing)
  - ❦ **Extroverti (e)** (Outgoing)

- **Fâché (e)** (Angry)
- **Faible** (Weak)
- **Fiable** (Reliable)
- **Fier/Fière** (Proud)
- **Fort (e)** (Strong)
- **Fou/Folle** (Crazy)
- **Généreux/-euse** (Generous)
- **Gentil/Gentille** (Kind, gentle)
- **Grand (e)** (Big, tall)
- **Gros, Grosse** (Fat, large)
- **Heureux/-euse** (Happy)
- **Honnête** (Honest)
- **Imaginatif/-ive** (Imaginative)
- **Impulsif/-ive** (Impulsive)
- **Indépendant (e)** (Independent)
- **Intelligent (e)** (Intelligent)
- **Intéressant (e)** (Interesting)
- **Intraverti (e)** (Introverted/shy)
  - ❦ **Introverti (e)** (Introverted/shy)
- **Joli (e)** (Pretty)
- **Laid (e)** (Ugly, awful)
- **Malade** (Sick)
- **Maladroit (e)** (Awkward, clumsy)
- **Malheureux/-euse** (Unhappy)
- **Mauvais (e)** (Bad)
- **Méchant (e)** (Mean, evil)

Vocabulaire

Les adjectifs
(Adjectives)

Chapter 7

- **Mignon, Mignonne** (Cute)
- **Mince** (Thin)
- **Mystérieux/-ieuse** (Mysterious)
- **Nerveux/-euse** (Nervous)
- **Nouveau/-elle** (New)
- **Paresseux/-euse** (Lazy)
- **Patient (e)** (Patient)
- **Petit (e)** (Small, short)
- **Poli (e)** (Polite)
- **Prudent (e)** (Careful)
- **Responsable** (Responsible)
- **Riche** (Rich)
- **Sensible** (Sensitive)
- **Sérieux/-euse** (Serious)
- **Sophistiqué (e)** (Sophisticated)
- **Spirituel/-elle** (Spiritual)
- **Spontané (e)** (Spontaneous)
- **Sportif/-ive** (Sportive/athletic)
- **Talentueux/-euse** (Talented)
- **Têtu (e)** (Stubborn)
- **Timide** (Shy)
- **Travailleur/-euse** (Hardworking)
- **Triste** (Sad)
- **Vieux, Vieille** (Old)

(Masculine words—
Feminine words ending in...)

masculine	feminine
• -if	• -ive
• -eux	• -euse
• -oux	• -ouse
• -ien	• -ienne
• -on	• -onne
• -el	• -elle
• -er	• -ère
• -et	• -ette, -ète
• -en	• -enne
• -eur	• -euse
• -teur	• -trice

Les adjectifs: masculin/féminin
(Masculine/Feminine forms of adjectives)

RallyCoach

Partners coach each other as they apply the masculine and feminine rules to adjectives.

Steps

Setup: Make sure partners have one pencil or pen to share.

1 Students Pair Up
Students sit in pairs and share one worksheet and one pen or pencil.

2 Work Together
Partner A completes the sentence by explaining aloud what he or she is doing and writing the correct form of the adjective on the line. Partner B coaches and praises. Partner A passes the worksheet and pencil or pen to Student B.

3 Next Sentence
Partner B completes the next sentence. Partner A coaches and praises.

4 Continue
Students continue taking turns writing the correct from of the adjective until they have reached the end of the page.

Les adjectifs: masculin/féminin
(Masculine/Feminine forms of adjectives)

Directions: One worksheet is provided per pair of students. Students apply masculine and feminine rules to adjectives. Partner A solves by talking aloud to his or her partner. Partner B coaches and praises. Roles are then reversed. Pairs continue until the page is complete.

Partner A ODD—Partner B EVEN

1. Il est _____.
(bavard)

2. Il est _____.
(comique)

3. Elle est _____.
(patient)

4. Elle est _____.
(calme)

5. Il est _____.
(sportif)

6. Paul est _____.
(talentueux)

7. Elle est _____.
(imaginatif)

8. Amélie est _____.
(malheureux)

9. Bernard est _____.
(vieux)

10. Patrick est _____.
(beau)

11. Angela est _____.
(vieux)

12. Pamela est _____.
(beau)

Les adjectifs: Comment sont-ils?

Les dialogues: Mes amis!
(Dialogues: My friends!)

Mix-Pair-Share

Students pair up with a partner who shares the same short dialogue. They read the two parts together. When done, they stand back-to-back and get ready to mix and find a new dialogue partner!

Steps

Setup: The teacher prepares the Dialogue Cards by copying each set on different colored paper. (There are six different dialogues.)

1 Students Mix
Each student receives a Dialogue Card. Students move around the room exchanging their cards with students they meet.

2 Teacher Calls, "Pair!"
Students pair up with the student who has the same color Dialogue Card.

3 Talk
Students decide who is Partner A and who is Partner B. Each reads their part of the dialogue, focusing on pronunciation.

4 Back-to-Back
Students stand back-to-back when done reading their dialogues.

5 Teacher Calls, "Mix!"
The teacher calls, "Mix!" Students thank their partner for sharing and then mix in the room, exchanging cards with students they meet.

6 Teacher Calls, "Pair!"
The teacher calls, "Pair!" again and students find a new dialogue partner.

7 Continue Process
The teacher decides how many times or dialogues students are going to share.

Les dialogues: Mes amis!
(Dialogues: My friends!)

Directions: Copy each set of *Les dialogues* cards on different colored paper. Distribute cards to students to read together. Students pair up with the person with the same color *Les dialogues* cards. When finished, students mix to find a new partner.

Partenaire A:
Connais-tu mon amie Brenda?

Partenaire B:
Oui! Elle aime aider ses amis!

Partenaire A:
Brenda est gentille.

Partenaire B:
Elle est sensible aussi.

Dialogue #1

Partenaire A:
Connais-tu mon amie Brenda?

Partenaire B:
Oui! Elle aime aider ses amis!

Partenaire A:
Brenda est gentille.

Partenaire B:
Elle est sensible aussi.

Dialogue #1

Les dialogues: Mes amis!
(Dialogues: My friends!)

Directions: Copy each set of *Les dialogues* cards on different colored paper. Distribute cards to students to read together. Students pair up with the person with the same color *Les dialogues* cards. When finished, students mix to find a new partner.

Dialogue #2

Partenaire A:
Connais-tu mon ami Stuart?

Partenaire B:
Non, comment est-il?

Partenaire A:
Stuart aime jouer aux sports: au basket-ball, au soccer, au baseball...

Partenaire B:
Il est vraiment sportif!

Dialogue #2

Partenaire A:
Connais-tu mon ami Stuart?

Partenaire B:
Non, comment est-il?

Partenaire A:
Stuart aime jouer aux sports: au basket-ball, au soccer, au baseball...

Partenaire B:
Il est vraiment sportif!

Les dialogues: Mes amis!
(Dialogues: My friends!)

Directions: Copy each set of *Les dialogues* cards on different colored paper. Distribute cards to students to read together. Students pair up with the person with the same color *Les dialogues* cards. When finished, students mix to find a new partner.

Partenaire A:
Est-ce que tu connais Anne?

Partenaire B:
Non, comment est-elle?

Partenaire A:
Elle aime tous les sports: elle joue au tennis, au soccer et aussi elle joue au volleyball!

Partenaire B:
Anne est vraiment sportive!

Dialogue #3

Partenaire A:
Est-ce que tu connais Anne?

Partenaire B:
Non, comment est-elle?

Partenaire A:
Elle aime tous les sports: elle joue au tennis, au soccer et aussi elle joue au volleyball!

Partenaire B:
Anne est vraiment sportive!

Dialogue #3

Les dialogues: Mes amis!

(Dialogues: My friends!)

Directions: Copy each set of *Les dialogues* cards on different colored paper. Distribute cards to students to read together. Students pair up with the person with the same color *Les dialogues* cards. When finished, students mix to find a new partner.

Partenaire A:
Est-ce que tu connais David?

Partenaire B:
Non, comment est-il?

Partenaire A:
Il aime dire des blagues. Il est comique!

Partenaire B:
Oh oui, il est un ami comique!

Dialogue #4

Partenaire A:
Est-ce que tu connais David?

Partenaire B:
Non, comment est-il?

Partenaire A:
Il aime dire des blagues. Il est comique!

Partenaire B:
Oh oui, il est un ami comique!

Dialogue #4

Les dialogues: Mes amis!

(Dialogues: My friends!)

Activity 2 — Mix-Pair-Share

Directions: Copy each set of *Les dialogues* cards on different colored paper. Distribute cards to students to read together. Students pair up with the person with the same color *Les dialogues* cards. When finished, students mix to find a new partner.

Dialogue #5

Partenaire A:
Connais-tu Isabelle.

Partenaire B:
Oui, elle est mon amie.

Partenaire A:
Elle aime faire de la photographie.

Partenaire B:
Oui, et elle adore faire de la peinture
et aussi elle joue du piano!

Partenaire A:
Isabelle est très active!

Dialogue #5

Partenaire A:
Connais-tu Isabelle.

Partenaire B:
Oui, elle est mon amie.

Partenaire A:
Elle aime faire de la photographie.

Partenaire B:
Oui, et elle adore faire de la peinture
et aussi elle joue du piano!

Partenaire A:
Isabelle est très active!

Les dialogues: Mes amis!
(Dialogues: My friends!)

Directions: Copy each set of *Les dialogues* cards on different colored paper. Distribute cards to students to read together. Students pair up with the person with the same color *Les dialogues* cards. When finished, students mix to find a new partner.

Partenaire A:
Est-ce que tu connais Benjamin?

Partenaire B:
Oui, il est un de mes amis!

Partenaire A:
Il est très patient.

Partenaire B:
Oui, il aime aider ses amis avec les devoirs.

Partenaire A:
Et aussi, il aide ses grands-parents!

Dialogue #6

Partenaire A:
Est-ce que tu connais Benjamin?

Partenaire B:
Oui, il est un de mes amis!

Partenaire A:
Il est très patient.

Partenaire B:
Oui, il aime aider ses amis avec les devoirs.

Partenaire A:
Et aussi, il aide ses grands-parents!

Dialogue #6

Activity 3

Les bonnes qualités!
(Good qualities!)

StandUp–HandUp–PairUp

Students pair up and take turns sharing ideas about the good qualities of friends.

Steps

1 **Students Pair Up**
Students StandUp–HandUp–PairUp to find a partner.

2 **Teacher Makes a Statement**
The teacher gives the statement and provides Think Time for students. *"Quelles sont les qualités d'un bon ami?"*

3 **Students Share**
The teacher assigns roles: Who is Partner A and Partner B (e.g., Partner A is the partner with the longest hair, wearing the most color blue, or with brown eyes, etc.). Partner A starts by providing one adjective describing a positive quality of a friend. Partner B continues by providing another adjective. Students continue RallyRobin, sharing adjectives until the teacher calls time or an allotted number of adjectives are shared.

4 **Celebrate**
Students thank their partners for sharing, and put their hands up to find another partner.

5 **A New Statement Is Provided**
The teacher provides another statement and assigns roles for partners to share a list of adjectives to describe the new topic. Ideas for sharing are on the next page.

(continued)

Les bonnes qualités!
(Good qualities!)

StandUp–HandUp–PairUp

Ideas for Sharing in Pairs

Teacher can ask students to:

- Describe the qualities of a good friend:
  "*Quelles sont les qualités d'un bon ami?*"

- Describe the qualities of a good baseball player:
  "*Quelles sont les qualités d'un bon joueur de baseball?*"

- Describe the qualities of a pet (dog, cat):
  "*Quelles sont les qualités d'un animal de compagnie/d'un chien/d'un chat?*"

- Describe the qualities of Santa Claus:
  "*Quelles sont les qualités du Père Noël?*"

- Describe the qualities of a famous person (athlete, celebrity, etc):
  "*Quelles sont les qualités d'un célèbre/d'un athlète professionnel, de Kristen Stewart, de Sponge Bob Square Pants?*"

- Pick something that they know about—some current famous person or character: The list is endless!

Les adjectifs!
(Adjectives!)

Quiz-Quiz-Trade

Students pair up and question each other about the adjective forms—giving the adjective in the opposite form, either masculine or feminine.

Steps

Setup: The teacher creates and laminates *Les adjectifs!* cards for students. An erasable marker is given to each student to write the answer on the back of the card before playing Quiz-Quiz-Trade.

1 **Distribute Cards**
The teacher distributes one laminated card to each student. Students write the opposite form of the adjective on the back of the card. **Hint:** This can be a team effort, checking each other's answers to make sure that they are written correctly before playing.

2 **Find a Partner**
With their card in hand, students pair up with another student from another team and stand shoulder to shoulder.

3 **Students Quiz Each Other**
To quiz a partner, students state the adjective on their card and their partner must state the adjective in the opposite form (masculine/feminine). Then, the other partner quizzes his or her partner about the partner's card. **Hint:** If his or her partner does not know the correct response, the answer is immediately shown to him or her and then questioned again.

4 **Trade Cards and Find New Partners**
After partners have asked and answered each other's questions, they give each other a high five, trade cards and find a new partner.

(continued)

Les adjectifs!
(Adjectives!)

Quiz-Quiz-Trade

Steps

5 Continue Quizzing
This activity can go on for an allotted amount of time, or for a number of trades.

Variations

• **Increase Difficulty.** Have students write the plural forms of the adjectives on the back of the card to trade with classmates.

• **Color-Code the Cards.** Copy the cards on different colored paper so the masculine forms are on one color and the feminine forms on another color to clearly differentiate the gender. Students will know what form to answer (masculine or feminine depending on what color the card is).

• **Color-Code According to Rules.** Cards can be color-coded according to the ways they change (e.g., *–if* to *–ive*, *-eux* to *–euse*, *-ien* to *–ienne*, etc.)

Les adjectifs masculins!
(Masculine adjectives!)

Directions: Cut out the *Les adjectifs masculins!* cards along the dotted line. Then fold the card in half so the question is on the front and the answer is on the back. Glue or tape cards together to keep the answers and questions on opposite sides.

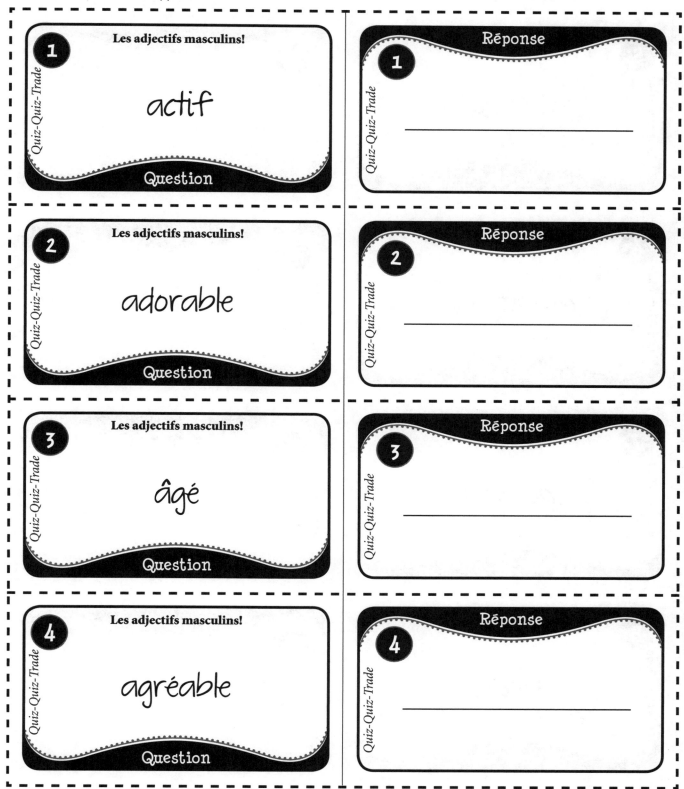

1 — Les adjectifs masculins! — Quiz-Quiz-Trade

actif

Question

1 — Réponse — Quiz-Quiz-Trade

_____

2 — Les adjectifs masculins! — Quiz-Quiz-Trade

adorable

Question

2 — Réponse — Quiz-Quiz-Trade

_____

3 — Les adjectifs masculins! — Quiz-Quiz-Trade

âgé

Question

3 — Réponse — Quiz-Quiz-Trade

_____

4 — Les adjectifs masculins! — Quiz-Quiz-Trade

agréable

Question

4 — Réponse — Quiz-Quiz-Trade

_____

Les adjectifs masculins!
(Masculine adjectives!)

Directions: Cut out the *Les adjectifs masculins!* cards along the dotted line. Then fold the card in half so the question is on the front and the answer is on the back. Glue or tape cards together to keep the answers and questions on opposite sides.

5 Les adjectifs masculins!

Quiz-Quiz-Trade

agressif

Question

5 Réponse

Quiz-Quiz-Trade

_____

6 Les adjectifs masculins!

Quiz-Quiz-Trade

ambitieux

Question

6 Réponse

Quiz-Quiz-Trade

_____

7 Les adjectifs masculins!

Quiz-Quiz-Trade

bavard

Question

7 Réponse

Quiz-Quiz-Trade

_____

8 Les adjectifs masculins!

Quiz-Quiz-Trade

beau

Question

8 Réponse

Quiz-Quiz-Trade

_____

Les adjectifs masculins!
(Masculine adjectives!)

Directions: Cut out the *Les adjectifs masculins!* cards along the dotted line. Then fold the card in half so the question is on the front and the answer is on the back. Glue or tape cards together to keep the answers and questions on opposite sides.

9 Quiz-Quiz-Trade — Les adjectifs masculins!

calme

Question

9 Quiz-Quiz-Trade — Réponse

_____

10 Quiz-Quiz-Trade — Les adjectifs masculins!

célèbre

Question

10 Quiz-Quiz-Trade — Réponse

_____

11 Quiz-Quiz-Trade — Les adjectifs masculins!

content

Question

11 Quiz-Quiz-Trade — Réponse

_____

12 Quiz-Quiz-Trade — Les adjectifs masculins!

courageux

Question

12 Quiz-Quiz-Trade — Réponse

_____

Les adjectifs masculins!
(Masculine adjectives!)

Directions: Cut out the *Les adjectifs masculins!* cards along the dotted line. Then fold the card in half so the question is on the front and the answer is on the back. Glue or tape cards together to keep the answers and questions on opposite sides.

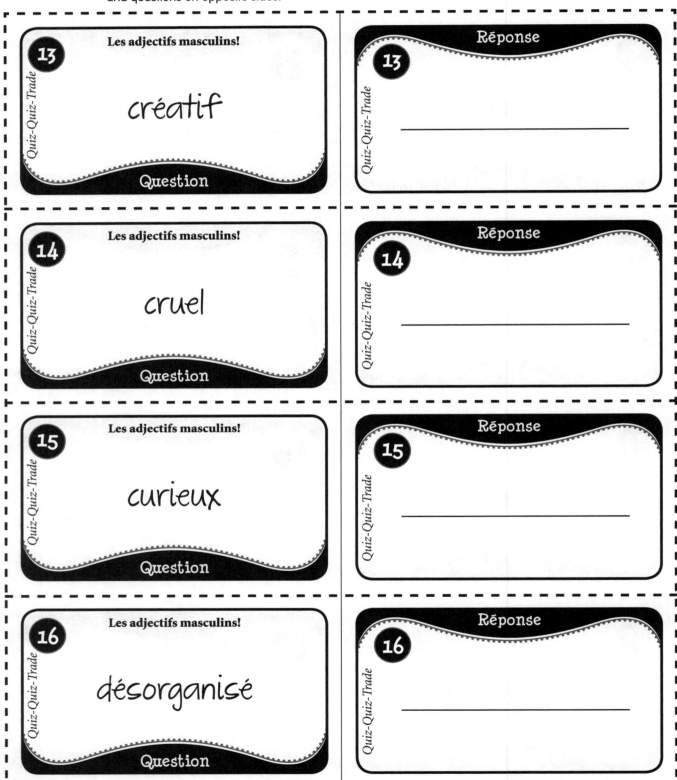

13 Les adjectifs masculins!
Quiz-Quiz-Trade

créatif

Question

Réponse
13
Quiz-Quiz-Trade

_____

14 Les adjectifs masculins!
Quiz-Quiz-Trade

cruel

Question

Réponse
14
Quiz-Quiz-Trade

_____

15 Les adjectifs masculins!
Quiz-Quiz-Trade

curieux

Question

Réponse
15
Quiz-Quiz-Trade

_____

16 Les adjectifs masculins!
Quiz-Quiz-Trade

désorganisé

Question

Réponse
16
Quiz-Quiz-Trade

_____

Les adjectifs masculins!
(Masculine adjectives!)

Directions: Cut out the *Les adjectifs masculins!* cards along the dotted line. Then fold the card in half so the question is on the front and the answer is on the back. Glue or tape cards together to keep the answers and questions on opposite sides.

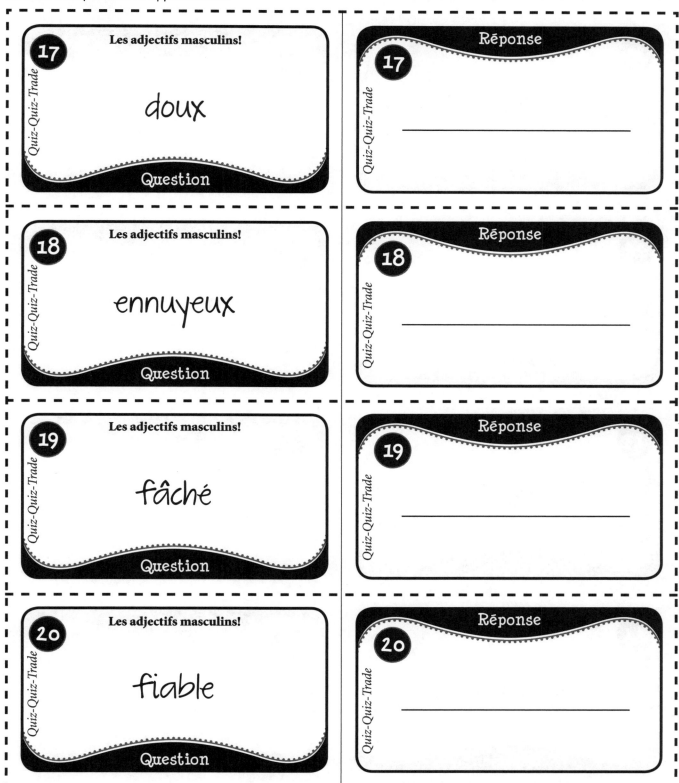

17 — Les adjectifs masculins! — Quiz-Quiz-Trade

doux

Question

17 — Réponse — Quiz-Quiz-Trade

_____

18 — Les adjectifs masculins! — Quiz-Quiz-Trade

ennuyeux

Question

18 — Réponse — Quiz-Quiz-Trade

_____

19 — Les adjectifs masculins! — Quiz-Quiz-Trade

fâché

Question

19 — Réponse — Quiz-Quiz-Trade

_____

20 — Les adjectifs masculins! — Quiz-Quiz-Trade

fiable

Question

20 — Réponse — Quiz-Quiz-Trade

_____

Les adjectifs masculins!
(Masculine adjectives!)

Directions: Cut out the *Les adjectifs masculins!* cards along the dotted line. Then fold the card in half so the question is on the front and the answer is on the back. Glue or tape cards together to keep the answers and questions on opposite sides.

21 Quiz-Quiz-Trade — Les adjectifs masculins! **fier** Question	Réponse **21** Quiz-Quiz-Trade _____
22 Quiz-Quiz-Trade — Les adjectifs masculins! **fou** Question	Réponse **22** Quiz-Quiz-Trade _____
23 Quiz-Quiz-Trade — Les adjectifs masculins! **fort** Question	Réponse **23** Quiz-Quiz-Trade _____
24 Quiz-Quiz-Trade — Les adjectifs masculins! **généreux** Question	Réponse **24** Quiz-Quiz-Trade _____

Les adjectifs masculins!
(Masculine adjectives!)

Directions: Cut out the *Les adjectifs masculins!* cards along the dotted line. Then fold the card in half so the question is on the front and the answer is on the back. Glue or tape cards together to keep the answers and questions on opposite sides.

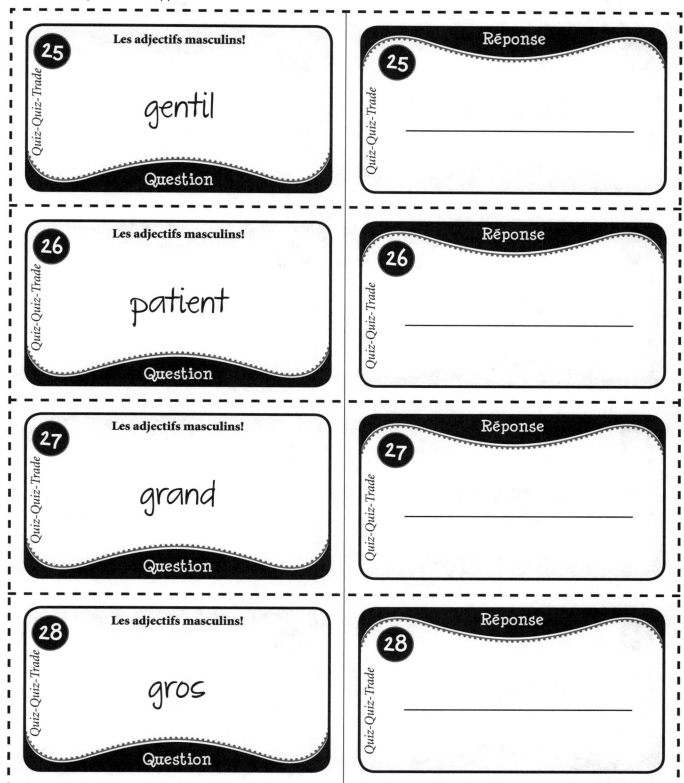

25 Les adjectifs masculins!

Quiz-Quiz-Trade

gentil

Question

Réponse
25

Quiz-Quiz-Trade

_____

26 Les adjectifs masculins!

Quiz-Quiz-Trade

patient

Question

Réponse
26

Quiz-Quiz-Trade

_____

27 Les adjectifs masculins!

Quiz-Quiz-Trade

grand

Question

Réponse
27

Quiz-Quiz-Trade

_____

28 Les adjectifs masculins!

Quiz-Quiz-Trade

gros

Question

Réponse
28

Quiz-Quiz-Trade

_____

Activity 4
Quiz-Quiz-Trade

Les adjectifs masculins!
(Masculine adjectives!)

Directions: Cut out the *Les adjectifs masculins!* cards along the dotted line. Then fold the card in half so the question is on the front and the answer is on the back. Glue or tape cards together to keep the answers and questions on opposite sides.

Quiz-Quiz-Trade

29 Les adjectifs masculins!

heureux

Question

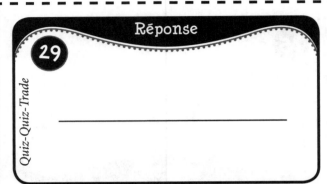

Quiz-Quiz-Trade

Réponse

29

_____

Quiz-Quiz-Trade

30 Les adjectifs masculins!

honnête

Question

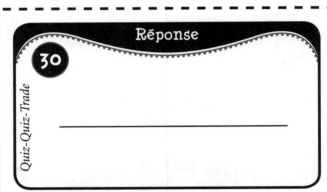

Quiz-Quiz-Trade

Réponse

30

_____

Quiz-Quiz-Trade

31 Les adjectifs masculins!

imaginatif

Question

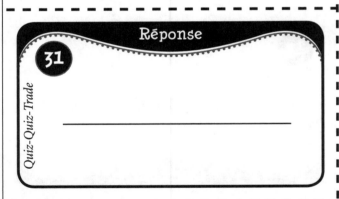

Quiz-Quiz-Trade

Réponse

31

_____

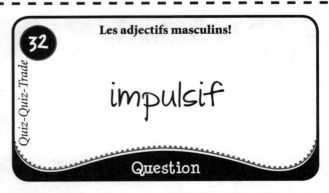

Quiz-Quiz-Trade

32 Les adjectifs masculins!

impulsif

Question

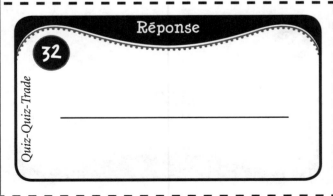

Quiz-Quiz-Trade

Réponse

32

_____

Les adjectifs masculins!
(Masculine adjectives!)

Directions: Cut out the *Les adjectifs masculins!* cards along the dotted line. Then fold the card in half so the question is on the front and the answer is on the back. Glue or tape cards together to keep the answers and questions on opposite sides.

33 Quiz-Quiz-Trade — Les adjectifs masculins! intéressant Question	**Réponse** 33 Quiz-Quiz-Trade _____
34 Quiz-Quiz-Trade — Les adjectifs masculins! laid Question	**Réponse** 34 Quiz-Quiz-Trade _____
35 Quiz-Quiz-Trade — Les adjectifs masculins! malade Question	**Réponse** 35 Quiz-Quiz-Trade _____
36 Quiz-Quiz-Trade — Les adjectifs masculins! malheureux Question	**Réponse** 36 Quiz-Quiz-Trade _____

Les adjectifs masculins!
(Masculine adjectives!)

Directions: Cut out the *Les adjectifs masculins!* cards along the dotted line. Then fold the card in half so the question is on the front and the answer is on the back. Glue or tape cards together to keep the answers and questions on opposite sides.

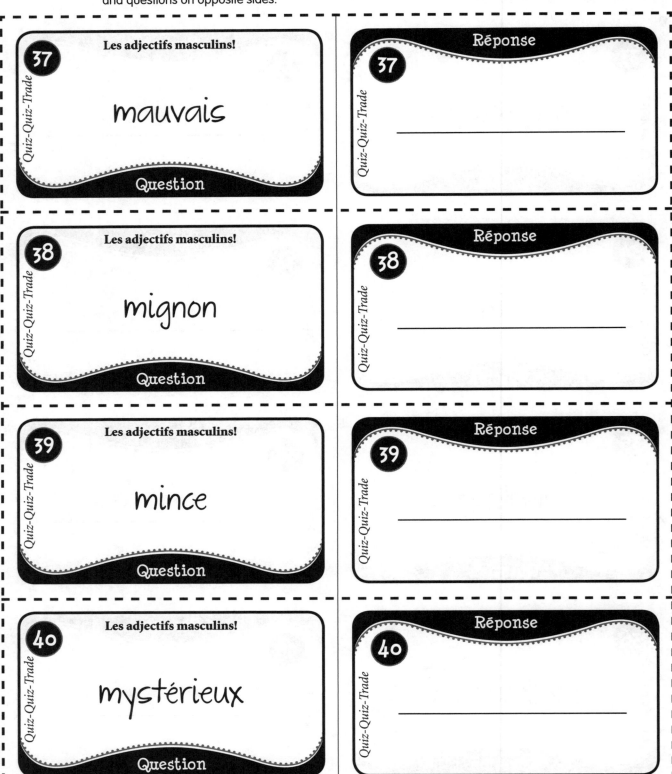

37 *Quiz-Quiz-Trade* — Les adjectifs masculins!

mauvais

Question

Réponse **37** *Quiz-Quiz-Trade* _____

38 *Quiz-Quiz-Trade* — Les adjectifs masculins!

mignon

Question

Réponse **38** *Quiz-Quiz-Trade* _____

39 *Quiz-Quiz-Trade* — Les adjectifs masculins!

mince

Question

Réponse **39** *Quiz-Quiz-Trade* _____

40 *Quiz-Quiz-Trade* — Les adjectifs masculins!

mystérieux

Question

Réponse **40** *Quiz-Quiz-Trade* _____

Les adjectifs masculins!
(Masculine adjectives!)

Directions: Cut out the *Les adjectifs masculins!* cards along the dotted line. Then fold the card in half so the question is on the front and the answer is on the back. Glue or tape cards together to keep the answers and questions on opposite sides.

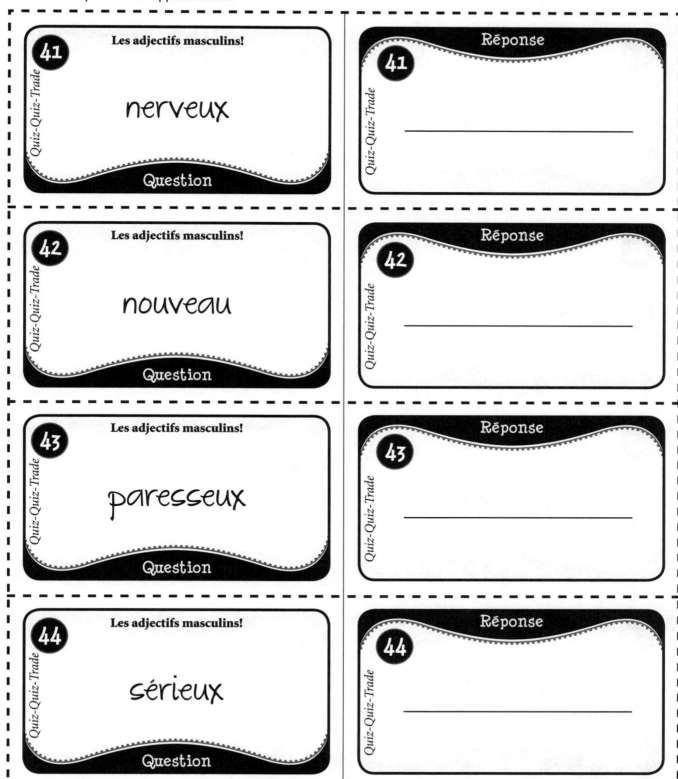

41 · Les adjectifs masculins! · Quiz-Quiz-Trade

nerveux

Question

41 · Réponse · Quiz-Quiz-Trade

_____

42 · Les adjectifs masculins! · Quiz-Quiz-Trade

nouveau

Question

42 · Réponse · Quiz-Quiz-Trade

_____

43 · Les adjectifs masculins! · Quiz-Quiz-Trade

paresseux

Question

43 · Réponse · Quiz-Quiz-Trade

_____

44 · Les adjectifs masculins! · Quiz-Quiz-Trade

sérieux

Question

44 · Réponse · Quiz-Quiz-Trade

_____

Les adjectifs masculins!
(Masculine adjectives!)

Directions: Cut out the *Les adjectifs masculins!* cards along the dotted line. Then fold the card in half so the question is on the front and the answer is on the back. Glue or tape cards together to keep the answers and questions on opposite sides.

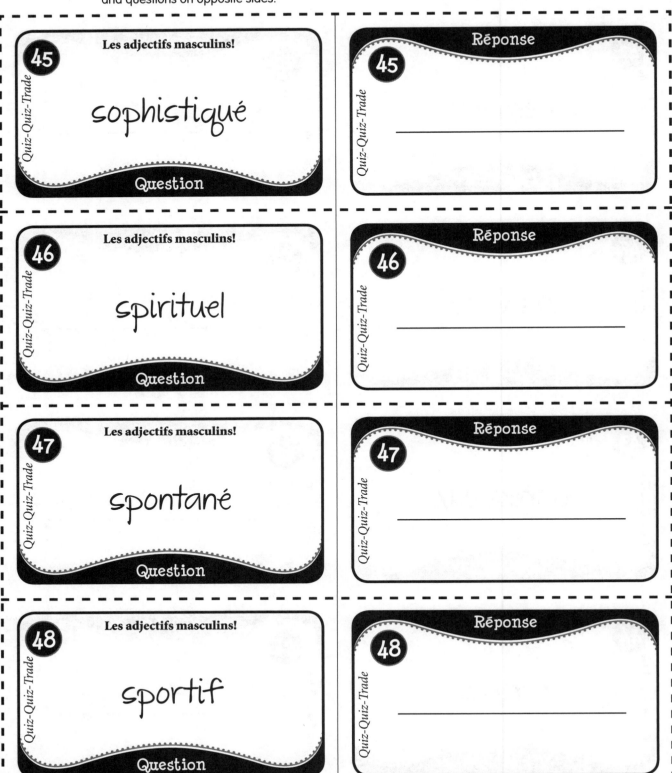

45 — Quiz-Quiz-Trade — Les adjectifs masculins!

sophistiqué

Question

45 — Quiz-Quiz-Trade — Réponse
_____

46 — Quiz-Quiz-Trade — Les adjectifs masculins!

spirituel

Question

46 — Quiz-Quiz-Trade — Réponse
_____

47 — Quiz-Quiz-Trade — Les adjectifs masculins!

spontané

Question

47 — Quiz-Quiz-Trade — Réponse
_____

48 — Quiz-Quiz-Trade — Les adjectifs masculins!

sportif

Question

48 — Quiz-Quiz-Trade — Réponse
_____

Les adjectifs masculins!
(Masculine adjectives!)

Directions: Cut out the *Les adjectifs masculins!* cards along the dotted line. Then fold the card in half so the question is on the front and the answer is on the back. Glue or tape cards together to keep the answers and questions on opposite sides.

Quiz-Quiz-Trade
49 — Les adjectifs masculins!
têtu
Question

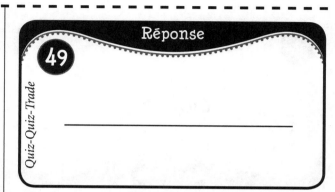

Quiz-Quiz-Trade
Réponse
49
_____

Quiz-Quiz-Trade
50 — Les adjectifs masculins!
timide
Question

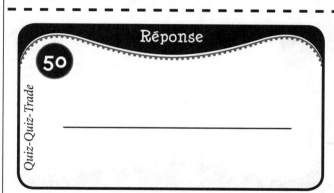

Quiz-Quiz-Trade
Réponse
50
_____

Quiz-Quiz-Trade
51 — Les adjectifs masculins!
travailleur
Question

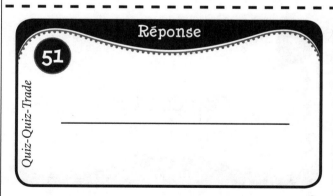

Quiz-Quiz-Trade
Réponse
51
_____

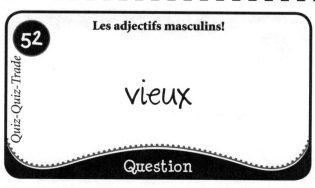

Quiz-Quiz-Trade
52 — Les adjectifs masculins!
vieux
Question

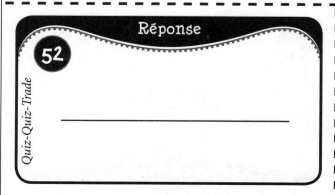

Quiz-Quiz-Trade
Réponse
52
_____

Les adjectifs féminins!
(Feminine adjectives!)

Directions: Cut out the *Les adjectifs féminins!* cards along the dotted line. Then fold the card in half so the question is on the front and the answer is on the back. Glue or tape cards together to keep the answers and questions on opposite sides.

Les adjectifs féminins!

1

Quiz-Quiz-Trade

active

Question

Réponse

1

Quiz-Quiz-Trade

_____

Les adjectifs féminins!

2

Quiz-Quiz-Trade

âgée

Question

Réponse

2

Quiz-Quiz-Trade

_____

Les adjectifs féminins!

3

Quiz-Quiz-Trade

agressive

Question

Réponse

3

Quiz-Quiz-Trade

_____

Les adjectifs féminins!

4

Quiz-Quiz-Trade

amiable

Question

Réponse

4

Quiz-Quiz-Trade

_____

Cooperative Learning & French • Chiupka-Jozin
Kagan Publishing • 1 (800) 933-2667 • www.KaganOnline.com

Les adjectifs féminins!
(Feminine adjectives!)

Directions: Cut out the *Les adjectifs féminins!* cards along the dotted line. Then fold the card in half so the question is on the front and the answer is on the back. Glue or tape cards together to keep the answers and questions on opposite sides.

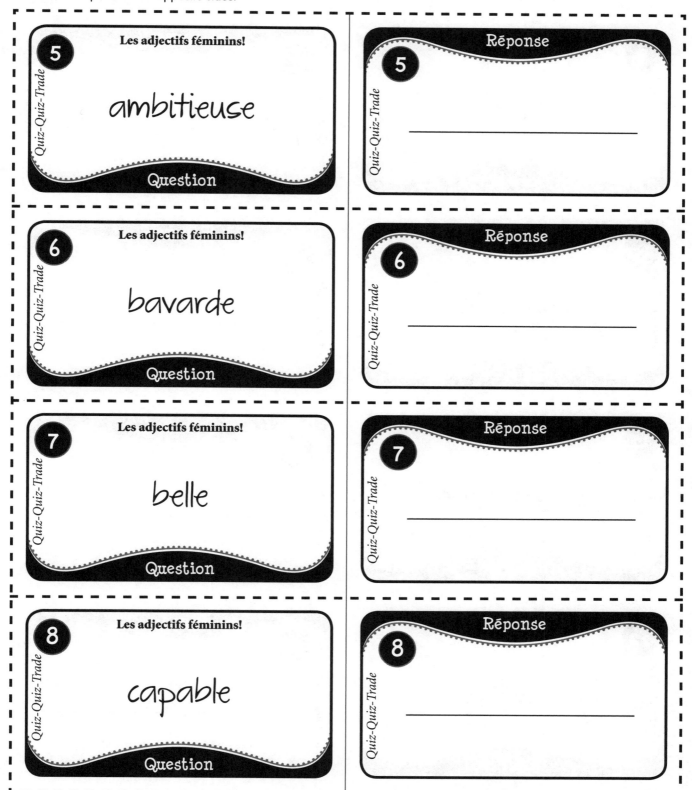

5 Les adjectifs féminins!

ambitieuse

Question

5 Réponse

_____

6 Les adjectifs féminins!

bavarde

Question

6 Réponse

_____

7 Les adjectifs féminins!

belle

Question

7 Réponse

_____

8 Les adjectifs féminins!

capable

Question

8 Réponse

_____

Les adjectifs féminins!
(Feminine adjectives!)

Directions: Cut out the *Les adjectifs féminins!* cards along the dotted line. Then fold the card in half so the question is on the front and the answer is on the back. Glue or tape cards together to keep the answers and questions on opposite sides.

9 — Quiz-Quiz-Trade — Les adjectifs féminins!

chic

Question

9 — Quiz-Quiz-Trade — Réponse

_____

10 — Quiz-Quiz-Trade — Les adjectifs féminins!

contente

Question

10 — Quiz-Quiz-Trade — Réponse

_____

11 — Quiz-Quiz-Trade — Les adjectifs féminins!

courageuse

Question

11 — Quiz-Quiz-Trade — Réponse

_____

12 — Quiz-Quiz-Trade — Les adjectifs féminins!

créative

Question

12 — Quiz-Quiz-Trade — Réponse

_____

Les adjectifs féminins!
(Feminine adjectives!)

Directions: Cut out the *Les adjectifs féminins!* cards along the dotted line. Then fold the card in half so the question is on the front and the answer is on the back. Glue or tape cards together to keep the answers and questions on opposite sides.

13
Quiz-Quiz-Trade
Les adjectifs féminins!

cruelle

Question

13
Quiz-Quiz-Trade
Réponse

_____

14
Quiz-Quiz-Trade
Les adjectifs féminins!

curieuse

Question

14
Quiz-Quiz-Trade
Réponse

_____

15
Quiz-Quiz-Trade
Les adjectifs féminins!

distraite

Question

15
Quiz-Quiz-Trade
Réponse

_____

16
Quiz-Quiz-Trade
Les adjectifs féminins!

douce

Question

16
Quiz-Quiz-Trade
Réponse

_____

Les adjectifs féminins!
(Feminine adjectives!)

Directions: Cut out the *Les adjectifs féminins!* cards along the dotted line. Then fold the card in half so the question is on the front and the answer is on the back. Glue or tape cards together to keep the answers and questions on opposite sides.

17 — Quiz-Quiz-Trade — **Les adjectifs féminins!**

énergique

Question

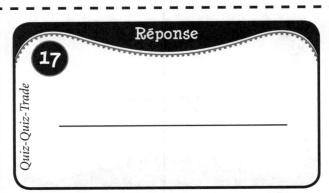

Réponse

17 — Quiz-Quiz-Trade

_____

18 — Quiz-Quiz-Trade — **Les adjectifs féminins!**

extraverti(e)

Question

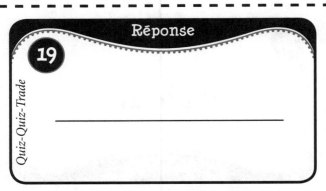

Réponse

18 — Quiz-Quiz-Trade

_____

19 — Quiz-Quiz-Trade — **Les adjectifs féminins!**

faible

Question

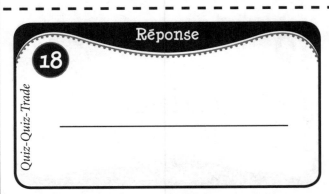

Réponse

19 — Quiz-Quiz-Trade

_____

20 — Quiz-Quiz-Trade — **Les adjectifs féminins!**

fière

Question

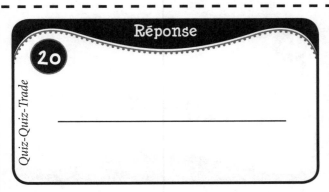

Réponse

20 — Quiz-Quiz-Trade

_____

Les adjectifs féminins!
(Feminine adjectives!)

Directions: Cut out the *Les adjectifs féminins!* cards along the dotted line. Then fold the card in half so the question is on the front and the answer is on the back. Glue or tape cards together to keep the answers and questions on opposite sides.

21 Quiz-Quiz-Trade — Les adjectifs féminins!

forte

Question

21 Quiz-Quiz-Trade — Réponse

_____

22 Quiz-Quiz-Trade — Les adjectifs féminins!

généreuse

Question

22 Quiz-Quiz-Trade — Réponse

_____

23 Quiz-Quiz-Trade — Les adjectifs féminins!

grosse

Question

23 Quiz-Quiz-Trade — Réponse

_____

24 Quiz-Quiz-Trade — Les adjectifs féminins!

honnête

Question

24 Quiz-Quiz-Trade — Réponse

_____

Activity 4 · Quiz-Quiz-Trade

Les adjectifs féminins!
(Feminine adjectives!)

Directions: Cut out the *Les adjectifs féminins!* cards along the dotted line. Then fold the card in half so the question is on the front and the answer is on the back. Glue or tape cards together to keep the answers and questions on opposite sides.

25 Les adjectifs féminins! — imaginative — Question

25 Réponse _____

26 Les adjectifs féminins! — impulsive — Question

26 Réponse _____

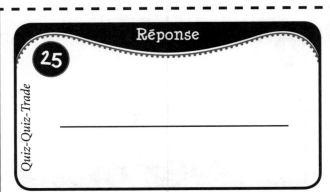

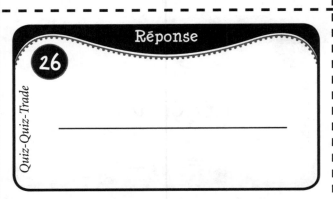

27 Les adjectifs féminins! — indépendante — Question

27 Réponse _____

28 Les adjectifs féminins! — intelligente — Question

28 Réponse _____

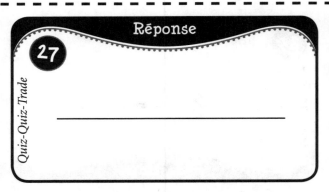

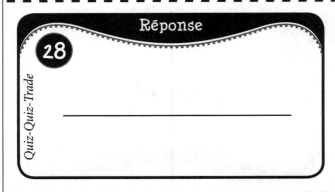

Cooperative Learning & French • Chiupka-Jozin
Kagan Publishing • 1 (800) 933-2667 • www.KaganOnline.com

Les adjectifs féminins!
(Feminine adjectives!)

Directions: Cut out the *Les adjectifs féminins!* cards along the dotted line. Then fold the card in half so the question is on the front and the answer is on the back. Glue or tape cards together to keep the answers and questions on opposite sides.

29 Quiz-Quiz-Trade — Les adjectifs féminins!

introvertie

Question

29 Quiz-Quiz-Trade — Réponse

_____

30 Quiz-Quiz-Trade — Les adjectifs féminins!

jolie

Question

30 Quiz-Quiz-Trade — Réponse

_____

31 Quiz-Quiz-Trade — Les adjectifs féminins!

maladroite

Question

31 Quiz-Quiz-Trade — Réponse

_____

32 Quiz-Quiz-Trade — Les adjectifs féminins!

malheureuse

Question

32 Quiz-Quiz-Trade — Réponse

_____

Les adjectifs féminins!
(Feminine adjectives!)

Directions: Cut out the *Les adjectifs féminins!* cards along the dotted line. Then fold the card in half so the question is on the front and the answer is on the back. Glue or tape cards together to keep the answers and questions on opposite sides.

33 Quiz-Quiz-Trade — Les adjectifs féminins! méchante Question	**33** Quiz-Quiz-Trade — Réponse _____
34 Quiz-Quiz-Trade — Les adjectifs féminins! mignonne Question	**34** Quiz-Quiz-Trade — Réponse _____
35 Quiz-Quiz-Trade — Les adjectifs féminins! mystérieuse Question	**35** Quiz-Quiz-Trade — Réponse _____
36 Quiz-Quiz-Trade — Les adjectifs féminins! nerveuse Question	**36** Quiz-Quiz-Trade — Réponse _____

Les adjectifs féminins!
(Feminine adjectives!)

Directions: Cut out the *Les adjectifs féminins!* cards along the dotted line. Then fold the card in half so the question is on the front and the answer is on the back. Glue or tape cards together to keep the answers and questions on opposite sides.

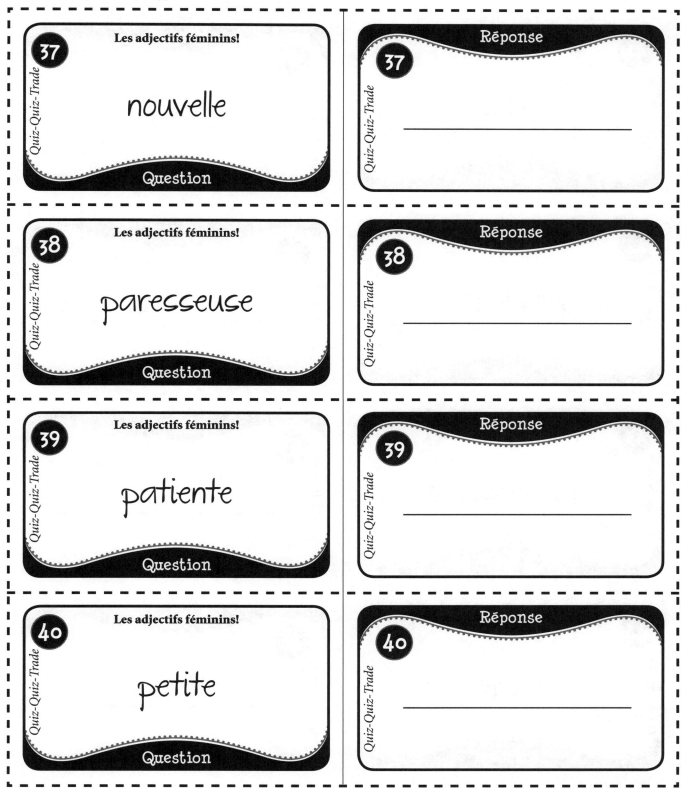

37 — Quiz-Quiz-Trade — Les adjectifs féminins!

nouvelle

Question

37 — Quiz-Quiz-Trade — Réponse

_____

38 — Quiz-Quiz-Trade — Les adjectifs féminins!

paresseuse

Question

38 — Quiz-Quiz-Trade — Réponse

_____

39 — Quiz-Quiz-Trade — Les adjectifs féminins!

patiente

Question

39 — Quiz-Quiz-Trade — Réponse

_____

40 — Quiz-Quiz-Trade — Les adjectifs féminins!

petite

Question

40 — Quiz-Quiz-Trade — Réponse

_____

Les adjectifs féminins!
(Feminine adjectives!)

Directions: Cut out the *Les adjectifs féminins!* cards along the dotted line. Then fold the card in half so the question is on the front and the answer is on the back. Glue or tape cards together to keep the answers and questions on opposite sides.

Les adjectifs féminins!

41 | Quiz-Quiz-Trade

polie

Question

Réponse

41 | Quiz-Quiz-Trade

_____

Les adjectifs féminins!

42 | Quiz-Quiz-Trade

prudente

Question

Réponse

42 | Quiz-Quiz-Trade

_____

Les adjectifs féminins!

43 | Quiz-Quiz-Trade

responsable

Question

Réponse

43 | Quiz-Quiz-Trade

_____

Les adjectifs féminins!

44 | Quiz-Quiz-Trade

riche

Question

Réponse

44 | Quiz-Quiz-Trade

_____

Les adjectifs féminins!
(Feminine adjectives!)

Directions: Cut out the *Les adjectifs féminins!* cards along the dotted line. Then fold the card in half so the question is on the front and the answer is on the back. Glue or tape cards together to keep the answers and questions on opposite sides.

45 — Les adjectifs féminins! — Quiz-Quiz-Trade

sensible

Question

45 — Réponse — Quiz-Quiz-Trade

_____

46 — Les adjectifs féminins! — Quiz-Quiz-Trade

sérieuse

Question

46 — Réponse — Quiz-Quiz-Trade

_____

47 — Les adjectifs féminins! — Quiz-Quiz-Trade

spirituelle

Question

47 — Réponse — Quiz-Quiz-Trade

_____

48 — Les adjectifs féminins! — Quiz-Quiz-Trade

sportive

Question

48 — Réponse — Quiz-Quiz-Trade

_____

Les adjectifs féminins!
(Feminine adjectives!)

Directions: Cut out the *Les adjectifs féminins!* cards along the dotted line. Then fold the card in half so the question is on the front and the answer is on the back. Glue or tape cards together to keep the answers and questions on opposite sides.

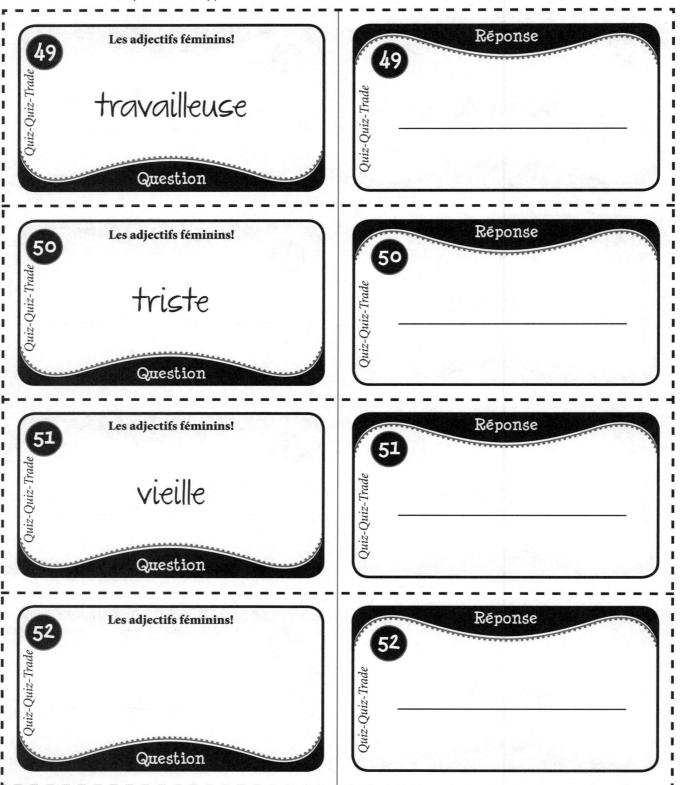

49 — Quiz-Quiz-Trade — Les adjectifs féminins!

travailleuse

Question

Réponse

49 — Quiz-Quiz-Trade

_____

50 — Quiz-Quiz-Trade — Les adjectifs féminins!

triste

Question

Réponse

50 — Quiz-Quiz-Trade

_____

51 — Quiz-Quiz-Trade — Les adjectifs féminins!

vieille

Question

Réponse

51 — Quiz-Quiz-Trade

_____

52 — Quiz-Quiz-Trade — Les adjectifs féminins!

Question

Réponse

52 — Quiz-Quiz-Trade

_____

Montrez-moi les adjectifs!
(Show me the adjectives!)

Showdown

Students practice writing the different forms of adjectives, seeing how well they remember the different forms. This is a great way to quickly assess their ability and understanding. This activity can be played in teams or as a whole class.

Steps

Setup: For the Showdown question cards, use the cards from Activity 4 *Les adjectifs!*, or use the cards from this activity. The teacher cuts out cards before distributing them to teams. Students can use dry erase boards to write their answers and erase them for the next round.

1 Distribute Question Cards
Each team receives a set of Adjective cards. The cards are placed in the center of the team table.

2 Read the Question
The Showdown Captain reads a card stating the form and what the teammates write down. (Students can be asked to write the opposite gender—masculine/feminine, or the plural form of the adjective.)

3 Think and Write Answers
Students work alone and write answers.

4 Signal When Ready
Teammates signal "thumbs up" when ready.

5 Montrez-Moi
The Showdown Captain calls, *"Showdown!"* or *"Montrez-moi!"* in French.

6 Teams Discuss
Teammates show and discuss their answers. If there is concern as to the correct answer, all members of the team must be in consensus and all must raise their hands. The teacher will then respond to their questions.

(continued)

5 Montrez-moi les adjectifs!
(Show me the adjectives!)

Showdown

7 Celebrate
Teammates celebrate or coach, discussing the correct form of the adjectives.

8 Start a New Round
A new Showdown Captain leads the next round, picking another Adjective Card and having teammates write down the correct form of the adjective.

Variations

• **Limit Cards.** Limit the cards distributed to each team.

• **Masculine or Feminine.** Chose only masculine or feminine cards for students to work with.

• **Choose Theme.** Decide in advance what the "theme of the game" will be: masculine form to feminine, feminine form to masculine, or plural forms.

• **Mix It Up.** Challenge students by giving them a variety of cards. They have to decide what teammates must write down.

Montrez-moi les adjectifs!
Show me the adjectives!

Directions: Cut out the *les adjectifs!* cards along the dotted line. Teams place cards in the center of the table. The Showdown Captain picks a card and reads it aloud. Teammates each write the correct form of the adjective. Students "showdown" to compare answers.

1 Showdown actif	**2** Showdown adorable
3 Showdown âgé	**4** Showdown agréable
5 Showdown agressif	**6** Showdown ambitieux
7 Showdown bavard	**8** Showdown beau

Montrez-moi les adjectifs!
Show me the adjectives!

Directions: Cut out the *les adjectifs!* cards along the dotted line. Teams place cards in the center of the table. The Showdown Captain picks a card and reads it aloud. Teammates each write the correct form of the adjective. Students "showdown" to compare answers.

9 Showdown calme	**10** Showdown célèbre
11 Showdown content	**12** Showdown courageux
13 Showdown créatif	**14** Showdown cruel
15 Showdown curieux	**16** Showdown désorganisé

Montrez-moi les adjectifs!
Show me the adjectives!

Directions: Cut out the *les adjectifs!* cards along the dotted line. Teams place cards in the center of the table. The Showdown Captain picks a card and reads it aloud. Teammates each write the correct form of the adjective. Students "showdown" to compare answers.

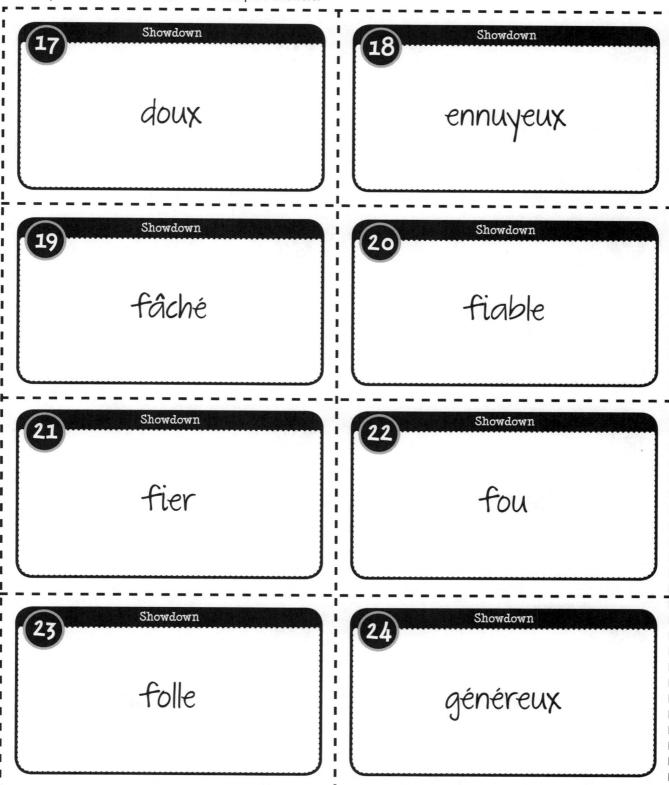

17 Showdown doux	**18** Showdown ennuyeux
19 Showdown fâché	**20** Showdown fiable
21 Showdown fier	**22** Showdown fou
23 Showdown folle	**24** Showdown généreux

Montrez-moi les adjectifs!
Show me the adjectives!

Directions: Cut out the *les adjectifs!* cards along the dotted line. Teams place cards in the center of the table. The Showdown Captain picks a card and reads it aloud. Teammates each write the correct form of the adjective. Students "showdown" to compare answers.

25 Showdown gentil	**26** Showdown gentille
27 Showdown grand	**28** Showdown gros
29 Showdown heureux	**30** Showdown heureuse
31 Showdown imaginatif	**32** Showdown impulsif

Montrez-moi les adjectifs!
Show me the adjectives!

Directions: Cut out the *les adjectifs!* cards along the dotted line. Teams place cards in the center of the table. The Showdown Captain picks a card and reads it aloud. Teammates each write the correct form of the adjective. Students "showdown" to compare answers.

33 Showdown intéressant	**34** Showdown laid
35 Showdown malade	**36** Showdown malheureux
37 Showdown mauvais	**38** Showdown mignon
39 Showdown mince	**40** Showdown mystérieux

Montrez-moi les adjectifs!
Show me the adjectives!

Directions: Cut out the *les adjectifs!* cards along the dotted line. Teams place cards in the center of the table. The Showdown Captain picks a card and reads it aloud. Teammates each write the correct form of the adjective. Students "showdown" to compare answers.

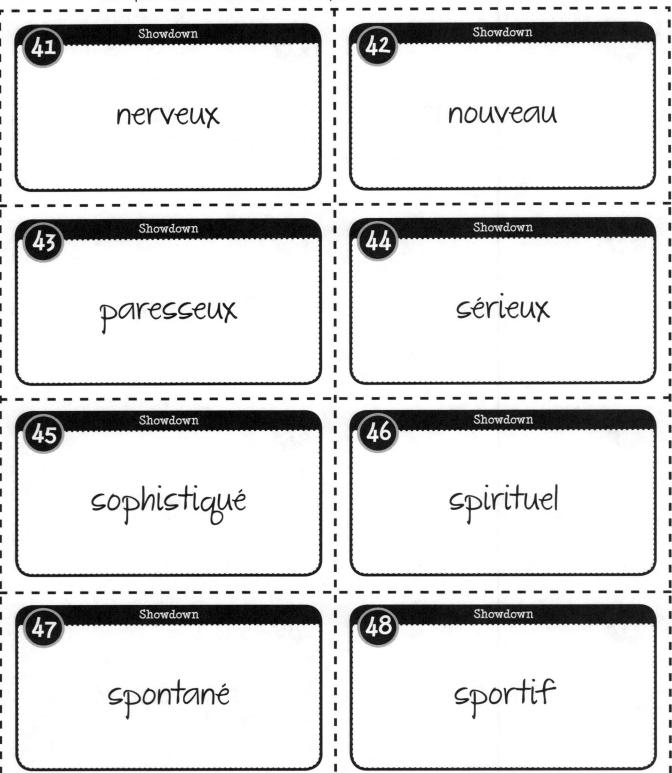

41 Showdown	42 Showdown
nerveux	nouveau

43 Showdown	44 Showdown
paresseux	sérieux

45 Showdown	46 Showdown
sophistiqué	spirituel

47 Showdown	48 Showdown
spontané	sportif

Montrez-moi les adjectifs!
Show me the adjectives!

Directions: Cut out the *les adjectifs!* cards along the dotted line. Teams place cards in the center of the table. The Showdown Captain picks a card and reads it aloud. Teammates each write the correct form of the adjective. Students "showdown" to compare answers.

49 Showdown têtu	**50** Showdown timide
51 Showdown travailleur	**52** Showdown vieux
53 Showdown active	**54** Showdown âgée
55 Showdown agressive	**56** Showdown amiable

Montrez-moi les adjectifs!
Show me the adjectives!

Directions: Cut out the *les adjectifs!* cards along the dotted line. Teams place cards in the center of the table. The Showdown Captain picks a card and reads it aloud. Teammates each write the correct form of the adjective. Students "showdown" to compare answers.

57 Showdown ambitieuse	**58** Showdown bavarde
59 Showdown belle	**60** Showdown capable
61 Showdown chic	**62** Showdown contente
63 Showdown courageuse	**64** Showdown créative

Montrez-moi les adjectifs!
Show me the adjectives!

Directions: Cut out the *les adjectifs!* cards along the dotted line. Teams place cards in the center of the table. The Showdown Captain picks a card and reads it aloud. Teammates each write the correct form of the adjective. Students "showdown" to compare answers.

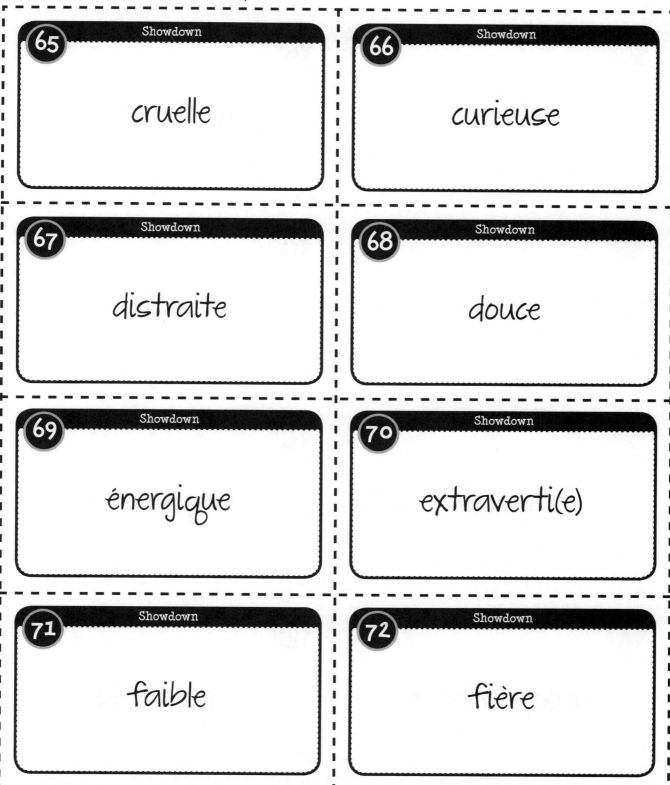

65 Showdown cruelle	**66** Showdown curieuse
67 Showdown distraite	**68** Showdown douce
69 Showdown énergique	**70** Showdown extraverti(e)
71 Showdown faible	**72** Showdown fière

Montrez-moi les adjectifs!
Show me the adjectives!

Directions: Cut out the *les adjectifs!* cards along the dotted line. Teams place cards in the center of the table. The Showdown Captain picks a card and reads it aloud. Teammates each write the correct form of the adjective. Students "showdown" to compare answers.

73 Showdown forte	**74** Showdown généreuse
75 Showdown grosse	**76** Showdown honnête
77 Showdown imaginative	**78** Showdown impulsive
79 Showdown indépendante	**80** Showdown intelligente

Montrez-moi les adjectifs!
Show me the adjectives!

Directions: Cut out the *les adjectifs!* cards along the dotted line. Teams place cards in the center of the table. The Showdown Captain picks a card and reads it aloud. Teammates each write the correct form of the adjective. Students "showdown" to compare answers.

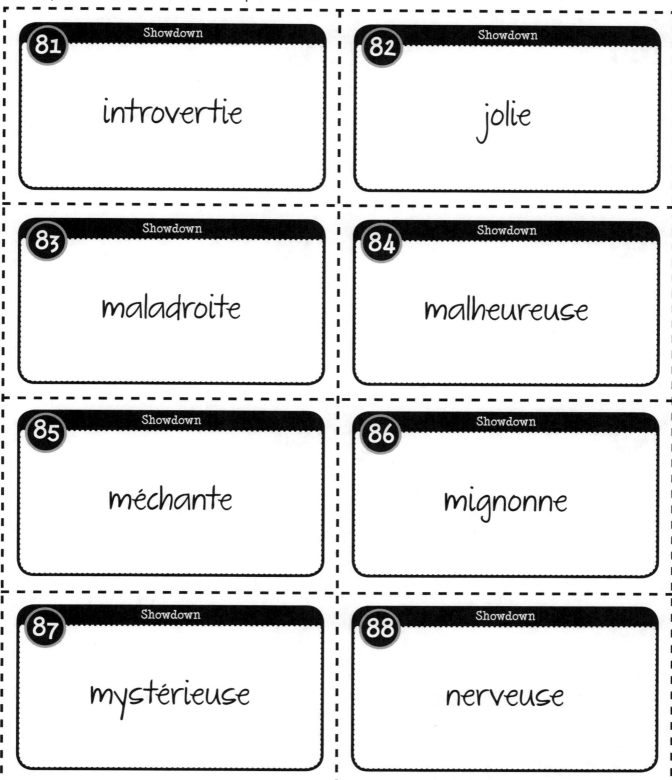

81 Showdown introvertie	**82** Showdown jolie
83 Showdown maladroite	**84** Showdown malheureuse
85 Showdown méchante	**86** Showdown mignonne
87 Showdown mystérieuse	**88** Showdown nerveuse

Montrez-moi les adjectifs!
Show me the adjectives!

Directions: Cut out the *les adjectifs!* cards along the dotted line. Teams place cards in the center of the table. The Showdown Captain picks a card and reads it aloud. Teammates each write the correct form of the adjective. Students "showdown" to compare answers.

89 Showdown nouvelle	**90** Showdown paresseuse
91 Showdown patiente	**92** Showdown petite
93 Showdown polie	**94** Showdown prudente
95 Showdown responsable	**96** Showdown riche

Montrez-moi les adjectifs!
Show me the adjectives!

Directions: Cut out the *les adjectifs!* cards along the dotted line. Teams place cards in the center of the table. The Showdown Captain picks a card and reads it aloud. Teammates each write the correct form of the adjective. Students "showdown" to compare answers.

97 Showdown sensible	**98** Showdown sérieuse
99 Showdown spirituelle	**100** Showdown sportive
101 Showdown travailleuse	**102** Showdown triste
103 Showdown vieille	**104** Showdown

Chapter 8
Ta journée
(Your day)

Structures & Activities

Vocabulaire

Ta journée
(Your day)

Les actions (Actions)

- **Je me baigne** (I go for a swim)
  Se baigner (To bathe)
- **Je me brosse** (I brush)
  Se brosser (To brush)
- **Je me coiffe** (I style)
  Se coiffer (To style)
- **Je me couche** (I go to bed)
  Se coucher (To go to bed)
- **Je me demande** (I ask myself)
  Se demander (To wonder)
- **Je me dépêche** (I hurry)
  Se dépêcher (To hurry)
- **Je me déshabille** (I undress)
  Se déshabiller (To undress)
- **Je me lave** (I wash)
  Se laver (To wash)
- **Je me lève** (I get up)
  Se lever (To get up)
- **Je me maquille** (I put on make-up)
  Se maquiller (Put on make up)
- **Je me mets en colère** (I get angry)
  Se mettre en colère (To get angry)
- **Je me moque de** (I make fun of)
  Se moquer de (To mock)
- **Je me peigne** (I comb)
  Se peigner (To comb)
- **Je me prépare** (I get ready)
  Se préparer (To prepare)

- **Je me promène** (I go for a walk)
  Se promener (To take a walk)
- **Je me rase** (I shave)
  Se raser (To shave)
- **Je me repose** (I rest)
  Se reposer (To rest)
- **Je me sèche** (I dry)
  Se sécher (To dry)
- **Je me sens** (I feel)
  Se sentir (To feel)
- **Je me souviens de** (I remember)
  Se souvenir de (To remember)
- **Je me tais** (I get quiet)
  Se taire (To be quiet)
- **Je m'amuse** (I have fun)
  S'amuser (To have fun)
- **Je m'assieds** (I sit down)
  S'assoir (To sit)
- **Je m'en vais** (I leave/go away)
  S'en aller (To leave)
- **Je m'endors** (I fall asleep)
  S'endormir (Go to sleep)
- **Je m'énerve** (I get upset)
  S'énerver (To irritate)
- **Je m'ennuie** (I get bored)
  S'ennuyer (To be bored)
- **Je m'habille** (I dress)
  S'habiller (To get dressed)

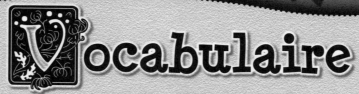

Vocabulaire

Ta journée
(Your day)

- **Je m'inquiète** (I get worried)
  S'inquieter (To worry)
- **Je m'inscris (à)** (I enroll in/join)
  S'inscrire (Enroll/To join)

Les parties du corps
(Parts of the body)

- **La figure** (Face)
- **Le visage** (Face)
- **Les cheveux** (Hair)
- **Les dents** (Teeth)
- **Les mains** (Hands)

Se laver (To wash)

- **Il/elle se lave**
  (He/she washes (him/herself))
- **Ils/Elles se lavent** (They wash themselves)
- **Je me lave** (I wash (myself))
- **Nous nous lavons** (We wash (ourselves))
- **Tu te laves** (You wash (yourself))
- **Vous vous lavez** (You wash (yourself))

Ce que je fais (What I am doing)

- **Je couche le bébé** (I put the baby to bed)
- **Je lave la bicyclette** (I wash the bicycle)
- **Je me couche** (I go to bed)
- **Je me lave les mains** (I wash my hands)
- **Je me promène** (I take a walk)
- **Je promène le chien** (I walk the dog)

Le matin, je me...: Les verbes réfléchis
(In the morning, I...: Reflexive verbs)

RallyCoach

Partners coach each other on sentences describing what they do in the morning.

Steps

Setup: The teacher copies one worksheet for partners to complete together. Students need only one pencil or pen to share.

1 Distribute Materials
Each pair of students needs one worksheet.

2 Partners Coach
Partner A completes the sentence by inserting the correct form of the reflexive verb; explaining aloud what he or she is doing. Partner B coaches and praises. Partner A passes the worksheet and pencil or pen to Partner B.

3 Next Sentence
Partner B completes the next sentence; Partner A coaches and praises.

4 Continue
Students continue working on sentences until they have reached the end of the page.

Le matin, je me...: Les verbes réfléchis

(In the morning, I...: Reflexive verbs)

Directions: One worksheet is provided per pair of students. Students write the reflexive verb in the sentence. Partner A solves by talking aloud to his or her partner. Partner B coaches and praises. Roles are then reversed. Pairs continue until the page is complete.

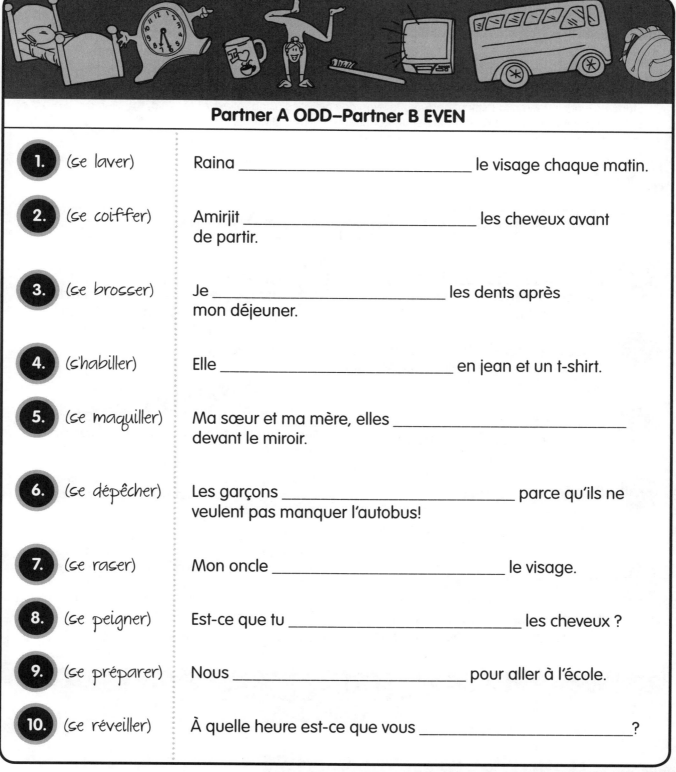

Partner A ODD–Partner B EVEN

1. (se laver)   Raina _____ le visage chaque matin.

2. (se coiffer)   Amirjit _____ les cheveux avant de partir.

3. (se brosser)   Je _____ les dents après mon déjeuner.

4. (s'habiller)   Elle _____ en jean et un t-shirt.

5. (se maquiller)   Ma sœur et ma mère, elles _____ devant le miroir.

6. (se dépêcher)   Les garçons _____ parce qu'ils ne veulent pas manquer l'autobus!

7. (se raser)   Mon oncle _____ le visage.

8. (se peigner)   Est-ce que tu _____ les cheveux ?

9. (se préparer)   Nous _____ pour aller à l'école.

10. (se réveiller)   À quelle heure est-ce que vous _____?

Les actions de tous les jours
(Everyday actions)

Think-Write-RoundRobin

Students work in teams to think of answers to everyday activities using reflexive verbs. Using the Think and Write Time before RoundRobin allows students to articulate their thoughts before they are asked to share them.

Steps

Setup: The teacher gives a blank piece of paper and a pen or pencil to record ideas.

1 Distribute Recording Paper
The teacher gives each student one recording sheet.

2 Teacher Reads First Question
The teacher reads the first question and provides Think Time.

3 All Write
Teammates record their answers on their own recording sheet.

4 Students Signal
Teammates signal with a "thumbs up" when they are ready to share their responses.

5 Students Respond
The teacher tells teams to begin sharing their responses. Teammates continue sharing until all have had their turn.

6 Continue
The teacher continues to ask each question. Students think, write an answer, and then RoundRobin-share with teammates.

Variations

- **Yes or No Questions.** Students can answer simple "yes or no" questions or the questions can be more involved as to the time or order of events. For example: *"Est-ce que tu te réveilles à 7 heures?" "Est-ce que tu te coiffes avant ou après que tu te brosses les dents?"*

- **Question Captain.** Teacher gives each team a question sheet. The sheet is cut into question strips. A "Question Captain" is chosen to read a question. Teammates think, write, then RoundRobin in response to the questions. A new "Question Captain" is chosen to read each question.

- **Oral, No Writing.** Use these as oral questions, asking and answering without the written steps.

Les actions de tous les jours

(Everyday actions)

Directions: Students are asked questions provided by the teacher or given on a worksheet. In teams, students write and then share answers with their teammates.

1. Est-ce que tu te laves les cheveux chaque matin?

2. Est-ce que tu te rases?

3. Est-ce que tu te maquilles?

4. Avec quoi est-ce que tu te coiffes: un peigne ou une brosse?

5. À quelle heure est-ce que tu te réveilles?

6. À quelle heure est-ce que tu te lèves?

7. À quelle heure est-ce que tu te couches?

8. À quelle heure est-ce que tu t'endors?

9. Qu'est-ce que tu fais quand tu te mets en colère?

10. Comment est-ce que tu te prépares pour aller à l'école?

Qu'est-ce que tu fais?
(What do you do?)

Find Someone Who

Students circulate around the classroom forming and re-forming pairs trying to "find someone who" can answer one of the questions about their daily routine.

Steps

Setup: The teacher prepares a worksheet for students to use.

1 Distribute the Worksheet
Students are given the worksheet to review.

2 Students Pair Up
Students circulate around the class. Students keep a hand raised until they find a partner.

3 Ask
In pairs, students take turns asking a question from the worksheet: Partner A asks Partner B—Partner B responds. Partner A records the answer on his or her own worksheet and expresses appreciation.

4 Check
Partner B checks and initials the answer.

5 Reverse Roles
Partner B now asks a question and Partner A responds. Partner B records the answer on his or her own worksheet and expresses appreciation.

6 Check
Partner A checks and initials the answer.

(continued)

Qu'est-ce que tu fais?
(What do you do?)

Find Someone Who

Steps

7 Praise and Part
Partners high five—and raise a hand as they search for a new partner.

8 Repeat
Students repeat the process until their worksheets are complete.

9 Experts
Experts are students who have completed their worksheets. Once their worksheets are complete, they return to their desks and can be approached by others as a resource.

activities

Qu'est-ce que tu fais?
(What do you do?)

Directions: Students circulate around the classroom forming and re-forming pairs trying to "find someone who" can answer one of the questions about their daily routine. Write the answer provided by your partner and have your partner initial the answer.

Est-ce que tu te laves les cheveux le matin ou le soir? _____ **1** Initials: _____	Est-ce que tu te brosses les dents trois fois par jour? _____ **2** Initials: _____	Est-ce que tu te peignes? _____ **3** Initials: _____
Est-ce que tu t'habilles dans la salle de bains? _____ **4** Initials: _____	Est-ce que tu te brosses les cheveux dans ta chambre ou dans la salle de bains? _____ **5** Initials: _____	À quelle heure est-ce que tu te réveilles? _____ **6** Initials: _____
À quelle heure est-ce que tu te couches? _____ **7** Initials: _____	Est-ce que tu te rases? _____ **8** Initials: _____	Est-ce que tu t'habilles dans ta chambre? _____ **9** Initials: _____
Est-ce que tu aimes te baigner? _____ **10** Initials: _____	Où est-ce que tu aimes te reposer? _____ **11** Initials: _____	Est-ce que tu t'amuses avec les amis d'école? _____ **12** Initials: _____

Je me prépare!
(I get ready!)

Find-the-Fiction

Students write four statements about their daily tasks. Classmates guess which one of the four statements is a fiction.

Steps

Setup: The teacher gives each student one piece of paper or worksheet to write down four statements about themselves.

1 Students Think
Teacher poses the question: *"What do you do each day?"* *"Qu'est-ce que tu fais chaque jour?"*

2 Students Write
Students write four statements about their daily tasks using reflexive verbs. One of the statements is a false statement (an activity they don't do, or one they rarely do).

3 Students Pair Up
Students stand, put a hand up and pair up with another student who has a hand raised. Partner A reads his or her statements and Partner B tries to decide which statement is false. Partner B guesses the false statement! If he or she guesses correctly, Partner A says,

"Oui! Très bien!" If Partner B does not guess the false statement, then Partner A says, *"Ah non! Ce n'est pas correcte!"*

4 Students Switch Roles
Students switch roles, with Partner A trying to guess Partner B's false statement. After Partner A guesses, Partner B responds.

5 Celebrate and Find a New Partner
Each student thanks the other for sharing and raises a hand in search of a new partner.

6 Continue Guessing
Students continue the activity until the teacher calls time.

Je me prépare!
(I get ready!)

Directions: Students write four things they do each day using reflexive verbs. One of the four statements must be fiction. Students pair up with classmates and partners guess which statement is false.

Que fais-tu chaque jour?

1

2

3

4

La journée de Monsieur Taillegrand!
(Mr. Taillegrand's day!)

Blind Sequencing

In teams, students receive cards with pictures of events in Mr. Taillegrand's day. Without seeing each other's cards, they must describe their events from the pictures and work together as a team to sequence the events, placing them face down on the table. When completed, they flip over the cards and check the sequence. Teammates discuss how effective they were in sequencing and then create strategies to improve sequencing.

Steps

Setup: The teacher makes copies of the Picture Cards and distributes all six to each team.

 1 Distribute Cards
Teammates cut out the Picture Cards. Teams divide the six Picture Cards evenly among teammates. For teams of four, two teammates will receive two cards.

 2 Teams Play
Students hide their cards from teammates. Starting with Student #1, teammates look at their own cards and describe in French what the man is doing. Student #2 continues by describing what is on his or her card.

 3 Sequence Cards
Teammates decide which picture goes first. After the team reaches consensus on the sequence of the card, the teammate places the card face down on the team table. No one can touch another teammate's card.

 4 Check and Celebrate
Teammates turn cards over to see if the team has communicated the correct order of the cards! The team celebrates if they have the correct sequence.

(continued)

La journée de Monsieur Taillegrand!
(Mr. Taillegrand's day!)

Blind Sequencing

Variations

- **Sequencing.** Teammates place cards on the table face up. Each student describes his or her card when placing it in the correct order where everyone can see it.

- **Line-Ups.** Students line up in the order in which the events occur in Mr. Taillegrand's day. One at a time, students describe what Mr. Taillegrand is doing on their card.

La journée de Monsieur Taillegrand!

(Mr. Taillegrand's day!)

Directions: Cut out the Picture Cards along the dotted line and distribute them equally among teammates. Take turns describing each card, and then decide as a team where the card belongs in the sequence. Remember, only you can see and touch your cards.

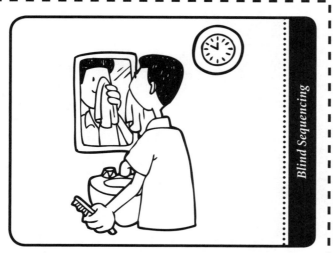

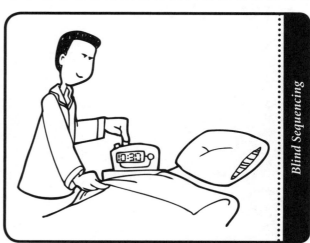

Chapter 9
Le monde: La géographie
(The world: Geography)

Structures & Activities

Vocabulaire

Le monde: La géographie
(The world: Geography)

Chapter 9

Les prépositions
(Prepositions)

- **À** (To: Used with towns, cities)
- **Au** (To: Used with masculine countries (and Mexico))
- **Aux** (To: Used with plural countries e.g., Aux États-Unis)
- **En** (To: Used with all continents and with feminine countries)
- **Je vais à...** (I am going to...)
- **Je viens de...** (I come from...)
- **Je voyage** (I am travelling)

Les villes (Cities)

- **d'Amsterdam** (From Amsterdam)
- **de New York** (From New York)
- **de Rome** (From Rome)
- **de Toronto** (From Toronto)

Les provinces et territoires
(Provinces and territories)

- **À Terre-Neuve** (To Newfoundland)
- **À l'île Prince Edouard** (To Prince Edward Island)
- **Au Manitoba** (To Manitoba)
- **Au Nouveau Brunswick** (To New Brunswick)
- **Au Nunavut** (To Nunavut)
- **Au Québec** (To Quebec)
- **Au Yukon** (To the Yukon)
- **Aux Territoires du Nord-Ouest** (To the Northwest Territories)
- **En Alberta** (To Alberta)
- **En Colombie Britannique** (To British Columbia)
- **En Nouvelle Écosse** (To Nova Scotia)
- **En Ontario** (To Ontario)

Vocabulaire

Le monde: La géographie
(The world: Geography)

Chapter 9

Les pays (Countries)

- **La Chine** (China)
- **La France** (France)
- **L'Allemagne** (Germany)
- **L'Angleterre** (England)
- **L'Espagne** (Spain)
- **L'Italie** (Italy)
- **Le Canada** (Canada)
- **Le Japon** (Japan)
- **Le Mexique** (Mexico)
- **Le Pérou** (Peru)
- **Les États-Unis** (United States)

Les continents (Continents)

- **L'Afrique** (Africa)
- **L'Amérique du nord** (North America)
- **L'Amérique du sud** (South America)
- **L'Asie** (Asia)
- **L'Europe** (Europe)

Moi, j'aimerais voyager...
(I would like to travel to...)

Talking Chips

Students have fun talking about places they would like to travel.

Steps

> **Setup:** The teacher gives each teammate an equal number of Talking Chips. These may be pieces of paper, bingo chips, or the ready-made Talking Chips provided.

1 Teacher Poses Question
The teacher asks the class the question: *"Où aimerais-tu voyager?"* *("Where would you like to travel?")*

2 Teams Begin
One teammate places a chip in the center to begin the discussion. They say: *"J'aimerais voyager…"* and complete the sentence with a place they would like to visit.

3 Keep the Discussion Going
Team members use chips to continue the discussion. Each time a member has an idea, he or she places one of his or her Talking Chips on the team table. Players can make as many statements as they have Talking Chips, but once they have used up their Talking Chips, they must wait until other team members have used up theirs.

4 Chips Used Up
Once all team Talking Chips have been placed on the team table, students collect chips and can continue their discussion. **Hint:** All students must have used up all of their Talking Chips before collecting chips and continuing the discussion.

(continued)

Moi, j'aimerais voyager...
(I would like to travel to...)

Talking Chips

Variations

- **Cities I've Visited.** Students can discuss different cities they have already visited. *"Où as-tu voyagé?"*

- **Different Continents.** Students can discuss different cities and/or countries on different continents! *"Quelles villes sont en Chine?/en Asie?" "Quels pays sont en Afrique?"*

- **Where My Family is From.** Students can discuss where their families are from! *"D'où vient ta famille?"*

Moi, j'aimerais voyager...
(I would like to travel to...)

Directions: Cut out the *Mon tour à parler* chips along the dotted line. Give a minimum of two chips to each student for discussion and to play *"Mon tour à parler."*

Les voyages qui ne coûtent pas un sou!
(Trips that don't cost a thing!)

Showdown

Teams practice telling where they are going based on the question cards.
Each teammate has an opportunity to share their response with the team!

Steps

Setup: The teacher prepares the Question Cards for each team. Cards are distributed to teams and students cut out the cards. Each teammate needs something to write on. This could be a dry erase board or pieces of paper.

1 Shuffle and Place the Cards
Question Cards are placed in the center of the team table.

2 Read Question
The Showdown Captain reads a question.

3 Think and Write
Students work alone and write answers.

4 Thumbs Up
Teammates signal when they're ready by raising their thumbs.

5 Show Your Response
The Showdown Captain calls *"Showdown"* (or *"Montrez-moi!"*).

6 Show and Discuss
Teammates show their responses and discuss the answers.

7 Celebrate
Teammates celebrate or coach if teammates need extra help.

8 Continue Playing
A new Showdown Captain leads the next round.

Les voyages qui ne coûtent pas un sou!
(Trips that don't cost a thing!)

Directions: Cut out the *Les voyages* cards along the dotted line. Teams place cards in the center of the table. The Showdown Captain picks a card and reads it aloud. Every student writes his or her own answer. Students "showdown" to compare answers.

---

1   Showdown

J'aime les endroits ensoleillés. J'aime la chaleur et la plage. J'aime me bronzer et nager dans l'océan. Où est-ce que je peux voyager?

---

2   Showdown

J'aime faire du ski! L'hiver c'est ma saison favorite! Je veux faire de la planche à neige aussi. Où est-ce que je peux voyager?

---

3   Showdown

J'aime l'histoire. J'aime les civilisations anciennes. Je veux faire une exploration! Où est-ce que je dois voyager?

---

4   Showdown

J'aime visiter les musées. Je veux voir les peintures d'autre temps. Les artistes m'intéressent beaucoup. Où est-ce que je dois voyager?

---

5   Showdown

Je n'ai pas visité tout mon pays natal. Je viens de Juneau en Alaska et je veux voir une autre partie de notre grand pays! Où est-ce que je peux voyager?

---

6   Showdown

J'aime manger du poisson. J'aime tous les fruits de mer! J'aime aussi surfer et faire de la natation. Je veux essayer de faire de la plongée sous-marine. Où est-ce que je dois voyager?

Où vont-ils?
(Where are they going?)

Numbered Heads Together

Students have an opportunity to think and write their responses before sharing with their teammates. One student from each team is chosen to share with the class. This is a great class challenge activity!

Steps

Setup: The teacher creates Country, City, and Continent Cards. Copy the cards and laminate them so students can write on the cards. Find a method, such as a spinner, for randomly selecting a student.

1 Distribute Cards
The teacher distributes the cards for students to write the answers on in Step 4.

2 Students Number Off
Each member of the team is assigned a number.

3 Teacher Poses a Question
The teacher shows the class the name of a city, country, or continent and asks, *"Where are they going?" "Où vont-ils?"*

4 Students Think and Write
Students think and write down their responses without discussing or showing their answers to teammates.

Use a dry erase marker to write the correct form of "to": *à, à la/l', au, aux, en* in front of the city name, country name, or continent name. No discussing or sharing ideas is permitted at this independent stage.

5 Heads Together
The teacher announces, *"Têtes ensembles!"* ("Heads together"). Students share and discuss their responses.

6 Teams Signal When Ready
When each team has completed their discussion and all teammates are in agreement and have recorded the same answer, they signal to the teacher they are ready (a simple "thumbs up" is good!)

(continued)

Où vont-ils?
(Where are they going?)

Numbered Heads Together

7 **Teacher Calls a Number**
The teacher randomly chooses a number. That teammate stands to share the team's response.

8 **Teams Celebrate**
Teams celebrate their awesome teamwork, or discuss how they might improve for the next round.

9 **Continue Play**
The teacher continues with the next question.

Variations

- **Where Are They From?** Students can work on *"D'où viennent-ils?"* *("where are they from?")* questions by using "from": *de, de la, des, du* instead of the forms of "to" *(à, aux, à la/l', en)*. Cards can be sorted by color—cities, countries, and continents—or different colors according to their masculine or feminine form.

- **Vont or Viennent.** Have students write a complete sentence starting with, *"Ils vont"* or *"Ils viennent."*

- **Allons or Venons.** Students could be asked, *"Où allez-vous?"* or *"D'où allez-vous?"*; to which they would respond with sentences beginning with *"Nous allons"* or *"Nous Venons."*

Où vont-ils?
(Where are they going?)

Directions: Cut out the *Où vont-ils?* cards along the dotted line. Students practice discussing and writing the correct form of "to" in front of the names of the cities, countries, and continents.

1 Numbered Heads Together

_____ Rome

2 Numbered Heads Together

_____ New York

3 Numbered Heads Together

_____ Toronto

4 Numbered Heads Together

_____ Alberta

5 Numbered Heads Together

_____ Ontario

6 Numbered Heads Together

_____ Québec

7 Numbered Heads Together

_____ Colombie Britannique

8 Numbered Heads Together

_____ île Prince Edouard

9 Numbered Heads Together

_____ Territoires du Nord-Ouest

10 Numbered Heads Together

_____ Canada

11 Numbered Heads Together

_____ États-Unis

12 Numbered Heads Together

_____ Mexique

Où vont-ils?
(Where are they going?)

Directions: Cut out the *Où vont-ils?* cards along the dotted line. Students practice discussing and writing the correct form of "to" in front of the names of the cities, countries, and continents.

13 *Numbered Heads Together* ____ France	**14** *Numbered Heads Together* ____ Angleterre
15 *Numbered Heads Together* ____ Allemagne	**16** *Numbered Heads Together* ____ Espagne
17 *Numbered Heads Together* ____ Italie	**18** *Numbered Heads Together* ____ Chine
19 *Numbered Heads Together* ____ Pérou	**20** *Numbered Heads Together* ____ Japon
21 *Numbered Heads Together* ____ Asie	**22** *Numbered Heads Together* ____ Europe
23 *Numbered Heads Together* ____ Afrique	**24** *Numbered Heads Together* ____ Amérique du nord

Où sommes-nous?
(Where are we?)

Mix-N-Match

Students repeatedly quiz each other on cities and countries.

Steps

Setup: The teacher creates two sets of cards: One for cities and another for the associated countries. The teacher models with the class how to match the cities with countries before playing so students are familiar with the vocabulary. This will help increase their knowledge!

1 Distribute Cards
Students receive either a Country Card or a City Card.

2 Students Mix and Pair
With a card in one hand, students stand up, put a hand up, and pair with a classmate.

3 Partners Quiz Each Other
Partners take turns quizzing each other. For example, if a student has the *Italie* card, he or she may ask his or her partner, *"What is a city in Italie?"* If a student has the *Rome* card, he or she may ask his or her partner, *"What country is Rome in?"* Partners quiz each other.

4 Partners Trade Cards
Partners thank each other, trade cards, and put a hand up to find a new partner.

5 Teacher Calls *"Freeze!"*
The teacher calls, *"Gelez!"* Students freeze and think about the card that matches their card. They move to the center of the room to find the classmate with a matching card.

(continued)

Où sommes-nous?
(Where are we?)

Mix-N-Match

Variations

• **Color-Code the Cards.** Copy the City Cards on one color and the Country Cards on another color. This is a great way for students to discover the names of cities and countries in French.

• **Research More.** Have students search and find their own pairs of cities and countries, states, provinces, etc!

Où sommes-nous?
(Where are we?)

Directions: Cut out the *Où sommes-nous?* cards along the dotted line. Give one card to each student. Distribute cards in sequence so for every student with a City Card, there is a student with a matching Country Card.

Mix-N-Match
Ottawa

Mix-N-Match
Washington, D.C.

Mix-N-Match
Londres

Mix-N-Match
Paris

Mix-N-Match
Tokyo

Mix-N-Match
Canberra

Mix-N-Match
Pékin

Mix-N-Match
Berlin

Mix-N-Match
Rome

Mix-N-Match
Lima

Mix-N-Match
Madrid

Mix-N-Match
Acapulco

Où sommes-nous?
(Where are we?)

Directions: Cut out the *Où sommes-nous?* cards along the dotted line. Give one card to each student. Distribute cards in sequence so for every student with a City Card, there is a student with a matching Country Card.

Mix-N-Match	*Mix-N-Match*
Canada	États-Unis
Mix-N-Match	*Mix-N-Match*
Angleterre	France
Mix-N-Match	*Mix-N-Match*
Japon	Australie
Mix-N-Match	*Mix-N-Match*
Chine	Allemagne
Mix-N-Match	*Mix-N-Match*
Italie	Pérou
Mix-N-Match	*Mix-N-Match*
Espagne	Mexique

Chapter 10
Quand?
(When?)

Structures & Activities

Vocabulaire

Quand?
(When?)

L'heure (Time)

- **À cinq heures moins le quart**
  (At 4:45)
  - 🍁 **À cinq heures moins quart**
    (At 4:45)
- **À cinq heures moins dix** (At 4:50)
- **À cinq heures moins vingt-cinq**
  (At 4:35)
- **À dix heures** (At ten o'clock)
- **À midi** (At noon)
- **À minuit** (At midnight)
- **À une heure** (At one o'clock)
- **Aujourd'hui** (Today)
- **Ce matin** (This morning)
- **Ce soir** (This evening)
- **Cet après-midi** (This afternoon)
- **Demain** (Tomorrow)
- **Demain matin (après-midi, soir)**
  (Tomorrow morning (afternoon, evening))
- **Et demie** (Half past)
- **Et quart** (Quarter past)
- **Le lendemain** (The day after tomorrow)
- **La semaine prochaine** (Next week)
- **Plus tard** (Later)
- **Tout de suite** (Right now)

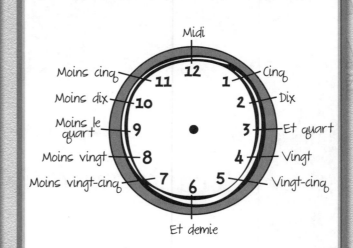

* **Moins quart (quarter to) is used in North America**

Vocabulaire

Quand?
(When?)

Chapter 10

Les mois (Months)

- **janvier** (January)
- **février** (February)
- **mars** (March)
- **avril** (April)
- **mai** (May)
- **juin** (June)
- **juillet** (July)
- **août** (August)
- **septembre** (September)
- **octobre** (October)
- **novembre** (November)
- **décembre** (December)
- **le premier...** (The first of...)
- **en janvier** (In January)

Les jours (Day)

- **dimanche** (Sunday)
- **lundi** (Monday)
- **mardi** (Tuesday)
- **mercredi** (Wednesday)
- **jeudi** (Thursday)
- **vendredi** (Friday)
- **samedi** (Saturday)

Les saisons (Seasons)

- **Au printemps** (In the spring)
- **En automne** (In the fall)
- **En été** (In the summer)
- **En hiver** (In the winter)

Note:
When ecpressing the date, there are two acceptable forms:
- *"C'est lundi le deux mai."* (It's Monday, the second of May.)
- *"C'est le lundi deux mai."* (It's Monday, May second.)
There are no commas when writing the date in French.

À quelle heure?
(At what time?)

Fan-N-Pick

Teams play Fan-N-Pick to ask teammates in French if they enjoy doing an activity pictured on a card at the time pictured on the card. For example, "Do you enjoy playing basketball at two o'clock?"

Steps

Setup: The teacher gives each team a set of Picture Cards.

1 Distribute Cards
Teams cut out the Picture Cards.

2 Fan Cards
Student #1 holds the cards in a fan and says, *"Choisis une carte!"*

3 Ask a Question
Student #2 (clockwise in the group) picks one card and asks the question written on the card. For example, *"À quelle heure est-ce qu'il joue au basketball?"* The student pauses to allow five seconds Think Time.

4 Respond
Student #3 answers the question based on the time shown on the card. For example, *"Il joue au basketball à deux heures."*

5 Praise
Student #4 praises Student #3's answer in French: *"Super!"*, *"Excellent!"*, etc.

6 Play Continues
Students rotate roles one person clockwise for each new round. Play continues until all students have answered a card or for an allotted amount of time/turns.

(continued)

À quelle heure?
(At what time?)

Fan-N-Pick

Variations

- **Write It Out.** Students can write out the questions and answers on a worksheet or response board.

- **Vary Difficulty.** Vary the difficulty by creating different types of questions based on the cards. For example:

  "Quand est-ce qu'on fait du kayak?" *(en été)*
  "Bon alors, à quelle heure?" (the time stated on the clock)
  Students can state the wrong time and ask, *"Est-ce qu'il joue au hockey à neuf heures?"*

À quelle heure?
(At what time?)

Directions: Copy a set of *À quelle heure?* cards for each team. Cut out each card along the dotted line. Give each team a set of cards so they can ask teammates if they enjoy doing the activity at the time given on the card.

1 — Fan-N-Pick

À quelle heure est-ce qu'il joue au basketball?

2:00

2 — Fan-N-Pick

À quelle heure est-ce qu'elle danse?

4:30

3 — Fan-N-Pick

À quelle heure est-ce qu'ils font leurs devoirs?

6:30

4 — Fan-N-Pick

À quelle heure est-ce qu'elles regardent la télévision?

8:00

5 — Fan-N-Pick

À quelle heure est-ce qu'ils jouent au hockey?

5:30

6 — Fan-N-Pick

À quelle heure est-ce qu'il se lève?

7:00

À quelle heure?
(At what time?)

Directions: Copy a set of *À quelle heure?* cards for each team. Cut out each card along the dotted line. Give each team a set of cards so they can ask teammates if they enjoy doing the activity at the time given on the card.

7 — *Fan-N-Pick*

À quelle heure est-ce qu'elle se maquille?

8:00

8 — *Fan-N-Pick*

À quelle heure est-ce qu'ils flânent?

9:30

9 — *Fan-N-Pick*

À quelle heure est-ce qu'ils jouent à des jeux vidéo?

9:00

1o — *Fan-N-Pick*

À quelle heure est-ce qu'elles jouent au baseball?

1:00

11 — *Fan-N-Pick*

À quelle heure est-ce qu'il fait du ski?

11:00

12 — *Fan-N-Pick*

À quelle heure est-ce qu'elle mange son dîner?

12:30

Quelle heure est-il?
(What time is it?)

RallyCoach

Students work in pairs solving and coaching different questions about telling time.

Steps

> **Setup:** The teacher prepares the *Quelle heure est-il?* worksheet for each pair of students.

1 **Students Sit in Pairs**
Students pair up. The teacher gives one worksheet to each pair.

2 **First Problem**
Partner A solves the first problem by finding the clock that matches the time stated. As Partner A draws a line to connect the clock and the written time, he or she tells Partner B what is being connected. For example, *"Il est deux heures. Voici la cloche."* (It's two o'clock. Here is the clock.) Partner B coaches and praises.

3 **Next Problem**
Partner B solves the next problem; Partner A coaches and praises.

4 **Continue Solving Problems**
Partners continue to take turns solving problems until all are solved.

Hints

- Have only one pen or pencil between the two partners. They keep the paper between them so both can see it, and pass the pencil when they are finished writing their answers.

- Be sure students read the times aloud on their turn.

Variations

- **Share Problems.** Have the non-writing partner ask, *"Quelle heure est-il?"* and the writing partner responds as they draw the line connecting the clock with the written time.

- **Write It.** Have students write the number of the correct time statement beside the matching clock.

Quelle heure est-il?

(What time is It?)

Directions: In pairs, students take turns connecting the clock with the written time, coaching and praising each other's answers.

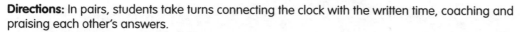

Partner A ODD—Partner B EVEN

1. Il est une heure.

2. Il est une heure et demie.

3. Il est deux heures.

4. Il est deux heures et quart.

5. Il est quatre heures et demie.

6. Il est quatre heures moins quart.

7. Il est sept heures et demie.

8. Il est sept heures vingt-cinq.

9. Il est cinq heures moins dix.

10. Il est dix heures et demie.

11. Il est dix heures.

12. Il est onze heures.

13. Il est minuit.

14. Il est minuit moins quart.

15. Il est neuf heures.

16. Il est neuf heures et demie.

17. Il est dix heures et quart.

18. Il est dix heures moins quart.

19. Il est dix heures moins dix.

20. Il est trois heures.

Quelle est la date?
(What's the date?)

Flashcard Game

Students practice saying dates from calendars. They proceed through three rounds as they quiz each other with flashcards, mastering the content to win cards.

Steps

Setup: The teacher gives each student his or her own set of flashcards.

1 **Pair Up**
In pairs, the Tutee gives his or her flashcards to the Tutor.

2 **Round 1: Maximum Cues**
The Tutor shows the picture on the first card and asks, *"Quelle est la date?"* and shows and reads the answer written on the back of the card. The Tutor then turns the card back over and again asks the question on the front of the card asking the Tutee to answer from memory.

3 **Tutee Answers**
If the correct answer is given, the Tutee wins the card back and receives praise from the Tutor. If wrong, the Tutor shows the Tutee the answer side of the card and coaches. The

card is then returned to the stack to try again later. **Hint:** The tutor can ask, *"How can I help you remember that?"* The pair can discuss ways of remembering answers.

4 **Switch**
When the Tutee wins all cards, partners switch roles. When the new Tutee wins all his or her cards, partners advance to Round 2.

5 **Round 2: Few Cues**
The process is repeated, except the Tutor shows only the question side of the card and asks the Tutee to answer from memory. If wrong, the Tutor shows the Tutee the answer side, and the card is returned to the stack to try again.

(continued)

Quelle est la date?
(What's the date?)

Flashcard Game

Steps

6 **Round 3: No Cues**
Again, the process is repeated, except the Tutor quizzes the Tutee on each question without showing the Tutee the flashcards.

Tip

Limit each round to no more than five cards. If a student has won all cards, he or she can add bonus cards.

Variation

Students can ask about dates before or after the date on the card.
- *"Quelle sera la date demain?"* (What will the date be tomorrow?)
- *"Quelle était la date hier?"* (What was the date yesterday?)

Quelle est la date?
(What's the date?)

Directions: Cut out *Quelle est la date?* cards along the dotted line. Then fold each card in half so the calendar is on the front and the written date is on the back.

1 — **Quelle est la date?**
Flashcard Game
décembre
20 lundi
Question

1 — **Quelle est la date?**
Flashcard Game
C'est lundi le vingt décembre.
Réponse

2 — **Quelle est la date?**
Flashcard Game
avril
12 mercredi
Question

2 — **Quelle est la date?**
Flashcard Game
C'est mercredi le douze avril.
Réponse

3 — **Quelle est la date?**
Flashcard Game
juillet
3 mercredi
Question

3 — **Quelle est la date?**
Flashcard Game
C'est mercredi le trois juillet.
Réponse

Quelle est la date?
(What's the date?)

Directions: Cut out *Quelle est la date?* cards along the dotted line. Then fold each card in half so the calendar is on the front and the written date is on the back.

4 — Quelle est la date? — Flashcard Game

juin
15 vendredi

Question

4 — Quelle est la date? — Flashcard Game

C'est vendredi le quinze juin.

Réponse

5 — Quelle est la date? — Flashcard Game

octobre
31 samedi

Question

5 — Quelle est la date? — Flashcard Game

C'est samedi le trente-et-un octobre.

Réponse

6 — Quelle est la date? — Flashcard Game

août
6 mardi

Question

6 — Quelle est la date? — Flashcard Game

C'est mardi le six août.

Réponse

Quelle est la date?
(What's the date?)

Directions: Cut out *Quelle est la date?* cards along the dotted line. Then fold each card in half so the calendar is on the front and the written date is on the back.

Quelle est la date?
(What's the date?)

Directions: Cut out *Quelle est la date?* cards along the dotted line. Then fold each card in half so the calendar is on the front and the written date is on the back.

10 — Quelle est la date?

Flashcard Game

Question

10 — Quelle est la date?

Flashcard Game

C'est vendredi
le quatorze février.

Réponse

11 — Quelle est la date?

Flashcard Game

Question

11 — Quelle est la date?

Flashcard Game

C'est dimanche
le vingt-neuf mars.

Réponse

12 — Quelle est la date?

Flashcard Game

Question

12 — Quelle est la date?

Flashcard Game

C'est jeudi
le quinze septembre.

Réponse

Quand?
(When?)

Think-Write-RoundRobin

Students are given discussion topics about when they like to do certain activities. They think, write down ideas to share, and then RoundRobin. Students respond by discussing which months or times (e.g., *en janvier, demain, en hiver,* etc.)

Steps

Setup: The teacher copies the *Quand?* question sheet. Each student needs a piece of paper to record his or her answers.

1 Distribute Recording Paper
The teacher gives each student one recording sheet.

2 Teacher Reads First Question
The teacher reads the first question and provides Think Time.

3 All Write
Teammates record their answers on their own recording sheet.

4 Students Signal
Teammates signal with a "thumbs up" when they are ready to share their responses.

5 Students Respond
The teacher tells teams to begin sharing their responses. Teammates continue sharing until all have had their turn.

6 Continue
The teacher continues to ask each question. Students think, write an answer, and then RoundRobin-share with teammates.

Variations

- **Yes or No Questions.** Students can answer simple "yes or no" questions or the questions can be more involved as to the time or order of events. For example: *"Est-ce que tu te réveilles à 7 heures?" "Est-ce que tu te coiffes avant ou après que tu te brosses les dents?"*

- **Question Captain.** Teacher gives each team a question sheet. The sheet is cut into question strips. A "Question Captain" is chosen to read a question. Teammates think, write, then RoundRobin in response to the questions. A new "Question Captain" is chosen to read each question.

- **Oral, No Writing.** Use these as oral questions, asking and answering without the written steps.

Quand?
(When?)

Directions: Students are asked questions provided by the teacher or stated on a worksheet. In teams, students write and then share answers with their teammates.

1. En quel mois peux-tu faire du ski?

2. En quel mois peux-tu faire de la bicyclette?

3. En quel mois peux-tu nager?

4. Quand est-ce qu'on peut faire de la motoneige?

5. Quand est-ce qu'on peut faire de la planche à roulettes?

6. Quand est-ce qu'on peut faire de la planche à neige?

7. En quel mois est-ce qu'on peut aller en vacances?

8. En quel mois est-ce que tu aimes voyager?

9. Quand est-ce que tu aimes flâner avec les amis?

10. Quand est-ce qu'on peut jouer au football?

11. En quel mois est-ce qu'on peut jouer au baseball?

12. Quand est-ce que tu rends visite á la famille ou les amis?

Chapter 11
Les verbes réguliers
(Regular verbs)

Structures & Activities

Vocabulaire

Les verbes réguliers
(Regular verbs)

Les verbes réguliers
(Regular verbs)

Les verbes en -ER

- **Écouter** (To listen to)
- **Flâner** (To hang out)
- **Jouer** (To play)
- **Parler** (To speak)
- **Téléphoner** (To telephone/call)
- **Tomber** (To fall)
- **Choisir** (To choose)

Les verbes en -IR

- **Finir** (To finish)
- **Grandir** (To grow)
- **Obéir** (To obey)
- **Remplir** (To fill)
- **Rougir** (To blush)

Les verbes en -RE

- **Attendre** (To wait)
- **Descendre** (To descend/go down)
- **Entendre** (To hear)
- **Perdre** (To lose)
- **Répondre** (To answer)
- **Vendre** (To sell)

Parler (To speak)

- **Je parle** (I speak)
- **Tu parles** (You speak)
- **Il/Elle parle** (He/she/it speaks)
- **Nous parlons** (We speak)
- **Vous parlez** (You speak)
- **Ils/Elles parlent** (They speak)

Finir (To finish)

- **Je finis** (He/she/it finishes)
- **Tu finis** (You finish)
- **Il/Elle finit** (He/she/it finishes)
- **Nous finissons** (We finish)
- **Vous finissez** (You finish)
- **Ils/Elles finissent** (They finish)

Entendre (To hear)

- **J'entends** (I hear)
- **Tu entends** (You hear)
- **Il/Elle entend** (He/she/it hears)
- **Nous entendons** (We hear)
- **Vous entendez** (You hear)
- **Ils/Elles entendent** (They hear)

Note:
- "Tu" means "you" in English when referring to someone you know personally, a friend, or someone younger.

- "Vous" means "you" in English when referring to one person, being polite: someone you don't know or would not use their first name (someone older or to whom you would refer to as Mr., Mrs., or Dr., in front of their name).

- "Vous" also means "you" in English when you are talking to a group of two or more people.

- The subject pronoun "on" literally means "one" or "people in general." It's often equivalent to the English passive voice. For example: *On parle français ici!* (One speaks/people speak French here). In addition, "on" is an informal replacement for "we," and is used more often in Canada to replace the subject pronoun *nous*. It is conjugated in the same manner as the *"il/elle"* form of verbs. *Qui (who)* is also conjugated the same as the *"il/elle"* form.

Les activités!
(Activities!)

Team Stand-N-Share

The teacher shows a picture of a scene to the class. Teams record as many activities they see people doing in the scene. Teams stand with the list of ideas to share using the regular verbs. The teacher selects one student to share an idea from the team list. Other teams either check the idea off their list or add it. Each team sits down when all items on their original list are shared.

Steps

Setup: The teacher shows the *Les activités!* scene so the whole class can see it. Each team has the *Les activités!* Recording Sheet and four pencils to record their answers using RoundTable.

1 Display Scene
The teacher explains that teams will record the activities they see in the scene displayed using their regular verb vocabulary. Depending on students' ability level, the teacher states if he or she would like full sentences or just verbs in the infinitive.

2 Teams Record
Each team, using RoundTable, records as many activities as they see being performed in the scene. Each student takes a turn recording something he or she sees in the scene, then passes the paper clockwise to the next teammate. Teammates can help each other if necessary.

3 Teams Share
Teams stand and one team member shares an item from his or her list. If the other teams have it, they check it off their list. If they don't have it, they add it to their list.

4 Continue Sharing
Teams take turns, sharing an item from their list until they have shared all of their ideas.

5 Teams Celebrate
Job well done! Look at all of the actions they knew how to talk/write about!

(continued)

Les activités!
(Activities!)

Team Stand-N-Share

Variations

- **Actions vs. Sentences:** The teacher asks students to write just the actions (verbs). The teacher asks students to write complete sentences using subject pronouns.

- **Write a Story!** Teams can write a story about the actions taking place in the scene. Who are the people? Where are they? Why are they doing those activities?

- **What Happens Next?** Teams can choose one character from the scene and write a short story about what that person is doing and what they will be doing next!

Les activités!
(Activities!)

Activity
1
Team
Stand-N-Share

Directions: Using this Les activités! scene, students record the activities they see on a separate worksheet.

la crème glacée

Les activités!
(Activities!)

Directions: Take turns in your team recording activities you see in the *Les activitiés* scene.

Les Activités que nous observons

1	
2	
3	
4	
5	
6	
7	
8	
9	
10	
11	
12	
13	
14	
15	

Les verbes réguliers!
(Regular verbs!)

Quiz-Quiz-Trade

This is a great way to practice and move these verbs into long-term memory. Students quiz a partner, get quizzed by a partner, and then trade their cards to repeat the process with a new partner.

Steps

> **Setup:** The teacher prepares a set of Verb Cards for the class.

1 **Distribute Cards**
The teacher cuts out the cards and distributes them to the class, one card per student.

2 **Students Pair Up**
Students stand up, hand up, pair up, and face each other.

3 **Students Quiz Each Other**
Students take turns asking questions about the card. Questions can be simply, *"Quel est le nom du verbe to talk en français?"*. His or her partner may respond, *"C'est le verbe parler."* Then, the other partner quizzes his or her partner about the card.

4 **Trade Cards and Find New Partners**
After partners have asked and answered each other's questions, they celebrate with a high five, trade cards, and find a new partner.

5 **Continue Quizzing**
This activity can go on for an allotted amount of time or for a number of trades.

(continued)

Les verbes réguliers!
(Regular verbs!)

Quiz-Quiz-Trade

Variations

• **Increase Difficulty.** More advanced students can create questions based on true and false or specific details on the card. For example:
  1. *"C'est le verbe _____"*.
  2. Multiple-choice response.
  3. Questions generated by students about what verb group: *-er*, *-ir*, or *-re* or the correct form based on a given subject or subject pronoun.
  4. Switch it up and have the students ask what the English form of the verb is when shown the French side of the card.

• **Hide the English.** To increase difficulty and avoid having students translate the vocabulary from English, hide the English terms by covering them up or whiting them out before copying the cards. If you cover up the English, be sure to teach students the French for each illustration in advance to ensure students know and use the target vocabulary.

• **Word Wall.** Enlarge the cards, cut them out, and post them on a classroom Word Wall to familiarize students with the chapter vocabulary.

Cooperative Learning & French • Chiupka-Jozin
Kagan Publishing • 1 (800) 933-2667 • www.KaganOnline.com

Les verbes réguliers!
(Regular verbs!)

Directions: Cut out the *Les verbes réguliers!* cards along the dotted line. Then fold the card in half so the question is on one side and the answer is on the back. Glue or tape cards together to keep the answers and questions on opposite sides.

1 Quiz-Quiz-Trade **Les verbes réguliers!**

To talk

Question

1 Quiz-Quiz-Trade Réponse

Parler

2 Quiz-Quiz-Trade **Les verbes réguliers!**

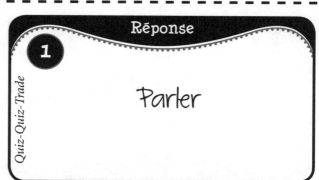

To listen to

Question

2 Quiz-Quiz-Trade Réponse

Écouter

3 Quiz-Quiz-Trade **Les verbes réguliers!**

To hang out

Question

3 Quiz-Quiz-Trade Réponse

Flâner

4 Quiz-Quiz-Trade **Les verbes réguliers!**

To telephone/call

Question

4 Quiz-Quiz-Trade Réponse

Téléphoner

Les verbes réguliers!
(Regular verbs!)

Directions: Cut out the *Les verbes reguliers!* cards along the dotted line. Then fold the card in half so the question is on one side and the answer is on the back. Glue or tape cards together to keep the answers and questions on opposite sides.

5

Les verbes réguliers!

Quiz-Quiz-Trade

To play

Question

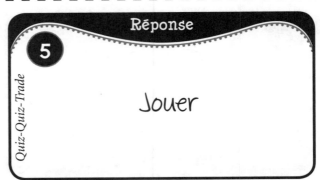

Réponse

5

Quiz-Quiz-Trade

Jouer

6

Les verbes réguliers!

Quiz-Quiz-Trade

To finish

Question

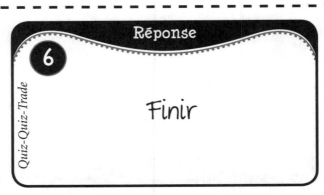

Réponse

6

Quiz-Quiz-Trade

Finir

7

Les verbes réguliers!

Quiz-Quiz-Trade

To choose

Question

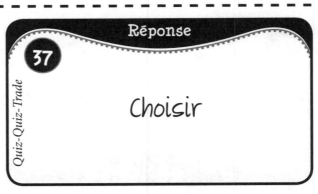

Réponse

37

Quiz-Quiz-Trade

Choisir

8

Les verbes réguliers!

Quiz-Quiz-Trade

To obey

Question

Réponse

8

Quiz-Quiz-Trade

Obéir

Les verbes réguliers!
(Regular verbs!)

Directions: Cut out the *Les verbes reguliers!* cards along the dotted line. Then fold the card in half so the question is on one side and the answer is on the back. Glue or tape cards together to keep the answers and questions on opposite sides.

Quiz-Quiz-Trade

9

Les verbes réguliers!

To blush

Question

Quiz-Quiz-Trade

Réponse

9

Rougir

Quiz-Quiz-Trade

10

Les verbes réguliers!

To hear

Question

Quiz-Quiz-Trade

Réponse

10

Entendre

Quiz-Quiz-Trade

11

Les verbes réguliers!

To sell

Question

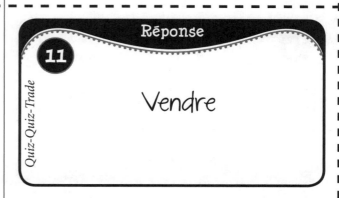

Quiz-Quiz-Trade

Réponse

11

Vendre

Quiz-Quiz-Trade

12

Les verbes réguliers!

To lose

Question

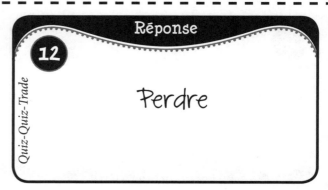

Quiz-Quiz-Trade

Réponse

12

Perdre

Les verbes réguliers!
(Regular verbs!)

Directions: Cut out the *Les verbes reguliers!* cards along the dotted line. Then fold the card in half so the question is on one side and the answer is on the back. Glue or tape cards together to keep the answers and questions on opposite sides.

13 Les verbes réguliers!
To answer
Question
Quiz-Quiz-Trade

Réponse
13
Répondre
Quiz-Quiz-Trade

14 Les verbes réguliers!
To grow
Question
Quiz-Quiz-Trade

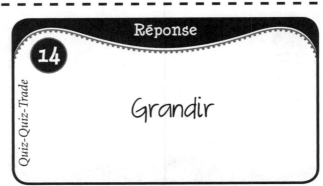

Réponse
14
Grandir
Quiz-Quiz-Trade

15 Les verbes réguliers!
To fill
Question
Quiz-Quiz-Trade

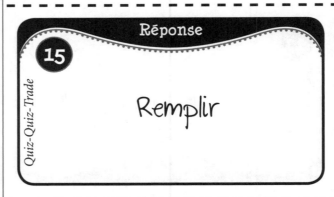

Réponse
15
Remplir
Quiz-Quiz-Trade

16 Les verbes réguliers!
To wait
Question
Quiz-Quiz-Trade

Réponse
16
Attendre
Quiz-Quiz-Trade

Les verbes réguliers!
(Regular verbs!)

Directions: Cut out the *Les verbes reguliers!* cards along the dotted line. Then fold the card in half so the question is on one side and the answer is on the back. Glue or tape cards together to keep the answers and questions on opposite sides.

17 — Quiz-Quiz-Trade

Les verbes réguliers!

Que font-ils?
They talk.

Question

Réponse

17 — Quiz-Quiz-Trade

Ils parlent.

---

18 — Quiz-Quiz-Trade

Les verbes réguliers!

Que fait-il?
He listens to music.

Question

Réponse

18 — Quiz-Quiz-Trade

Il écoute
la musique.

---

19 — Quiz-Quiz-Trade

Les verbes réguliers!

Que font-ils?
They hang out together.

Question

Réponse

19 — Quiz-Quiz-Trade

Ils flânent
ensemble.

2o — Quiz-Quiz-Trade

Les verbes réguliers!

Que fait-elle?
She calls her friend.

Question

Réponse

2o — Quiz-Quiz-Trade

Elle téléphone
à son ami.

Les verbes réguliers!
(Regular verbs!)

Directions: Cut out the *Les verbes reguliers!* cards along the dotted line. Then fold the card in half so the question is on one side and the answer is on the back. Glue or tape cards together to keep the answers and questions on opposite sides.

21 | Quiz-Quiz-Trade | Les verbes réguliers!

Que font-ils?
They play baseball.

Question

---

21 | Quiz-Quiz-Trade | Réponse

Ils jouent au baseball.

---

22 | Quiz-Quiz-Trade | Les verbes réguliers!

Que fait-il?"
He finishes the race.

Question

---

22 | Quiz-Quiz-Trade | Réponse

Il finit la course.

---

23 | Quiz-Quiz-Trade | Les verbes réguliers!

Que fait-elle?
She chooses ice cream.

Question

---

23 | Quiz-Quiz-Trade | Réponse

Elle choisit une crème glacée.

---

24 | Quiz-Quiz-Trade | Les verbes réguliers!

Que fait le chien?
The dog obeys the boy.

Question

---

24 | Quiz-Quiz-Trade | Réponse

Le chien obéit le garçon.

Les verbes réguliers!
(Regular verbs!)

Directions: Cut out the *Les verbes reguliers!* cards along the dotted line. Then fold the card in half so the question is on one side and the answer is on the back. Glue or tape cards together to keep the answers and questions on opposite sides.

---

25 — Quiz-Quiz-Trade

Les verbes réguliers!

Que fait-elle?

She blushes.

Question

---

25 — Quiz-Quiz-Trade

Réponse

Elle rougit.

---

26 — Quiz-Quiz-Trade

Les verbes réguliers!

Que font-elles?

They hear a noise.

Question

---

26 — Quiz-Quiz-Trade

Réponse

Elles entendent un bruit!

---

27 — Quiz-Quiz-Trade

Les verbes réguliers!

Que font-ils?

They sell lemonade.

Limonade

Question

---

27 — Quiz-Quiz-Trade

Réponse

Ils vendent de la limonade.

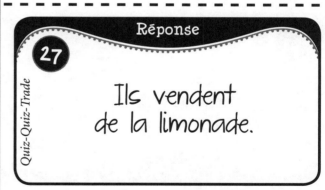

---

28 — Quiz-Quiz-Trade

Les verbes réguliers!

Qu'est-ce qui arrive?

He lost his dog.

Question

---

28 — Quiz-Quiz-Trade

Réponse

Le garçon perd son chien.

Les verbes réguliers!
(Regular verbs!)

Directions: Cut out the *Les verbes reguliers!* cards along the dotted line. Then fold the card in half so the question is on one side and the answer is on the back. Glue or tape cards together to keep the answers and questions on opposite sides.

29 · Quiz-Quiz-Trade · Les verbes réguliers!
Que fait-il?
He answers the door.
Question

Réponse
29 · Quiz-Quiz-Trade
Il répond à la porte.

30 · Quiz-Quiz-Trade · Les verbes réguliers!
Que fait-elle?
She is growing.
Question

Réponse
30 · Quiz-Quiz-Trade
Elle grandit.

31 · Quiz-Quiz-Trade · Les verbes réguliers!
Que font-ils?
They wait for the bus.
Question

Réponse
31 · Quiz-Quiz-Trade
Ils attendent l'autobus.

32 · Quiz-Quiz-Trade · Les verbes réguliers!
Que fait-il?
He falls down.
Question

Réponse
32 · Quiz-Quiz-Trade
Il tombe.

Que font-ils?
(What are they doing?)

Talking Chips

Students discuss what they see in the scene provided to them (use the scene on page 245). Students take turns sharing ideas using their Talking Chips to indicate it's their turn to talk! When all of the chips are in the middle of the table, students collect their chips and continue their discussion.

Steps

Setup: The teacher gives each teammate an equal number of Talking Chips. These may be pieces of paper, bingo chips, or the ready-made Talking Chips provided.

1 Provide a Topic
The teacher provides a topic by asking, *"Que font-ils?"* and gives time for students to think how they would answer.

2 Begin Talking
One student places a chip in center, begins the discussion, stating one activity he or she sees occuring in the scene (e.g., *"Les enfants jouent dans le parc."*).

3 Continue Discussion
Students use chips to continue the discussion, placing one of their own chips in the center of the team table. There is no given order. If they want to talk, they must place one of their chips. All students must place all of their chips in the center of the team table.

4 All Chips in the Center
A round is done when all of the chips are in the center of the team table. Students collect chips and continue their discussion until a set number of rounds or time is up.

(continued)

Que font-ils?
(What are they doing?)

Directions: Cut out the *Mon tour à parler* chips along the dotted line. Give a minimum of two chips to each student for discussion to play *"Mon tour à parler."*

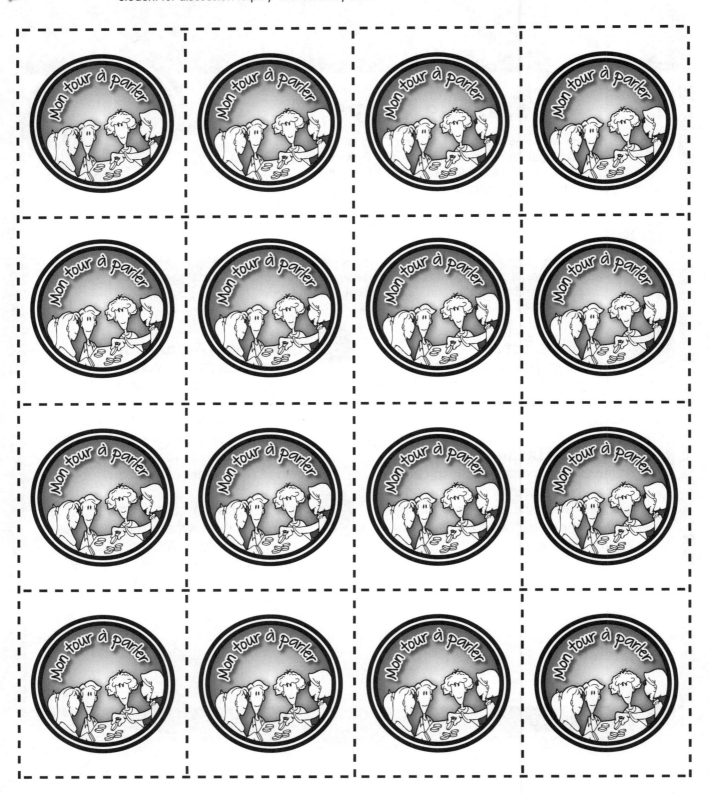

Au négatif!
(In the negative!)

Telephone

One student per team leaves the room during instructions on how to write sentences in the negative form. When students return, teammates provide instruction on the information missed.

Steps

1 **Learners Leave**
One student from each team, the Learner, is selected to leave the room.

2 **Teachers Learn**
Remaining students, the Teachers, receive instruction on how to write sentences in the negative form. The students will already be familiar with how to conjugate regular verbs in the three groups *(-ER,-IR, -RE)*. Include verbs from the regular groups as well as verbs which begin with a vowel (causing elision of *ne + vowel = n'*). For example, students will have to negate the following sentences:
- *J'aime la glace. (Je n'aime pas la glace.)*
- *Il finit ses devoirs. (Il ne finit pas ses devoirs.)*
- *Nous vendons la maison. (Nous ne vendons pas la maison.)*

3 **Teachers Plan**
The Teachers plan how to best instruct the Learner, making sure each Teacher has a part in the teaching, deciding on which verbs to use and the pronouns they will include. They will make sure they understand where the *ne/n'* and *pas* go in the sentence. If they struggle, the classroom teacher may provide a sample of sentences. The Teachers decide how they will check for understanding.

4 **Learners Reenter the Room**
Learners return to their teams and Teachers each teach their part of the content, with teammates expanding on the information as necessary. They then check for understanding.

(continued)

Au négatif!
(In the negative!)

Telephone

Steps

5 **Check**
The Learners may take a practice test.

6 **Reflect**
How did the Teachers do? Did they miss anything in their instruction? What could they have done differently? Have teams reflect on the process and how they could have done things differently.

Variation

• **Switch Teams.** Have a student from a different team come and be the Learner. Are the learning results the same?

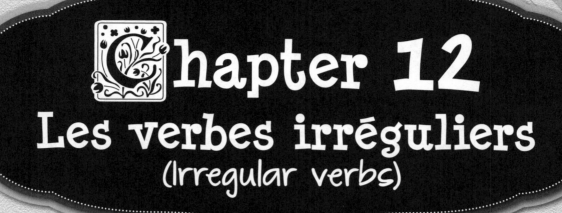

Chapter 12
Les verbes irréguliers
(Irregular verbs)

Structures & Activities

FRANCE

Vocabulaire

Les verbes irréguliers
(Irregular verbs)

Les verbes irréguliers
(Irregular verbs)

- **Aller** (To go)
- **Avoir** (To have)
- **Devenir** (To become)
- **Devoir** (To have to/must)
- **Écrire** (To write)
- **Être** (To be)
- **Faire** (To do/make)
- **Lire** (To read)
- **Mettre** (To put)
- **Pouvoir** (To be able to/can)
- **Savoir** (To know)
- **Venir** (To come)
- **Vouloir** (To want)

Aller (To go)

- **Je vais** (I go)
- **Tu vas** (You go)
- **Il/elle va** (He/she/it goes)
- **Nous allons** (We go)
- **Vous allez** (You go)
- **Ils/elles vont** (They go)

Avoir (To have)

- **J'ai** (I have)
- **Tu as** (You have)
- **Il/elle a** (He/she/it has)
- **Nous avons** (We have)
- **Vous avez** (You have)
- **Ils/elles ont** (They have)

Devenir (To become)

- **Je deviens** (I become)
- **Tu deviens** (You become)
- **Il/elle devient** (He/she/it becomes)
- **Nous devenons** (We become)
- **Vous devenez** (You become)
- **Ils/elles deviennent** (They become)

Devoir (To have to/must)

- **Je dois** (I have to/I must)
- **Tu dois** (You have to/you must)
- **Il/elle doit** (He/she/it has to/must)
- **Nous devons** (We have to/must)
- **Vous devez** (You have to/must)
- **Ils/elles doivent** (They have to/must)

Vocabulaire

Les verbes irréguliers
(Irregular verbs)

Écrire (To write)

- **J'écris** (I write)
- **Tu écris** (You write)
- **Il/elle écrit** (He/she/it writes)
- **Nous écrivons** (We write)
- **Vous écrivez** (You write)
- **Ils/elles écrivent** (They write)

Être (To be)

- **Je suis** (I am)
- **Tu es** (You are)
- **Il/elle est** (He/she/it is)
- **Nous sommes** (We are)
- **Vous êtes** (You are)
- **Ils/elles sont** (They are)

Faire (To do/to make)

- **Je fais** (I do/I make)
- **Tu fais** (You do/you make)
- **Il/elle fait** (He/she does/makes)
- **Nous faisons** (We do/make)
- **Vous faites** (You do/make)
- **Ils/elles font** (They do/make)

Lire (To read)

- **Je lis** (I read)
- **Tu lis** (You read)
- **Il/elle lit** (He/she/it reads)
- **Nous lisons** (We read)
- **Vous lisez** (You read)
- **Ils/elles lisent** (They read)

Mettre (To put)

- **Je mets** (I put)
- **Tu mets** (You put)
- **Il/elle met** (He/she/it puts)
- **Nous mettons** (We put)
- **Vous mettez** (You put)
- **Ils/elles mettent** (They put)

Pouvoir (Can/to be able to)

- **Je peux** (I can/I am able to)
- **Tu peux** (You can/you are able to)
- **Il/elle peut** (He/she/it can/is able to)
- **Nous pouvons** (We can/are able to)
- **Vous pouvez** (You can/are able to)
- **Ils/elles peuvent** (They can/are able to)

Vocabulaire

Les verbes irréguliers
(Irregular verbs)

Savoir (To know (how to do something or some information))

- **Je sais** (I know)
- **Tu sais** (You know)
- **Il/elle sait** (He/she/it knows)
- **Nous savons** (We know)
- **Vous savez** (You know)
- **Ils/elles savent** (They know)

Venir (To come)

- **Je viens** (I come)
- **Tu viens** (You come)
- **Il/elle vient** (He/she/it comes)
- **Nous venons** (We come)
- **Vous venez** (You come)
- **Ils/elles viennent** (They come)

Vouloir (To want)

- **Je veux** (I want)
- **Tu veux** (You want)
- **Il/elle veut** (He/she/it wants)
- **Nous voulons** (We want)
- **Vous voulez** (You want)
- **Ils/elles veulent** (They want)

Note:
- *"Tu"* means "you" in English when referring to someone you know personally, a friend, or someone younger.
- *"Vous"* means "you" in English when referring to one person, being polite: someone you don't know or would not use their first name (someone older or to whom you would refer to as Mr., Mrs., or Dr., in front of their name).
- *"Vous"* also means "you" in English when you are talking to a group of two or more people.
- The subject pronoun "on" literally means "one" or "people in general." It's often equivalent to the English passive voice. -For example: *On parle français ici!* (One speaks/people speak French here). In addition, "on" is an informal replacement for "we," and is used more often in Canada to replace the subject pronoun *nous*. It is conjugated in the same manner as the *"il/elle"* form of verbs. *Qui (who)* is also conjugated the same as the *"il/elle"* form.

Je...Nous...
(I...We...)

Simultaneous RoundTable

Students write sentences based on the teacher's prompt. Teams share their sentences with the class at the end of the activity!

Setup: The teacher gives each student paper and a pencil.

 1 **Set the Stage**
The teacher assigns the class the task of completing one of the following sentences:

- *Je vais…*
- *Je sais…*
- *Je veux…*
- *Je lis…*
- *J'écris…*
- *Je peux…*

The class brainstorms information that they can add to these sentence starters: for example—infinitive verbs to go with *je vais, je sais, je veux, je peux (aller, voyager, lire, marcher, assister)*, nouns that could follow *je lis* and *j'écris (un livre, une magazine, le journal, mon courriel, un message texte,* etc.).

The class also comes up with lists of details *with whom? when? where?* so that each student has a variety of possible details to add to complete the team's sentence. The teacher writes the responses on the board in columns under the questions.

 2 **Students Write**
Students write one sentence on their paper, each student adding an additional detail. For example, Student A begins the task by writing *"Je vais …voyager."*

 3 **Pass Papers**
Everyone passes their paper to the next person on their left in the team. Student B continues the phrase by adding another detail.

(continued)

Je...Nous...
(I...We...)

Simultaneous RoundTable

Steps

 Continue Passing
Students continue to Pass-N-Add until the teacher decides time is up or an allotted number of passes has expired (e.g., Everyone passes once around or twice around the team table). In our example from the previous page, Student A started the sentence with *"Je vais...voyager,"* Student B added *"...en Europe"*, Student C continued by adding *"en juillet,"* and Student D added *"avec ma famille."*

5 Discuss Ideas
Students then discuss their ideas and come up with statements based on things they do: e.g., *Nous allons...*
- *Nous savons...*
- *Nous voulons...*
- *Nous lisons...*
- *Nous écrivons...*
- *Nous pouvons...*

6 Share Statements with Class
Teams Stand-N-Share their responses!

Variations

- **RoundTable**

  Setup: Teams have one piece of paper on which to record all answers.

  Steps: 1. **Set the Stage:** Teacher assigns a statement to complete. The teacher gives Think Time.

  2. **Say, Write, and Pass:** Team members each make a statement, write it on the paper, and then pass the paper to the next team member (one paper—one pencil).

Je...Nous...

(I...We...)

Directions: Each team member writes sentences based on the teacher's prompt using the worksheet and pen or pencil. Team members write, and then pass to the next team member on their team.

1. _____
2. _____
3. _____
4. _____
5. _____
6. _____
7. _____
8. _____
9. _____
10. _____
11. _____
12. _____
13. _____
14. _____
15. _____

Les verbes irréguliers!
(Irregular verbs!)

Flashcard Game

Partners proceed through three rounds as they quiz each other with flashcards, mastering the content to win cards.

Steps

Setup: The teacher gives students their own set of flashcards. The teacher laminates cards so students can write the correct responses on the back of their cards (this could be the name of the verb in English or the correct form given a specific subject pronoun, or the past participle of the verb).

1 Pair Up
In pairs, the Tutee gives his or her flashcards to the Tutor.

2 Round 1: Maximum Cues
The Tutor shows the verb on the front of the card, then shows and reads the answer written on the back of the card. The Tutor then turns the card back over and again shows the verb on the front of the card and asks the Tutee to answer from memory.

3 Tutee Answers
If the correct answer is given, the Tutee wins the card back and receives delightful praise from the Tutor. If wrong, the Tutor shows the Tutee the answer side of the card and coaches. The card is then returned to the stack to try again later. **Hint:** Tutor can ask, *"How can I help you remember that?"* The pair can discuss ways of remembering answers.

4 Switch
When the Tutee wins all cards, partners switch roles. When the new Tutee wins all of his or her cards, partners advance to Round 2.

(continued)

2

Les verbes irréguliers!
(Irregular verbs!)

Flashcard Game

Steps

5 **Round 2: Few Cues**
The process is repeated, except the Tutor shows only the verb side of the card and asks the Tutee to answer from memory. If wrong, the Tutor shows the Tutee the answer side, and the card is returned to the stack to try again.

6 **Round 3: No Cues**
Again, the process is repeated, except the Tutor quizzes the Tutee on each question by stating the verb on the card without showing the Tutee the flashcards.

Hints

- Limit each round to no more than five cards. If a student has won all of the cards, he or she can add bonus cards.

- The tutor can show the "answer" side of the card and the Tutee must provide the correct infinitive of the verb!

Les verbes irréguliers!
(Irregular verbs!)

Directions: Cut out the *Les verbes irréguliers!* cards along the dotted line. Then fold each in half so the verb is on the front and the correct response is on the back. Keep verb and the correct response on opposite sides.

1 — *Les verbes irréguliers!*

Flashcard Game

Aller

Question

1 — Flashcard Game

_____

Réponse

2 — *Les verbes irréguliers!*

Flashcard Game

Avoir

Question

2 — Flashcard Game

_____

Réponse

3 — *Les verbes irréguliers!*

Flashcard Game

Devenir

Question

3 — Flashcard Game

_____

Réponse

4 — *Les verbes irréguliers!*

Flashcard Game

Écrire

Question

4 — Flashcard Game

_____

Réponse

Les verbes irréguliers!
(Irregular verbs!)

Directions: Cut out the *Les verbes irréguliers!* cards along the dotted line. Then fold each in half so the verb is on the front and the correct response is on the back. Keep verb and the correct response on opposite sides.

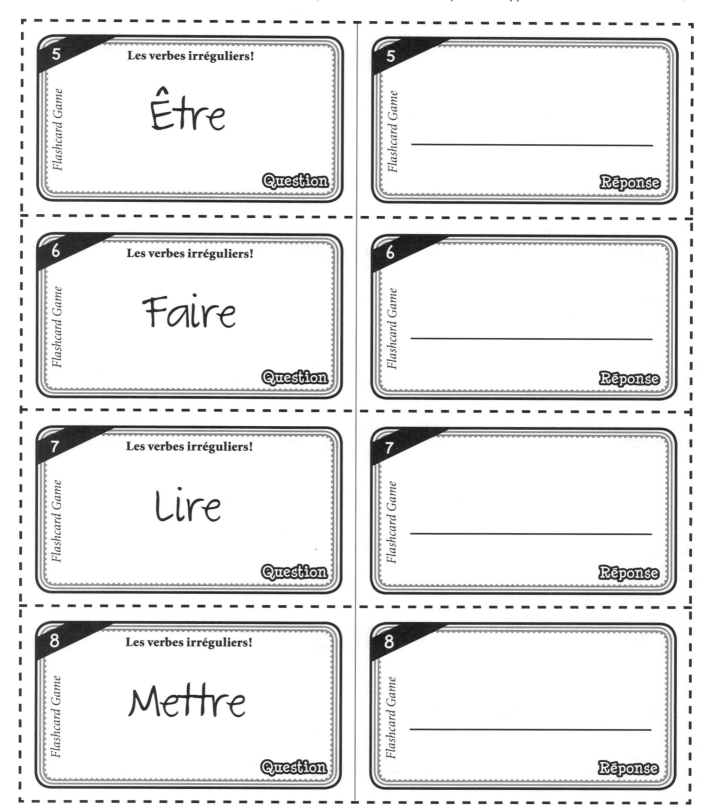

5 | Flashcard Game | **Les verbes irréguliers!**

Être

Question

5 | Flashcard Game

_____

Réponse

6 | Flashcard Game | **Les verbes irréguliers!**

Faire

Question

6 | Flashcard Game

_____

Réponse

7 | Flashcard Game | **Les verbes irréguliers!**

Lire

Question

7 | Flashcard Game

_____

Réponse

8 | Flashcard Game | **Les verbes irréguliers!**

Mettre

Question

8 | Flashcard Game

_____

Réponse

Les verbes irréguliers!
(Irregular verbs!)

Directions: Cut out the *Les verbes irréguliers!* cards along the dotted line. Then fold each in half so the verb is on the front and the correct response is on the back. Keep verb and the correct response on opposite sides.

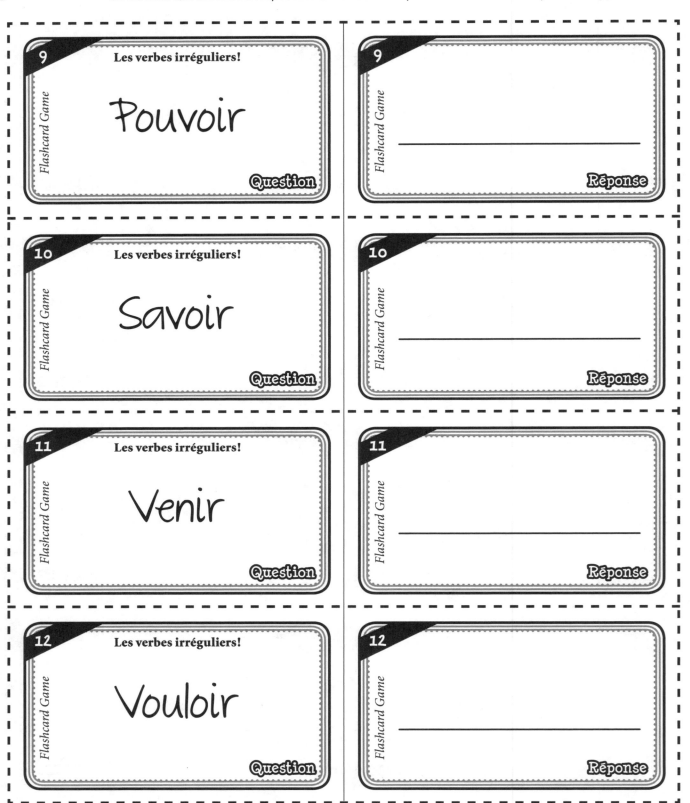

9 Les verbes irréguliers! Flashcard Game Pouvoir Question	**9** Flashcard Game _____ Réponse
10 Les verbes irréguliers! Flashcard Game Savoir Question	**10** Flashcard Game _____ Réponse
11 Les verbes irréguliers! Flashcard Game Venir Question	**11** Flashcard Game _____ Réponse
12 Les verbes irréguliers! Flashcard Game Vouloir Question	**12** Flashcard Game _____ Réponse

Ce qu'on fait!
(What we do!)

Pairs Compare

Pairs create a list of possible ideas or answers to a question or statement posed to them by the teacher. Pairs pair and compare their answers with another pair. Finally, pairs work as a team to create additional answers or ideas.

Steps

1 **Teacher Provides a Question**
The teacher provides a question/ statement that has multiple responses and provides Think Time. The teacher states how long students will have to record responses.
Questions may include:

- *Qu'est-ce que tu vas faire cet été?*
- *Qu'est-ce que tu veux pour Noël?*
- *Qu'est-ce que tu peux jouer en hiver?*
- *Qu'est-ce que tu dois faire pour conjuguer un verbe irrégulier?*

2 **RallyTable**
Shoulder partners share answers with each other: One partner writes a response on his or her Recording Sheet. The other partner then records a response. Partners continue sharing and recording as many responses as they can. Pairs keep their answers "secret" from other pairs.

3 **Teacher Calls Time**
When time is up, the teacher asks pairs to form teams of four.

4 **Pairs Compare**
Pairs pair and share their answers using RoundRobin. The other pair either adds the answer to their list or checks it off if they already have it.

5 **Team Challenge**
As a team, students generate new answers, taking turns within pairs recording answers on their pair list.

Ce qu'on fait!
(What we do!)

Directions: In pairs, take turns creating a list of *Ce qu'on fait!* items. Compare your list with another pair and see if you come up with the same items. Then, as a team, see if you can all come up with new *Ce qu'on fait!* items.

Teacher Question or Statement: _____

_____

_____

Réponses

1. _____

2. _____

3. _____

4. _____

5. _____

6. _____

7. _____

8. _____

9. _____

10. _____

11. _____

12. _____

13. _____

14. _____

15. _____

On s'entraîne!
(In training!)

RallyCoach

Students work with partners to practice conjugating irregular verbs and putting them in correct sentences.

Steps

Setup: The teacher gives each pair of students a list of sentences to complete. Partner A receives list A and Partner B receives list B.

1 Pair Up
Students sit in pairs. Students receive the worksheet. They can fold it or cut it in half so each partner has half the problems.

2 Partner A Writes
Partner A completes the first sentence on his or her list, talking through the process of what he or she is doing; Partner B coaches if necessary and praises when correct.

3 Partner B Writes
Partner B completes the first statement from his or her list, again talking through the process. Partner A coaches and praises.

4 Keep Talking and Writing
Pairs continue completing the sentences from each of the students' part of the page!

On s'entraîne!
(In training!)

Directions: One worksheet is provided per pair of students. Students fold or cut the paper so they only work on one half at a time. Partner A solves by talking aloud to his or her partner. Partner B coaches and praises. Roles are then reversed. Pairs continue until the page is complete.

On s'entraîne!
Complétez les phrases suivantes en utilisant la bonne forme du verbe!

Partenaire A _____	Partenaire B _____
(partenaire B-l'entraîneur _____)	(partenaire A-l'entraîneur _____)

1 Est-ce que tu _____ (vouloir) du chocolat?

1 Est-ce que tu _____ (lire) des bandes dessinées?

2 Il _____ (devenir) Superman avec son capuchon rouge.

2 Quand est-ce qu'elle _____ (devoir) rentrer?

3 Pourquoi est-ce que vous _____ (aller) à Toronto?

3 Nous _____ (écrire) des lettres à nos grands-parents.

4 Elles _____ (faire) de la motoneige en hiver.

4 Est-ce que vous _____ (mettre) du ketchup sur votre hamburger?

5 Où est-ce qu'on _____ (pouvoir) faire de la natation en été?

5 Je _____ (savoir) la date de ton anniversaire!

Trouve l'erreur!
(Find the mistake!)

Find-the-Fiction

Students write three sentences using the irregular verbs and read them to teammates. Teammates try to "find" which of the three statements is the "fiction." This is a great activity to first do as a class so students understand the process and will be able to generate their own statements.

Steps

1 Teacher States the Topic
The teacher announces the question to which students will write their statements. Here are some possible questions based on irregular verbs:
- *Qu'est-ce que tu peux faire?*
- *Qu'est-ce que tu vas faire ce soir?*
- *Qu'est-ce que tu sais faire?*
- *Qu'est-ce que tu dois faire chez toi?*
- *Qu'est-ce que tu aimes lire?*
- *Quels livres as-tu lus?*
- *Où est-ce que tu es allé hier soir/Où es-tu allé hier soir?*

2 Students Write
Teammates each write three statements responding to the question: Two true, one false, attempting to trick their teammates.

3 Stand and Share
One student on each team stands and reads his or her statements to teammates.

4 Teammates Think and Write
Without consulting teammates, each student writes down his or her own best guess which statement is false.

5 Teams Discuss
Teammates RoundRobin and defend their "best guess." (**Note:** The teacher may or may not ask teams to attempt to reach consensus).

6 Announce the Fiction
Teammates state their guess(es).

7 Reveal
The standing student announces the false statement.

(continued)

Trouve l'erreur!
(Find the mistake!)

Find-the-Fiction

Steps

8 **Celebrate**
Students celebrate: The standing student congratulates teammates who guessed correctly. Teammates who were fooled congratulate the standing student.

9 **Continue Playing**
The next teammate stands to share. The process is repeated.

Variations

- **Class Find-the-Fiction.** Find-the-Fiction may be played with the whole class. The teacher or a student may attempt to outwit the whole class.

- **Find the Error.** Students can write three statements, one containing a misspelled verb form. Students StandUp–HandUp–PairUp. In pairs, students have to figure out which is incorrect.

- **Fact-or-Fiction:** This variation of Find-the-Fiction is used on an occasional basis to spice up a review. In Fact-or-Fiction, students state a true-or-false statement, and it is up to teammates to decide if the statement is either a fact or fiction. Fact-or-Fiction is easier for young students because they only need to deal with one statement at a time.

Trouve l'erreur!
(Find the mistake!)

Directions: Students write three statements using the irregular verbs. One of the three statements must be fiction. Teammates guess which statement is the fiction.

1

2

3

Chapter 13
La musique
(Music)

Structures & Activities

Vocabulaire

La musique
(Music)

Chapter 13

Les styles de musique
(Music styles)

- **C'est de la bombe!** (That rocks!)
- **Cool/super!** (Cool, great, hot!)
- **Doué(e)** (Gifted)
- **L'opéra** (Opera)
- **La chanson** (Song)
- **La danse** (Dance music)
- **La musique alternative** (Alternative music)
- **La musique classique** (Classical music)
- **La musique traditionnelle** (Traditional music)
- **Le CD (disque compacte)** (CD)
- **Le chanteur/la chanteuse** (Singer)
- **Le choeur** (Choir)
- **Le country** (Country)
- **Le folk** (Folk music)
- **Le groupe** (Music group)
- **Le heavy metal** (Heavy metal)
- **Le hip hop** (Hip hop)
- **Le jazz** (Jazz)

- **Le palmarès** (The hit parade)
- **Le pop** (Pop music)
- **Le rap** (Rap)
- **Le reggae** (Reggae)
- **Le rock** (Rock)
- **Le rythme** (Rhythm)
- **Le techno** (Techno)
- **Les fans** (Fans)
- **Les paroles** (Lyrics)

Vocabulaire

La musique
(Music)

Les adjectifs
(Adjectives)

- **Agréable** (Nice)
- **Bon/bonne** (Good)
- **Branché/branchée** (In style)
- **Calmant/calmante** (Calm)
- **Captivant/captivante** (Captivating)
- **Choquant/choquante** (Shocking)
- **Créatif/créative** (Creative)
- **Électrifiant/électrifiante** (Electrifying)
- **Émouvant/émouvante** (Moving/emotional)
- **Énergique** (Energetic)
- **Ennuyeux/ennuyeuse** (Boring)
- **Génial/géniale** (Nice)
- **Irritant/irritante** (Irritating)
- **Magnifique** (Magnificent)
- **Mauvais/mauvaise** (Bad/poor)
- **Mélodieux/mélodieuse** (Melodious)
- **Offensif/offensive** (Offensive)

- **Passionant/passionante** (Passionate)
- **Populaire** (Popular)
- **Remarquable** (Remarkable)
- **Rythmé/rythmée** (Rythmic)
- **Talentueux/talentueuse** (Talented)
- **Touchant/touchante** (Touching)
- **Typique** (Typical)

Trouve quelqu'un qui...
(Find someone who...)

Find Someone Who

Students circulate around the classroom forming and re-forming pairs trying to "find someone who" can correctly answer one of the questions.

Steps

Setup: The teacher prepares the *Trouve quelqu'un qui…* worksheet for students to use.

---

1 **Distribute the Worksheet**
Students are given the worksheet to review.

2 **Students Pair Up**
Students circulate around the class. Students keep a hand raised until they find a partner.

3 **Ask**
In pairs, students take turns asking a question from the worksheet: Partner A asks Partner B. Partner B responds. Partner A records the answer on his or her own worksheet and expresses appreciation.

4 **Check**
Partner B checks and initials the answer.

5 **Reverse Roles**
Partner B now asks a question and Partner A responds. Partner B records the answer on his or her own worksheet and expresses appreciation.

6 **Check**
Partner A checks and initials the answer.

(continued)

Trouve quelqu'un qui...
(Find someone who...)

Find Someone Who

Steps

7 **Praise and Part**
Partners high five and raise a hand as they search for a new partner.

8 **Repeat**
Students repeat the process until their worksheets are complete.

9 **Experts**
Experts are students who have completed their worksheets. Once their worksheet is completed, they return to their desks and can be approached by others as a resource.

Trouve quelqu'un qui...
(Find someone who...)

Directions: Students circulate around the classroom forming and re-forming pairs trying to "find someone who" can answer the question. Have your partner initial the answer.

1 Est-ce que tu aimes la musique rap?

Initials: _____

Oui, j'aime la musique rap!

2 Est-ce que tu écoutes de la musique country?

Initials: _____

Oui, j'écoute de la musique country.

3 Est-ce que tes parents aiment le jazz?

Initials: _____

Oui, ils aiment le jazz.

4 Est-ce que tu écoutes de la musique classique?

Initials: _____

Oui, j'écoute de la musique classique.

5 Est-ce que tu as une chanson favorite?

Initials: _____

Oui, j'ai une chanson favorite!

6 Est-ce que tu n'aimes pas la musique techno?

Initials: _____

Je n'aime pas la musique techno.

7 Est-ce que tu n'aimes pas la musique d'opéra?

Initials: _____

Je n'aime pas la musique d'opéra.

8 Est-ce que tu aimes la musique latino?

Initials: _____

Oui, j'aime la musique latino.

9 Est-ce que tu aimes la musique danse?

Initials: _____

Oui, j'aime la musique danse.

10 Est-ce que tes parents écoutent du heavy metal?

Initials: _____

Oui, mes parents écoutent du heavy metal.

11 Est-ce que tu chantes dans un choeur?

Initials: _____

Oui, je chante dans un choeur.

12 Est-ce que tu aimes le rock?

Initials: _____

Non, je n'aime pas le rock.

On aime la musique!
(We like music!)

Pairs Compare

Pairs create a list of possible ideas or answers to a question or statement posed to them. Pairs pair and compare their answers with another pair. Finally, pairs work as a team to create additional answers or ideas.

Steps

1 **Teacher Provides a Question**
The teacher provides a question/statement that has multiple responses and provides Think Time. The teacher states how long students will have to record responses.
Examples:
- *La musique qu'on aime écouter, c'est la musique…*
- *Quel style de musique est-ce que tu aimes écouter quand tu fais tes devoirs?*
- *Quel style de musique est-ce que tes parents écoutent?*
- *Les chansons à la radio….*
- *La musique des émissions de télévision.*
- *Les annonces publicitaires avec la musique.*

2 **RallyTable**
Shoulder partners share answers with each other: One partner states a response, then writes it on the Recording Sheet. Then, the other partner states a response and records it. Pairs keep their answers "secret" from other pairs.

3 **Teacher Calls Time**
When time is up, the teacher asks pairs to form teams of four.

4 **Pairs Compare**
Pairs pair and share their answers using RoundRobin. The other pair either adds the answer to their list or checks it off if they already have it.

5 **Team Challenge**
As a team, students generate new answers, taking turns within pairs recording answers on their pair list.

On aime la musique!
(We like music!)

Directions: In pairs, take turns creating a list of answers to the question or statement. Compare your list with another pair and see if you come up with the same answers. Then, as a team, see if you can all come up with new answers.

Teacher Question or Statement: _____

_____

_____

Réponses

1. _____

2. _____

3. _____

4. _____

5. _____

6. _____

7. _____

8. _____

9. _____

10. _____

11. _____

12. _____

13. _____

14. _____

15. _____

On aime la musique!
(We like music!)

Poems for Two Voices (Song/Rap)

Partners create and present a poem they recite using one voice, each taking turns, or both together.

Steps

1 **The Theme Is Set**
The teacher assigns each pair a poem topic (e.g., instruments used in country music, qualities of rock music, music with rhythm, music that has good lyrics, etc.).

2 **Think Time**
Students are given Think Time and write down as many words in French that come to mind based on the given theme. The teacher shows the chapter vocabulary to encourage use of the vocabulary words.

3 **Write a Poem**
Partners work together to write their poem.

4 **Label the Poem**
Partners label each line of their poem, A, B, or AB, representing who will read each line. **Note:** Creating a rhyming poem may be too difficult for many students. It is okay if students' poems don't rhyme.

5 **Practice Reading**
Pairs rehearse their poems.

6 **Presentation of Poem**
Pairs recite their poems to another pair or to the class.

Variations

• **Recite a Poem.** The teacher writes a poem using the chapter vocabulary and provides the AB scripting. Pairs recite the poem.

• **Pairs Script It.** The teacher provides the poem and the pairs do their own AB scripting. They recite it as they have it scripted.

On aime la musique!
(We like music!)

Directions: Partners create and present a poem they recite. They label each line A, B, or AB representing if Partner A, Partner B, or both partners will read the line as they recite the poem.

Partenaire: _____

_____ _____
(label)

_____ _____
(label)

_____ _____
(label)

_____ _____
(label)

_____ _____
(label)

_____ _____
(label)

_____ _____
(label)

_____ _____
(label)

_____ _____
(label)

Un nouveau groupe!
(A new group/band!)

Carousel Feedback (Music Poster)

Teams create a poster about a new band performing in their community. Students circulate in the class and provide comments about each of the posters.

Steps

Setup: The teacher gives each team an *Un nouveau groupe!* sheet. Teams need writing materials and poster paper to draw on. The teacher provides a Comment/Recording Sheet for the final presentation of posters.

1 Set the Stage

The teacher announces the topic: A new band is coming to their community to perform a concert. Their job as a team is to create an eye-catching poster. Students are given time to think about and discuss what type of group/band, names of songs, date and time of the concert, band/group member names and the instruments they play.

2 Students Record Information

In teams using RoundTable Consensus, students record information on their sheets. When it is their turn to record a new idea, they must receive consensus from teammates before they write.

3 Create Poster

Teams work to create their team posters. They ensure everyone participates by either taking turns using RoundTable, or they divide the poster evenly among teammates and work on it simultaneously.

4 Display Posters

Finished posters are displayed around the classroom, either on walls or on team tables. A Comment/Recording Sheet is placed near the poster for other teams to record their comments.

(continued)

Un nouveau groupe!
(A new group/band!)

Carousel Feedback (Music Poster)

Steps

 5 Teams Rotate

Teams rotate around the class looking at other team posters. One teammate will write down comments about the poster! (The teacher explains that comments are positive and helpful to the other teams. Encourage teams to use the chapter vocabulary for their comments.)

 6 Move Again

After an allotted amount of time, or when all teams indicate they have written their comments, they rotate to the next poster. A new writer is selected to record the team's comments for that poster.

Un nouveau groupe!

(A new group/band!)

Directions: In teams, create a poster about a new band performing in your community. Students circulate around the room and provide feedback about each of the posters. Use this sheet to plan team posters.

Activity 4

Carousel Feedback

____

(Nom du groupe)

____

(Style de musique)

En vedette

(Noms des membres du groupe et leurs instruments/rôles)

____

____

____

____

____

(Chansons)

____

(Date du concert)

____

(Heure du concert)

____

(Lieu)

Un nouveau groupe!
(A new group/band!)

Directions: Teams use this Comment/Recording Sheet when rotating from project to project to leave feedback for other teams about their poster.

Commentaires

Chapter 14
Au cinéma
(At the movies)

Structures & Activities

Vocabulaire

Au cinéma
(At the movies)

Les films (Movies)

- **Aller chercher** (To pick someone up)
- **Arrêter manger quelque part** (To stop and eat somewhere)
- **En groupe** (As a group)
- **Flâner** (To hang out)
- **La rangée** (The row)
- **Le billet** (The ticket)
- **Le couvre-feu** (Curfew)
- **Le film** (The movie)
- **Le spectacle** (The show, play, performance)
- **Rigoler** (To have fun, to joke around)
- **S'amuser** (To have a good time/ to have fun)
- **S'éclater** (To have a lot of fun (lit: to explode))
- **Sympa/sympathique** (Nice/kind)
- **Un dessin-animé** (A cartoon)
- **Un drâme** (A drama)
- **Un film d'horreur** (A horror movie)
- **Un film de famille** (A family movie)
- **Un film musical** (A musical movie)
- **Un policier** (A police show)
- **Un spectacle** (A play (theatre production)

- **Une comédie** (A comedy)
- **Une fête de famille** (A family celebration)
- **Une spectacle musicale** (A musical)

Pour décrire des artistes
(To describe artists)

- **Exubérante (e)** (High-spirited, fun)
  - 🍁 **Fringant (e)** (High-spirited, fun)
- **Plein (e) d'énergie** (Full of energy)
- **Plein(e) de talent** (Full of talent, talented)
- **Provocant (e)** (Provocative, stimulating)
- **Sensass** (Sensational)
- **Unique** (Original)

Vocabulaire

Au cinéma
(At the movies)

Les classements de film
(Movie ratings)

- **U** *(Tout public)*—valid for all audiences.

- **10** *(Déconseillé aux moins de 10 ans)*—unsuitable for children younger than 10 (this rating is only used for TV), on movies, it's *"avertissement"* (warning). It means that some scenes may disturb young children and sensitive people, and on DVDs, it's written *"accord parental"* (parental guidance).

- **12** *(Interdit aux moins de 12 ans)*—unsuitable for children younger than 12 or forbidden in movies for under 12.

- **16** *(Interdit aux moins de 16 ans)*—unsuitable for children younger than 16 or forbidden in movies for under 16.

- **18** *(Interdit aux mineurs)*—unsuitable for children younger than 18 or forbidden in movies for under 18.

- **E** *(exempt)*—not rated.

Note:
French and Canadian Movie Ratings are different than U.S. Ratings.

Allons au cinéma!
(Let's go to the movies!)

Three-Step Interview

Students spend an allotted amount of time talking about going to the movies, what kind of movies they like to see, a recently viewed movie, or what they do while at the movie theatre. Students interview their partner and then each share with teammates what they learned.

Steps

Setup: The teacher gives each student one Interview Sheet.

1 Provide the Interview Topic
The teacher provides the interview topic:
- *Quel film veux-tu voir?*
- *Quel genre de films aimes-tu le plus?*
- *Quel film as-tu vu récemment?*
- *Que fais-tu au cinéma?*

Hint: These questions can be discussed as a class to prepare students as to what questions they can ask and even suggest sentence starters for answers.

2 Set the Time Limit
The teacher states how long pairs will have to interview each other, and provides Think Time.

3 Pairs Interview
In pairs, Partner A interviews Partner B. Students listen very carefully to the interviewee and may even take notes because after the interview, they will share what they heard.

4 Pairs Switch Roles
Partner B interviews Partner A.

5 RoundRobin
Pairs pair up to form groups of four. Each student, in turn, shares with the team what he or she learned in the interview.

Allons au cinéma!
(Let's go to the movies!)

Directions: Partners interview each other about movies and then share what they learned. Students use this Interview Sheet to record what they learned from their partner and the other two teammates.

Les notes de l'entrevue avec mon/ma partenaire

Mon/Ma partenaire s'appelle _____

Ce que j'ai appris du membre de mon équipe

Nom du membre de mon équipe _____

Ce que j'ai appris du membre de mon équipe

Nom du membre de mon équipe _____

Les films favoris!
(Favorite movies!)

One Stray

Students think about movie themes and titles. Teams share ideas and write down responses. One teammate "strays" from his or her team to a new team to share or gather information.

Steps

Setup: The teacher gives each team one Recording Sheet.

 1 ### Announce the Theme
The teacher announces the theme to the class. Here are some possible themes:

- *Les films d'horreur*
- *Les dessins-animés*
- *Les films de famille*
- *Un film qui a gagné un prix Grammy*
- *Un titre pour un nouveau film de...(famille, comédie, d'horreur, etc)*

 2 ### Students Think and Write
Students are given Think Time. Using RoundTable, teams record their ideas on the Recording Sheet. One teammate records an idea and the sheet is passed clockwise for the next teammate to record the next idea.

 3 ### Students Stand and Find a New Team
When teams are about halfway finished recording ideas, the teacher stops the class. The teacher calls one teammate's number (for example, Student #3) and that student from each team stands up. The remaining three teammates remain seated but raise their hands. Teacher calls *"stray."* Standing students take their group's list and stray to a team whose hands are raised. Teams lower their hands when a new member joins them.

(continued)

2

Les films favoris!
(Favorite movies!)

One Stray

 4

New Teammates Share Information

When the new teammate sits down, he or she shares ideas that his or her original team came up with which are different from the ideas the new team already has. The team records the additional ideas.

Optional

The group shares their list with the new teammate. The teacher announces the end of the sharing session. The new teammate thanks the team and then returns to their original teams to share what they have learned when they strayed.

Variations

• **Return and Report.** After the straying student shares ideas with the new team that his or her original team came up with, the new team shares the ideas they've come up with so far. The straying student returns to his original team and reports what he learned.

• **Multiple Strays.** After the straying, one teammate shares ideas with the new team, the teacher calls another number and that teammate strays to any team except the team where his or her teammate is already. This teammate shares ideas and the RoundTable continues.

Les films favoris!
(Favorite movies!)

Directions: Students think about movie themes and titles of the movie. Teams share ideas and then write responses. One teammate "strays" from his or her team to find a new team to share or gather information.

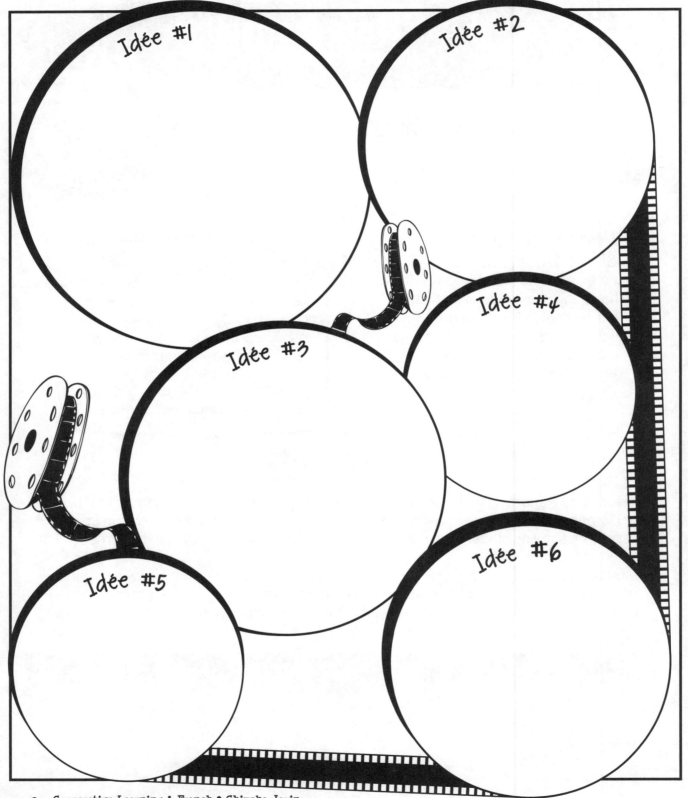

Idée #1

Idée #2

Idée #3

Idée #4

Idée #5

Idée #6

Les films
(Movies)

Find Someone Who

Students move around the classroom finding classmates to answer their questions about movies from their worksheet.

Steps

> **Setup:** The teacher makes copies of the *Les films* worksheet for each student in the classroom. The teacher may spend time going over questions so that all students understand what is being asked of them and how they will answer.

1 Form Pairs
Students take their worksheets, stand up, hand up, pair up to find a partner to answer one of the questions from their sheet.

2 Ask and Answer
Partner A asks a question that is on his or her worksheet and Partner B responds. Partner A records the answer on his or her own worksheet.

3 Check and Initial
Partner B checks and initials the answer.

4 Reverse Roles
Partner B asks Partner A a question that is on his or her worksheet and Partner A responds. Partner B now records the answer on his or

her own worksheet and expresses appreciation.

5 Check and Initial
Partner B checks and initials the answer.

6 Find a New Partner
Partners high five and raise a hand as they search for a new partner and repeat the process until their worksheets are complete.

7 Experts
Experts are students who have completed their worksheets. Once their worksheet is completed, they return to their desks and can be approached by others as a resource.

8 Teams Compare
Teams compare and discuss answers.

Les films
(Movies)

Directions: Students circulate around the classroom forming and re-forming pairs trying to "find someone who" can answer their question about movies. Record the answer provided by your partner and have your partner initial the answer.

1 Que fais-tu en groupe?

Initials: _____

2 Comment achètes-tu ton billet de cinéma?

Initials: _____

3 Quel est ton film favori?

Initials: _____

4 Qu'est-ce que tu aimes manger quand tu regardes un film au cinéma?

Initials: _____

5 Qu'est-ce que ta famille fait ensemble?

Initials: _____

6 Aimes-tu les films policiers ou les films d'horreur?

Initials: _____

7 Quelle comédie as-tu vue récemment?

Initials: _____

8 C'est quand ton couvre-feu?

Initials: _____

9 Où aimes-tu flâner avec tes amis?

Initials: _____

10 Quel acteur/Quelle actrice est plein(e) de talent?

Initials: _____

On parle des films
(Talking about movies)

Quiz-Quiz-Trade

Students create question cards, quiz a partner, get quizzed by a partner, and then trade their cards to repeat the process with a new partner.

Steps

Setup: The teacher prepares a set of blank Question Cards for the class.

1 Distribute Cards
The teacher cuts out the cards and distributes them to the class. (Alternatively, each student has one blank piece of note paper.)

2 Students Think and Write
Students write the name of a popular movie on one side of their card/paper and the genre of movie as the answer on the back. **Hint:** This can be a team effort, checking each other's cards/papers to make sure they are written correctly before playing.

3 Students Pair Up
Students stand up, hand up, pair up, and face their new partners.

4 Students Quiz Each Other
Students take turns asking questions about the card. Questions can be simply, *"C'est quel genre du film?"* His or her partner may respond *"C'est un film d'horreur… "*. Then, the other partner quizzes his or her partner about the card.

5 Trade Cards and Find New Partners
After partners have asked and answered each other's questions, they give each other a high five, trade cards, raise their hand, and find a new partner.

6 Continue Quizzing
This activity can go on for an allotted amount of time or number of trades.

(continued)

On parle des films
(Talking about movies)

Quiz-Quiz-Trade

Variations

- **Question Bank.** Work with the class to come up with questions they can ask each other about their movie cards. Post the question on the board so students can ask one of the questions as they pair up.

- **Increase Difficulty.** More advanced students can create questions based on true and false or specific details on the card. For example:
    1. *Est-ce que c'est un film de comédie?/C'est une comédie?*
    2. Multiple-choice response.
    3. Questions generated by students about what the movie is about or major actor/actresses.

- **The Other Side.** The teacher fills out one side of the card only with either the film names or the genres. Students must fill out the other side.

On parle des films
(Talking about movies)

Directions: Cut out the *On parle des films* cards along the dotted line. Then fold the card in half so the question is on the one side and the answer is on the back. Glue or tape cards together to keep the answers and questions on opposite sides.

1 — On parle des films — Quiz-Quiz-Trade

_____

(Le titre du film)

Question

1 — Réponse — Quiz-Quiz-Trade

_____

(Le genre du film)

2 — On parle des films — Quiz-Quiz-Trade

_____

(Le titre du film)

Question

2 — Réponse — Quiz-Quiz-Trade

_____

(Le genre du film)

3 — On parle des films — Quiz-Quiz-Trade

_____

(Le titre du film)

Question

3 — Réponse — Quiz-Quiz-Trade

_____

(Le genre du film)

4 — On parle des films — Quiz-Quiz-Trade

_____

(Le titre du film)

Question

4 — Réponse — Quiz-Quiz-Trade

_____

(Le genre du film)

On aime regarder des films!
(We like watching movies!)

Talking Chips

Students are given a topic to discuss. With their teams and personal chips, they contribute to the discussion until all of their chips are in the middle of the team table. When everyone has placed their chips, they are returned to their owners and the discussion continues!

Steps

Setup: The teacher places students into teams and each is given an equal number of chips or markers they can identify as their own (e.g., different shapes or colors, their name written on pieces of paper, chips provided, etc.).

 1 **Teacher Provides a Topic**
The teacher poses a question or topic to be discussed by the team.
Topics can include:
- *Qui est le meilleur acteur? Pourquoi?*
- *Qui est la meilleure actrice? Pourquoi?*
- *Quel est ton film favori? Pourquoi?*
- *Nommez des films recents.*
- *Nommez des acteurs.*
- *Nommez des films Disney.*
- *Préfères-tu regarder des films chez toi ou au théâtre?*

2 **Discussion Begins**
One student places a chip in the center and begins the discussion.

 3 **Continue Talking**
Students use chips to continue the discussion. There is no given order. Students must place one of their chips in the middle of the team table when they want to talk. If they have used up all of their chips, they must wait until everyone has placed all the chips in the middle before being able to continue the discussion.

 4 **Chips Used Up**
Students collect chips and continue their discussion.

On aime regarder des films!
(We like watching movies!)

Directions: Cut out the *Mon tour à parler* chips along the dotted line. Give a minimum of two chips to each student for discussion to play *"Mon tour à parler."*

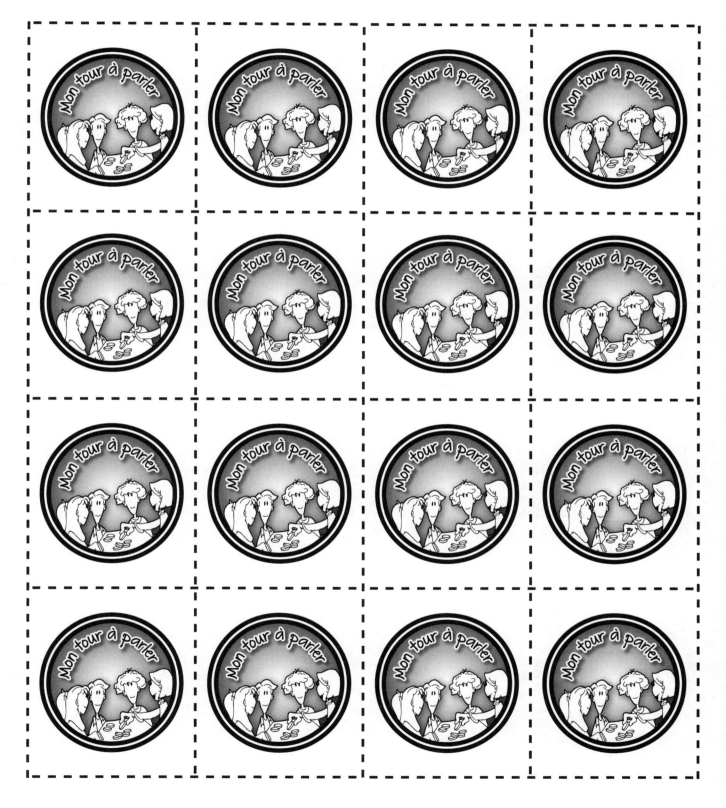

Chapter 15
Les Sports
(Sports)

Vocabulaire

Les Sports
(Sports)

Les activités sportives
(Sports activities)

- **Le badminton** (Badminton)
- **Le baseball** (Baseball)
- **Le basket-ball** (Basketball)
  - 🍁 **Le balon-panier** (Basketball)
- **La course automobile** (Car racing)
- **La course en fauteuil roulant** (Wheelchair racing)
- **Lacrosse** (Lacrosse)
- **Le cyclisme** (Cycling)
- **Le football** (Football)
- **La gymnastique** (Gymnastics)
- **Le hockey** (Hockey)
- **L'escalade** (Climbing (rock))
- **Le jogging** (Jogging)
- **Le karaté** (Karate)
- **La lutte** (Wrestling)
- **Le marathon** (Marathon (race))
- **La nage synchronisée** (Synchronized swimming)
- **La natation** (Swimming)
- **Le patin à roues alignées** (Inline skating (roller blading))
- **Le patinage** (Skating (ice))
- **Le patinage artistique** (Figure skating)
- **Le patinage de vitesse** (Speed skating)

- **La planche à neige** (Snowboarding)
- **La planche à roulettes** (Skateboarding)
- **Le plongeon** (Diving)
- **La randonnée pedestre** (Hiking)
- **Le saut en hauteur** (High jump)
- **Le saut en longueur** (Long jump)
- **Le ski acrobatique** (Acrobatic skiing)
- **Le ski alpin** (Downhill skiing)
- **Le ski de fond** (Cross-country skiing)
- **Le tennis** (Tennis)
- **Le vélo** (Cycling)
- **Le volley-ball** (Volleyball)
  - 🍁 **Le balon-volant** (Volleyball)

Les termes sportifs (Sports terms)

- **À toute vitesse** (At full speed)
- **Un arbitre** (Referee)
- **Un bâton** (Stick)
- **Un bonnet** (Cap (swimming))
- **Un casque** (Helmet)
- **Un cavalier/une cavalière** (Horseback rider)
- **Un certificat** (Certificate)
- **Un chandail** (A sweater)
- **Contre** (Against)
- **Un cycliste** (Cyclist)
- **En première place** (First place)

Cooperative Learning & French • Chiupka-Jozin
Kagan Publishing • 1 (800) 933-2667 • www.KaganOnline.com

Vocabulaire

Les Sports
(Sports)

- **L'entraînement** (Training)
- **Les épaulières** (Shoulder pads)
- **Une équipe** (Team)
- **Le gagnant, la gagnante** (The winner)
- **Un joueur, une joueuse** (A player)
- **Un gant** (Glove)
- **Les jambières** (Shinpads)
- **Un jeu** (Game)
- **Des lunettes (de nage)** (Glasses/goggles (swimming))
- **Un match** (Game)
- **Un maillot de bain/de lutte** (Bathing suit/wrestling singlet)
- **Une médaille (d'or, d'argent, de bronze)** (Medal (gold, silver, bronze))
- **Un nageur, une nageuse** (Swimmer)
- **Un objet souvenir** (Keepsake)
- **Des patins** (Skates)
- **Une rondelle** (Puck)
- **Un ruban** (Ribbon)
- **Un skieur, une skieuse** (Skier)
- **Un tournoi** (Tournament)
- **Un trophée** (Trophy)
- **Faire de l'alpinisme** (To mountain climb)
- **Faire des arts martiaux** (To do martial arts)
  - **Faire de l'athlétisme** (To do track and field)

- **Faire de la boxe** (To box)
- **Faire de la chasse** (To hunt)
- **Faire du canotage** (To canoe)
- **Faire de l'équitation** (To horseback ride)
- **Faire de l'escalade** (To rock climb)
- **Faire de la lutte** (To wrestle)
- **Faire de la natation** (To swim)
- **Faire de la plongée sous-marine** (To deep sea dive)
- **Faire du ski** (To ski)
- **Faire du ski alpin** (To downhill ski)
- **Jouer au badminton** (To play badminton)
- **Jouer au baseball** (To play baseball)
- **Jouer au basketball** (To play basketball)
- **Jouer au football** (To play football/*soccer (Europe))
- **Jouer au hockey** (To play hockey)
- **Jouer à la crosse** (To play lacrosse)
- **Jouer au soccer** (To play soccer)
- **Jouer au tennis** (To play tennis)

* Faire de la, Faire du (de+le is changed to 'du'), Faire de l', Faire des = to do a sport
* When you don't play the sport, you 'do' it in French!
* Jouer à la, Jouer au (à + le changes to au), Jouer à l', Jouer aux = to play a sport

Comparative and superlative forms of the adjective "good":
- Bon/bonne/bons/bonne (Good)
- Meilleur (e/s/es) (Better)
- Le meilleur/la meilleure/les meilleur(e)s (The best)

Comparative and superlative of adverb well:
- Bien (Well)–Mieux (Better)–Le mieux (The best)

On se prépare à jouer!
(Getting ready to play!)

Blind Sequencing

Teammates receive a set of six Picture Cards with an athlete getting ready to play. The first card shows the player with the least equipment and the last shows the player with the most equipment. Because only the student with the card can see the picture on the card, students must carefully describe each card for the team to correctly sequence the cards.

Steps

 1 **Distribute Cards**
Teammates cut out the cards and divide the six Picture Cards evenly amongst members. For teams of four, two teammates receive two cards.

 2 **Teams Play**
Students hide their cards from teammates. Starting with Student #1, teammates look at their own cards and describe them in French according to what the player is wearing. Student #2 continues by describing what is on his or her card.

 3 **Sequence Cards**
Teammates decide which picture goes first. After the team reaches consensus on the sequence of the card, the teammate places the card face down on the team table. No one can touch another teammate's card.

4 **Check and Celebrate**
Teammates turn cards over to see if the team has communicated the correct order of the cards! The team celebrates if they have the correct sequence.

(continued)

On se prépare à jouer!
(Getting ready to play!)

Blind Sequencing

Variations

- **Sequencing.** Teammates place cards on the table face up. Students describes their cards as they place them in the correct order where everyone can see.

- **Line-Ups.** Students line up in the order in which the player is dressed. One at a time, students describe the player on their card.

Activity 1 Vocabulary

- **Des épaulières** (Shoulder pads)
- **Des chaussettes** (Socks)
- **Des gants** (Gloves)
- **Des jambières** (Knee pads)
- **Un pantalon de hockey** (Hockey pants)
- **Un chandail de hockey** (Hockey jersey/ sweater)
- **Un casque de hockey/football/ baseball** (Helmet (hockey/football/baseball))
- **Un bâton de hockey** (Hockey stick)
- **Un gant de baseball** (Baseball glove)

- **Un ballon de soccer** (Soccer ball)
- **Un ballon de football** (Football)
- **Un bâton de baseball** (Baseball bat)
- **Une chemise de baseball/ basketball/football** (Shirt/jersey (baseball/basketball/football))
- **Des souliers** (Shoes)
- **Des lunettes (de ski, de natation)** (Goggles (ski/swim))
- **Un maillot de bain** (Swimsuit)
- **Un maillot de lutte** (Wrestling suit)

On se prépare à jouer!
(Getting ready to play!)

Directions: Cut out the *On se prépare à jouer!* cards along the dotted line and distribute equally among team members. Team members take turns describing each card, and then decide as a team where the card belongs in the sequence. Remember, only the team member can see and touch his or her cards.

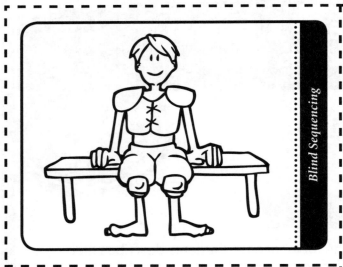

Blind Sequencing

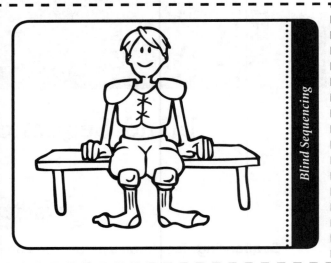

Blind Sequencing

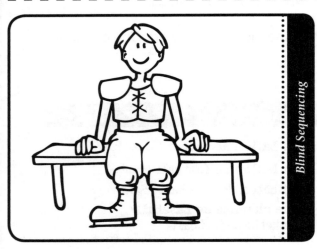

Blind Sequencing

Blind Sequencing

Blind Sequencing

Blind Sequencing

On se prépare à jouer!
(Getting ready to play!)

Directions: Cut out the *On se prépare à jouer!* cards along the dotted line and distribute equally among team members. Team members take turns describing each card, and then decide as a team where the card belongs in the sequence. Remember, only the team member can see and touch his or her cards.

On se prépare à jouer!
(Getting ready to play!)

Directions: Cut out the *On se prépare à jouer!* cards along the dotted line and distribute equally among team members. Team members take turns describing each card, and then decide as a team where the card belongs in the sequence. Remember, only the team member can see and touch his or her cards.

Blind Sequencing

Blind Sequencing

Blind Sequencing

Blind Sequencing

Blind Sequencing

Blind Sequencing

On habille le joueur—Un nouveau sport!
(Dress the player—A new sport!)

Match Mine!

Partners sit on opposite sides of a barrier. Both partners have identical game boards (a page with a player in his boxers!) and game pieces (sports clothing and equipment). One partner (the Sender) dresses the player with clothing and equipment and then must describe to the other partner (the Receiver) how the player is dressed. Their goal is to use chapter vocabulary and clear communication to make a match.

Steps

1 **Students Pair Up**
The teacher creates a barrier between two students (this can be two folders connected by paper clips so that partners cannot see each other's creations).

2 **Distribute Materials**
Each partner needs one game board (the player) and a sheet with the game pieces (equipment). Students cut out the equipment so each student has an identical set of pieces.

3 **Dress the Player**
Behind the barrier, Partner A (the Sender) uses the game pieces to dress the player.

4 **Make a Match**
Partner A describes the uniform to Partner B (Receiver). Partner A must clearly describe his or her information so that Partner B can match the player's uniform exactly!

5 **Check and Celebrate**
Once the pair thinks it has a match, the pair compares players. They celebrate if they made a match.

6 **Switch Roles**
Partners switch roles so that Partner B (the Sender) now creates a new uniform. Partner A is the Receiver.

(continued)

On habille le joueur—Un nouveau sport!
(Dress the player-A new sport!)

Match Mine!

Variations

- **Play as Partners:** Two players play together on one side of the barrier and two players play on the other side.

- **RoundTable:** As a team, students decide what the player will wear by taking turns adding on items. They verbalize each item as they place it on the player.

- **RoundTable Consensus:** Teams come up with the name of the sport and four rules by using RoundTable Consensus. All must contribute an idea and the team must all agree with the idea before they proceed. Other teammates can coach, helping with the French sentences!

On habille le joueur–Un nouveau sport!
(Dress the player–A new sport!)

Directions: Make one copy of the game board for each student playing (two game boards per pair).

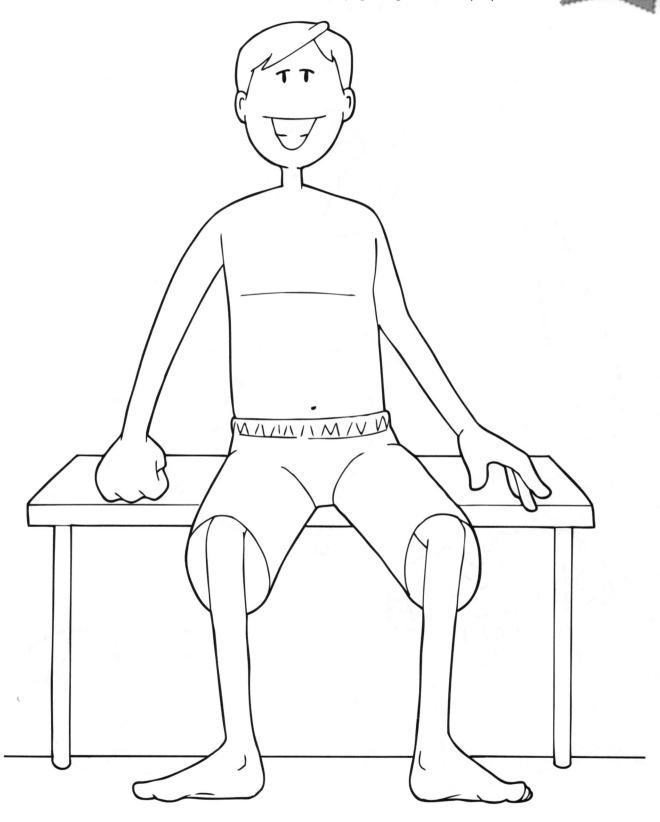

On habille le joueur–Un nouveau sport!

(Dress the player–A new sport!)

Directions: The teacher makes a copy of identical game pieces for each partner. Students cut out game pieces along the dotted line, making sure each partner has one of each piece.

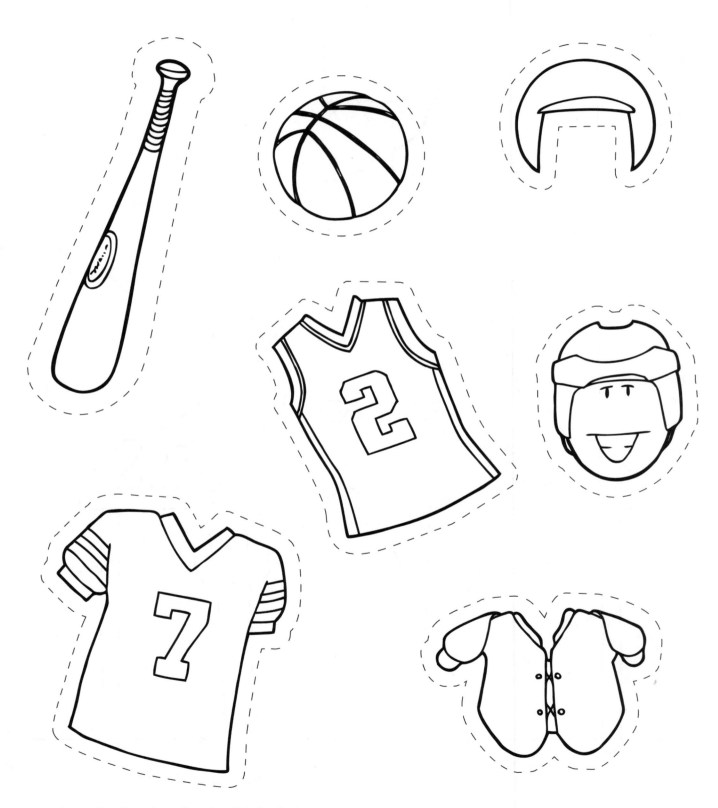

On habille le joueur—Un nouveau sport!
(Dress the player—A new sport!)

Directions: The teacher makes a copy of identical game pieces for each partner. Students cut out game pieces along the dotted line, making sure each partner has one of each piece.

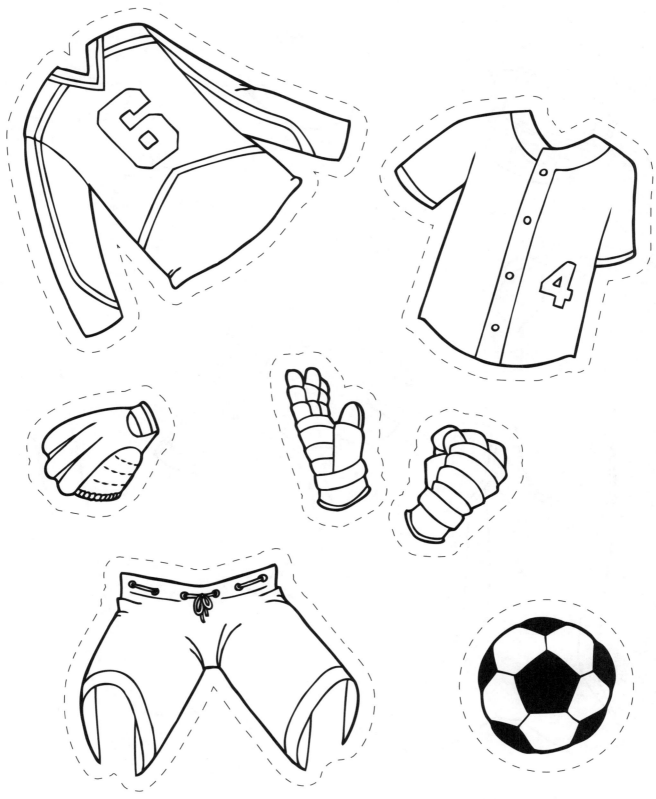

On habille le joueur–Un nouveau sport!
(Dress the player–A new sport!)

Directions: The teacher makes a copy of identical game pieces for each partner. Students cut out game pieces along the dotted line, making sure each partner has one of each piece.

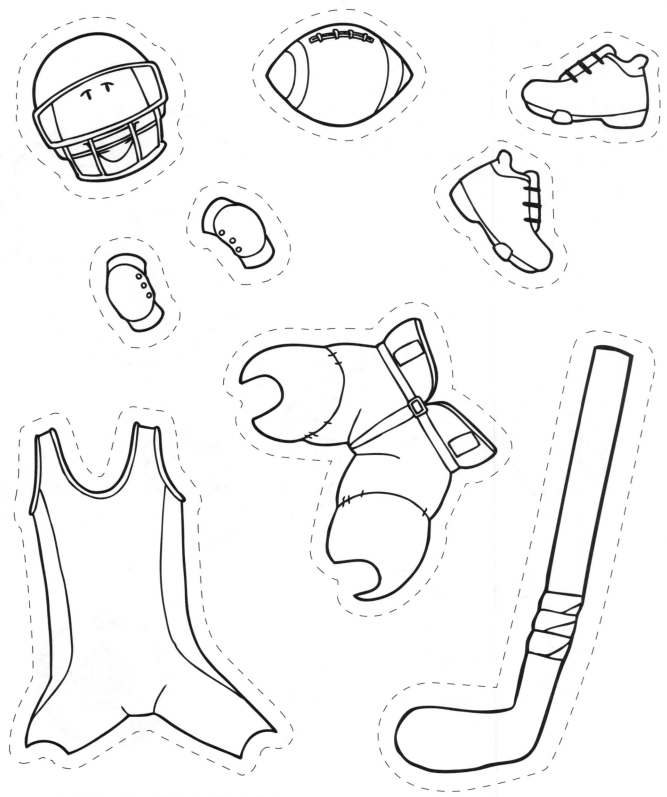

Est-ce que tu aimes...?
(Do you like...?)

Fan-N-Pick

Teams play Fan-N-Pick to ask teammates if they enjoy playing the sport on the card: *"Est-ce que tu aimes jouer au hockey?" "Oui, j'aime jouer au hockey."* Or, *"Non, je n'aime pas jouer au hockey."* Students practice using the verbs *jouer* and *faire*, depending on the sport selected.

Steps

Setup: The teacher gives each team a set of Picture Cards.

1 Distribute Cards
Teams cut out the Picture Cards.

2 Fan Cards
Student #1 holds the cards in a fan and says, *"Choisis une carte!"*

3 Ask a Question
Student #2 (clockwise in the group) picks one card and creates the question aloud based on the picture of the player: *"Est-ce que tu aimes jouer au hockey?"* The student pauses to allow five seconds Think Time.

4 Respond
Student #3 answers the question using *"Oui"* or *"Non"*: *"Non, je n'aime pas jouer au hockey."* (If needed, the student responding can look at the card.)

5 Praise
If the answer is correct, Student #4 praises Student #3's answer in French: *"Bravo!" "Bonne réponse!"* etc. If the answer is incorrect, Student #4 gives Student #3 the correct answer. Student #3 repeats the correct answer, then Student #4 praises in French.

6 Play Continues
Players rotate roles one person clockwise for each new round. Play continues until all players have answered a predetermined number of cards or for an allotted amount of time/turns. **Note:** When expressing the negative of an activity using the verb *"faire,"* the preposition *de la, de l'* and *du* change to *de/d'* (e.g., *"Je ne fais pas de kayak." "Je ne fais pas de gymnastique. Il ne fait pas d'escalade."*)

(continued)

Est-ce que tu aimes...?
(Do you like...?)

Fan-N-Pick

Tips

- **Write It Out.** Students can write out the questions and answers on a worksheet or response board.

- **Vary Difficulty.** Vary the difficulty by having student create different types of questions based on the cards.

  For example:
  - *Qui est le meilleur joueur de basketball?*
  - *Qui fait du ski alpin le mieux?*
  - *Quand est-ce qu'on fait du kayak?* *(en été)*

Est-ce que tu aimes...?

(Do you like...?)

Directions: Copy a set of *Est-ce que tu aimes?* cards for each team. Cut out each card along the dotted line. Give each team a set of cards so they can ask each other if they enjoy playing the sport on the card.

Est-ce que tu aimes...?
(Do you like...?)

Directions: Copy a set of *Est-ce que tu aimes?* cards for each team. Cut out each card along the dotted line. Give each team a set of cards so they can ask each other if they enjoy playing the sport on the card.

7   *Fan-N-Pick*

8   *Fan-N-Pick*

9   *Fan-N-Pick*

10   *Fan-N-Pick*

11   *Fan-N-Pick*

12   *Fan-N-Pick*

Jouer ou faire?
(Play or do?)

Find Someone Who

Students circulate around the classroom forming and re-forming pairs trying to "find someone who" can answer one of the questions on the worksheet. To answer, students name the sport and state if the verb *jouer* or *faire* is used.

Steps

Setup: The teacher prepares the *Jouer ou faire?* worksheet for students to use.

1 Distribute the Worksheet
Students are given the worksheet to review.

2 Students Pair Up
Students circulate around the class. Students keep a hand raised until they find a partner (who is not a teammate).

3 Ask
In pairs, students take turns asking a question from the worksheet: Partner A asks Partner B—Partner B responds. For example, for the basketball player the corret response is, *"Jouer au basketball."* Partner A records the answer on his or her own worksheet. and expresses appreciation.

4 Check
Partner B checks and initials the answer.

5 Reverse Roles
Partner B now asks a question and Partner A responds. Partner B records the answer on his or her own worksheet and expresses appreciation.

6 Check
Partner A checks and initials the answer.

7 Praise and Part
Partners high five and raise a hand as they search for a new partner.

(continued)

Jouer ou faire?
(Play or do?)

Find Someone Who

 8 **Repeat**
Students repeat the process until their worksheets are complete.

 9 **Experts**
Experts are students who have completed their worksheets. They sit at their desks and can be approached by others as a resource.

 10 **Teams Compare**
Students compare answers in teams. If there is a disagreement or uncertainty, students can check the chapter vocabulary or can simultaneously raise hands to ask a team question. The teacher responds to a team question.

Variations

Create Your Own!

• **Labeling Pictures:** Teacher distributes the worksheet having highlighted different parts/equipment on the picture. Students are asked to identify the equipment.

• **Likes/Plays Certain Sports…in Winter, Spring, Summer, and Fall:** Teacher asks students to answer according to when that sport is played (e.g., *On joue au baseball en été.* We play baseball in the summer.) There is more "correct answers" for students with this activity since this could depend on whether or not it is a sport played inside or outside!

• **Students Answer Questions About Sport Preferences.** Teacher directs students to ask if their partners like to play the sports on the Activity handout. Teachers can review the sports and students can write down key words. When they circulate around the classroom they can ask if their partner likes to play the sport, if they do, they will initial that picture.

Jouer ou faire?
(Play or do?)

Directions: Students circulate around the classroom forming and re-forming pairs trying to "find someone who" can correctly name the sport and determine if the verb *jouer* or *faire* is used. Record the answer provided by your partner and have your partner initial the answer.

Qu'est-ce que c'est?
(What is it?)

Quiz-Quiz-Trade

Students quiz a partner, get quizzed by a partner, and then trade their cards to repeat the process with a new partner.

Steps

Setup: The teacher prepares a set of Questions Cards for the class.

1 Distribute the Cards
The teacher cuts out the cards and distributes them to the class, one per student.

2 Students Pair Up
Students stand up, hand up, pair up, and face each other.

3 Students Quiz Each Other
Students take turns asking questions about the card. Questions can be simply, *"Qu'est-ce que c'est?"* His or her partner may respond *"C'est un joueur de hockey."* Students quiz and respond with each pairing.

4 Trade Cards and Find New Partners
After partners have asked and answered each other's questions, they give each other a high five, trade cards, and find a new partner.

5 Continue Quizzing
This activity can go on for an allotted amount of time or for a number of trades.

(continued)

Qu'est-ce que c'est?
(What is it?)

Quiz-Quiz-Trade

Tip

- **Increase Difficulty.** More advanced students can create questions based on true and false, or specific details on the card. For example:
  1. *"C'est un…"* The picture on the card of a piece of sports equipment or a player in a sport
  2. Multiple-choice response.
  3. Questions generated by students about what the players/picture is about—or detail on the picture

Qu'est-ce que c'est?
(What is It?)

Directions: Cut out the *Qu'est-ce que c'est?* cards along the dotted line. Then fold the card in half so the question is on one side and the answer is on the back. Glue or tape cards together to keep the answers and questions on opposite sides.

1 · Quiz-Quiz-Trade

Qu'est-ce que c'est?

Hockey player

Question

1 · Quiz-Quiz-Trade

Réponse

C'est un joueur de hockey.

2 · Quiz-Quiz-Trade

Qu'est-ce que c'est?

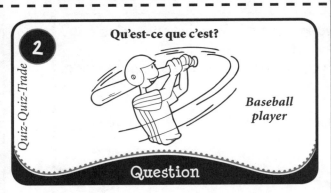

Baseball player

Question

2 · Quiz-Quiz-Trade

Réponse

C'est un joueur de baseball.

3 · Quiz-Quiz-Trade

Qu'est-ce que c'est?

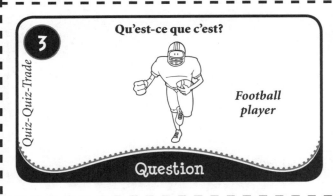

Football player

Question

3 · Quiz-Quiz-Trade

Réponse

C'est un joueur de football (américain).

4 · Quiz-Quiz-Trade

Qu'est-ce que c'est?

Karate

Question

4 · Quiz-Quiz-Trade

Réponse

Il fait du karaté.

Qu'est-ce que c'est?
(What is It?)

Directions: Cut out the *Qu'est-ce que c'est?* cards along the dotted line. Then fold the card in half so the question is on one side and the answer is on the back. Glue or tape cards together to keep the answers and questions on opposite sides.

5 · Quiz-Quiz-Trade

Qu'est-ce que c'est?

Cyclist

Question

Réponse

5 · Quiz-Quiz-Trade

C'est un cycliste.

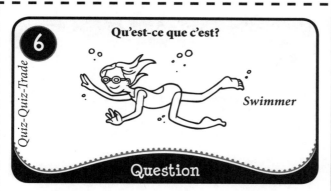

6 · Quiz-Quiz-Trade

Qu'est-ce que c'est?

Swimmer

Question

Réponse

6 · Quiz-Quiz-Trade

C'est une nageuse.

7 · Quiz-Quiz-Trade

Qu'est-ce que c'est?

Gymnast

Question

Réponse

7 · Quiz-Quiz-Trade

C'est une gymnaste.

8 · Quiz-Quiz-Trade

Qu'est-ce que c'est?

Boxing gloves

Question

Réponse

8 · Quiz-Quiz-Trade

Ce sont des gants de boxe.

Qu'est-ce que c'est?
(What is It?)

Directions: Cut out the *Qu'est-ce que c'est?* cards along the dotted line. Then fold the card in half so the question is on one side and the answer is on the back. Glue or tape cards together to keep the answers and questions on opposite sides.

9 Quiz-Quiz-Trade | Qu'est-ce que c'est?

Boxer

Question

Réponse

9 Quiz-Quiz-Trade

C'est un boxeur.

---

10 Quiz-Quiz-Trade | Qu'est-ce que c'est?

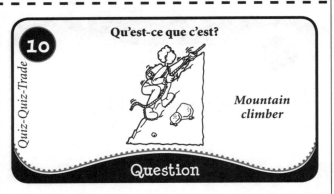

Mountain climber

Question

Réponse

10 Quiz-Quiz-Trade

C'est une alpiniste de montagne.

---

11 Quiz-Quiz-Trade | Qu'est-ce que c'est?

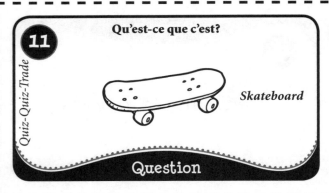

Skateboard

Question

Réponse

11 Quiz-Quiz-Trade

C'est une planche à roulettes.

---

12 Quiz-Quiz-Trade | Qu'est-ce que c'est?

Lacrosse player

Question

Réponse

12 Quiz-Quiz-Trade

C'est une joueuse de la crosse.

Qu'est-ce que c'est?

(What is It?)

Directions: Cut out the *Qu'est-ce que c'est?* cards along the dotted line. Then fold the card in half so the question is on one side and the answer is on the back. Glue or tape cards together to keep the answers and questions on opposite sides.

Quiz-Quiz-Trade | 13 | Qu'est-ce que c'est? | Canoe | Question

Réponse | 13 | Quiz-Quiz-Trade | Il fait du canotage.

Quiz-Quiz-Trade | 14 | Qu'est-ce que c'est? | Soccer ball | Question

Réponse | 14 | Quiz-Quiz-Trade | C'est une balle de soccer/foot(ball).

Quiz-Quiz-Trade | 15 | Qu'est-ce que c'est? | Wrestler | Question

Réponse | 15 | Quiz-Quiz-Trade | C'est un lutteur.

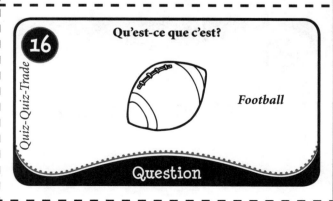

Quiz-Quiz-Trade | 16 | Qu'est-ce que c'est? | Football | Question

Réponse | 16 | Quiz-Quiz-Trade | C'est une balle de football (américain).

Qu'est-ce que c'est?
(What is It?)

Directions: Cut out the *Qu'est-ce que c'est?* cards along the dotted line. Then fold the card in half so the question is on one side and the answer is on the back. Glue or tape cards together to keep the answers and questions on opposite sides.

---

17 Qu'est-ce que c'est?

Quiz-Quiz-Trade

Diver

Question

Réponse

17

Quiz-Quiz-Trade

C'est une plongeuse.

---

18 Qu'est-ce que c'est?

Quiz-Quiz-Trade

Skates

Question

Réponse

18

Quiz-Quiz-Trade

Ce sont des patins.

---

19 Qu'est-ce que c'est?

Quiz-Quiz-Trade

Gymnast

Question

Réponse

19

Quiz-Quiz-Trade

C'est une gymnaste.

---

20 Qu'est-ce que c'est?

Quiz-Quiz-Trade

Horseback rider

Question

Réponse

2o

Quiz-Quiz-Trade

C'est une cavalière.

Qu'est-ce que c'est?
(What is It?)

Directions: Cut out the *Qu'est-ce que c'est?* cards along the dotted line. Then fold the card in half so the question is on one side and the answer is on the back. Glue or tape cards together to keep the answers and questions on opposite sides.

21 Qu'est-ce que c'est?

Skier

Quiz-Quiz-Trade

Question

21 Réponse

Quiz-Quiz-Trade

C'est une skieuse.

---

22 Qu'est-ce que c'est?

Trophy

Quiz-Quiz-Trade

Question

22 Réponse

Quiz-Quiz-Trade

C'est un trophée.

---

23 Qu'est-ce que c'est?

Bicycle

Quiz-Quiz-Trade

Question

23 Réponse

Quiz-Quiz-Trade

C'est une bicyclette.

---

24 Qu'est-ce que c'est?

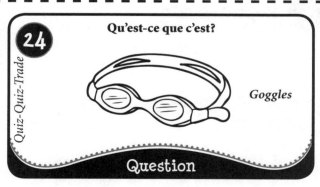

Goggles

Quiz-Quiz-Trade

Question

24 Réponse

Quiz-Quiz-Trade

Ce sont des lunettes de nage.

Soyez logique!/Mettez vous en rang!
(Be logical!/Line up!)

Logic Line-Ups

Teammates each role play a different sports player and use deduction to sequence themselves.

Steps

Setup: The teacher distributes four cards with sports players to each team. The teacher holds the Problem Cards to read to the class.

1 Line Up
Teammates line up shoulder to shoulder each holding a card with a player on it.

2 Choose a Leader
Each team selects a Logic Leader.

3 Give a Clue
The teacher reads the first statement from one of the Problem cards.

4 Start Line Up
The Logic Leader verbalizes how teammates should line up, according to what he or she can understand from the clue.

5 Agree
If teammates agree, they line up; if not, they discuss until they reach a consensus and then line up.

6 Next Clue
The teacher reads the next statement. The team adjusts their order as necessary. The Logic Leader unifies their sequence and directs the team to make any additional changes if necessary.

7 Repeat
Repeat steps 4 and 5 until all clues for a problem are acted upon.

8 Repeat Again.
Teacher repeats all clues so that students can check their order.

(continued)

Soyez logique!/Mettez vous en rang!
(Be logical!/Line up!)

Logic Line-Ups

9 **Teams Check**
The teacher can call one team (which is in the correct order) to show or announce their line-up order. The other teams check for correctness.

10 **Teams Celebrate**
If the team is in the wrong order, they correct themselves and then celebrate.

11 **Play Again**
Another Logic Leader is chosen and another round is played using a different *"problème."*

Tips

• **Teams Check.** For Step 8, where teams are checking their order by looking at one team, the class can announce the answer using choral response.

• **Laminate Cards.** Laminate the cards for future use.

• **Different Sports.** To create more Logic Line-Ups activities, create four different sports cards. Substitute sports on the clue cards or make up your own clues.

Soyez logique!/Mettez vous en rang!

(Be logical!/Line up!)

Directions: The teacher describes each order clue, and then students deduce together where they are to stand.

Problème #1

Le joueur de hockey est la seule personne à côté de la patineuse. Le skieur est deuxième de la gauche.

Problème #2

Le skieur est à la droite. Le cycliste n'est pas à côté du skieur ni du joueur de hockey.

Problème #3

Le cycliste n'est pas au debut, ni à la fin. Le joueur de hockey est entre le cycliste et le skieur. La patineuse est à la gauche.

Problème #4

La patineuse est à la gauche. Le skieur n'est pas à côté du joueur de hockey qui est à la droite.

ANSWERS

Réponse #1: Cycliste, Skieur, Patineuse, Joueur de hockey
Réponse #2: Cycliste, Patineuse, Joueur de hockey, Skieur
Réponse #3: Patineuse, Cycliste, Joueur de hockey, Skieur
Réponse #4: Patineuse, Skieur, Cycliste, Joueur de hockey

Soyez logique!/Mettez vous en rang!
(Be logical!/Line up!)

Directions: Cut out cards along the dotted line. Distribute a set of four cards to each team to play Logic Line-Ups. Students use deduction to sequence themselves.

Logic Line-Ups

Cycliste

Soyez logique!/Mettez vous en rang!
(Be logical!/Line up!)

Directions: Cut out cards along the dotted line. Distribute a set of four cards to each team to play Logic Line-Ups. Students use deduction to sequence themselves.

Logic Line-Ups

Skieur

Soyez logique!/Mettez vous en rang!

(Be logical!/Line up!)

Directions: Cut out cards along the dotted line. Distribute a set of four cards to each team to play Logic Line-Ups. Students use deduction to sequence themselves.

Logic Line-Ups

Patineuse

Soyez logique!/Mettez vous en rang!
(Be logical!/Line up!)

Directions: Cut out cards along the dotted line. Distribute a set of four cards to each team to play Logic Line-Ups. Students use deduction to sequence themselves.

Logic Line-Ups

Joueur de hockey

Cooperative Learning & French • Chiupka-Jozin
Kagan Publishing • 1 (800) 933-2667 • www.KaganOnline.com

On parle des sports!
(Talk about sports!)

Jot Thoughts

The teacher asks a sports-related quesiton, such as, *"Que sont les sports d'equipe?"* Teammates "cover the table," with sports that fit the teacher's question.

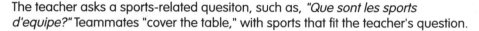

Steps

> **Setup:** The teacher gives each student many slips of paper and a pen or pencil.

1 Get Ready
The teacher asks a question to which the answer can include many different sports. Question ideas are in the box. The teacher sets a time limit (or designates the number of pieces of paper/responses from team/student), and provides Think Time.

2 Students Say and Write
Students say the sport and then write it on one slip of their paper. They are to write as many ideas as they can in the allotted time, one idea per slip of paper. No duplicate ideas!

3 Show Your Responses
Students place their papers in the center of the table. Students attempt to "cover the table" with no slips of paper overlapping.

Questions

Here are some possible questions for Jot Thoughts.

- *Que sont les sports d'équipe?* (Which sports are team sports?)
- *Que sont les sports individuels?* (Which sports are individual sports?)
- *Quels sports utilisent une balle?* (Which sports use a ball?)
- *Quels sports sont dans l'eau?* (Which sports are in the water?)
- *Que sont les sports d'hiver?* (Which sports are winter sports?)

(continued)

Activity **7**

On parle des sports!
(Talk about sports!)

Jot Thoughts

Tips

- **Lots of Paper.** Make sure each player has lots of slips of paper so teams can generate many ideas.

- **Talk About It.** After students brainstorm ideas, have them do a RoundRobin discussion to talk in French about the topic. For example, if they brainstorm team sports, ask the question, *"What is your favorite team sport and why?"* *("Quel est ton sport d'équipe préféré et pourquoi?")* Students each take a turn responding to the question in French.

- **Say It, Write It, Place It.** Teach students to say their idea out loud, write it down, and then place it on the team table. That way, they won't have duplicates and it also encourages students to practice saying and hearing the vocabulary.

- **Create a Collage.** Teams can create a team collage of favorite sports, labeling the sports in French.

otes

Notes